W9-AER-693

Gramley Library
Salem Academy and College
Winston-Salem, N.C. 27108

601

DIGITAL DILEMMAS

Gramley Library
Salem Academy and College
Winston-Salem, N.C. 27108

NEW DIRECTIONS IN INTERNATIONAL STUDIES

PATRICE PETRO, SERIES EDITOR

New Directions in International Studies expands cross-disciplinary dialogue about the nature of internationalism and globalization. The series highlights innovative new approaches to the study of the local and global as well as multiple forms of identity and difference. It focuses on transculturalism, technology, media, and representation and features the work of scholars who explore various components and consequences of globalization, such as the increasing flow of peoples, ideas, images, information, and capital across borders.

Under the direction of Patrice Petro, the series is sponsored by the Center for International Education at the University of Wisconsin–Milwaukee. The center seeks to foster interdisciplinary and collaborative approaches to international education by transcending traditional professional and geographic boundaries and by bringing together international and Milwaukee-based scholars, artists, practitioners, and educators. The center's book series originates from annual scholarly conferences that probe the political, economic, artistic, and social processes and practices of our time—especially those defining internationalism, cultural identity, and globalization.

MARK PHILIP BRADLEY AND PATRICE PETRO, eds.
Truth Claims: Representation and Human Rights

MARCUS BULLOCK AND PETER Y. PAIK, eds.
Aftermaths: Exile, Migration, and Diaspora Reconsidered

ELIZABETH SWANSON GOLDBERG
Beyond Terror: Gender, Narrative, Human Rights

LINDA KRAUSE AND PATRICE PETRO, eds.
Global Cities: Cinema, Architecture, and Urbanism in a Digital Age

ANDREW MARTIN AND PATRICE PETRO, eds.
Rethinking Global Security: Media, Popular Culture, and the "War on Terror"

TASHA G. OREN AND PATRICE PETRO, eds.
Global Currents: Media and Technology Now

PETER PAIK AND MARCUS BULLOCK, eds.
Aftermaths: Exile, Migration, and Diaspora Reconsidered

FREYA SCHIWY
Indianizing Film: Decolonization, the Andes, and the Question of Technology

CRISTINA VENEGAS
Digital Dilemmas: The State, the Individual, and Digital Media in Cuba

DIGITAL DILEMMAS

THE STATE, THE INDIVIDUAL, AND DIGITAL MEDIA IN CUBA

CRISTINA VENEGAS

Bramley Library
Salem Academy and College
Winston-Salem, N.C. 27108

RUTGERS UNIVERSITY PRESS

New Brunswick, New Jersey, and London

LIBRARY OF CONGRESS CATALOGING-IN-PUBLICATION DATA

Venegas, Cristina, 1959–
   Digital dilemmas : the state, the individual, and digital media in Cuba / Cristina Venegas.
     p. cm. — (New directions in international studies)
   Includes bibliographical references and index.
   ISBN 978–0–8135–4686–5 (hardcover : alk. paper) — ISBN 978–0–8135–4687–2 (pbk. : alk. paper)
    1. Mass media—Political aspects—Cuba. 2. Digital media—Political aspects—Cuba.
3. Internet—Political aspects—Cuba. 4. Mass media policy—Cuba. 5. Cuba—Politics and government—1990– 6. Social change—Cuba. 7. Mass media—Social aspects—Cuba.
8. Digital media—Social aspects—Cuba. 9. Internet—Social aspects—Cuba. 10. Cuba—Social conditions—1959– I. Title.
   P92.C9V46 2010
   302.23′1097291—dc22   2009006046

A British Cataloging-in-Publication record for this book is available from the British Library.

Copyright © 2010 by Cristina Venegas

All rights reserved
No part of this book may be reproduced or utilized in any form or by any means, electronic or mechanical, or by any information storage and retrieval system, without written permission from the publisher. Please contact Rutgers University Press, 100 Joyce Kilmer Avenue, Piscataway, NJ 08854–8099. The only exception to this prohibition is "fair use" as defined by U.S. copyright law.

Visit our Web site: http://rutgerspress.rutgers.edu

Manufactured in the United States of America

For Emi

And in memory of Germán Guzmán Campos and Antonio Zapata

CONTENTS

ILLUSTRATIONS

ACKNOWLEDGMENTS

I had no way of knowing, when I arrived in Cuba in 1992, that my teaching trips to the Escuela Internacional de Cine y Televisión in San Antonio de los Baños would result in this book. Nor could I guess the depth and value of the friendships I made there as they evolved over the years. Subsequently, many people have contributed to what is now the final text. Marsha Kinder encouraged me from the beginning to pursue a path of research that I then thought premature. Her sage advice and support were invaluable as I found my way through tumultuous historical events. I have depended on her steadfast commitment and friendship throughout the years, and it has proven a constant well of inspiration.

The research was carried out under difficult circumstances and over a period of many years. It would not have been possible without the people in Cuba who have helped me the most, Dolores "Lola" Calviño and Julio García Espinosa. They have devoted their lives to promoting film culture in Cuba and in Latin America. They encouraged me to pursue my own obsessions, and helped me to "connect the dots." Whether facilitating contacts, introducing me to friends and colleagues, or navigating Cuban bureaucracy, Lola Calviño would join in my investigations as we tried to understand the *special period* through the changing atmosphere of technology. Her tenacity and warmth taught me invaluable lessons about Cuba, its contradictory nature, its history, and its humor. My long conversations with respected filmmaker and theorist Julio García Espinosa about new technology, neorealism, television, or rumba have been both enlightening and entertaining. Together, these two persons are responsible for opening many doors to me and for expanding the context of my project.

I also benefited from long discussions with other Cuban colleagues. Victor Fowler found a most poetic way to describe my inquiry about Cuban digital communities, reminding me that the seeds for understanding these new formations in Cuba could be found in the biography of Julián del Casal, a nineteenth-century Cuban poet. Manuel Calviño provided astute observations about Cuban society and its complex layers, ideas he usually put forward over delicious meals. Film critic and historian Juan Antonio García Borrero included an early version of chapter 4 in an edited volume dedicated to García Espinosa, and Rufo Caballero was an astute listener. I am grateful to others in Cuba who so readily put aside their complicated schedules to talk candidly, and as often as was necessary: Jesús Martinez Alfonso, Beatriz Alonso, Jorge Barata, Roberto Cabada, Gerardo Chijona, Arnaldo Coro, Alfredo Luis del Valle, Carlos Diaz Arenas, Daniel Díaz Torres, Enrique Gonzalez-Manet, Jorge Hernandez, Manuel Herrera, Celina Morales, Blanca Patalla, Enrique Pineda Barnet, Pedro Urra, Naghim Vazquez, Berta Verdura, and Miguel Coyula. At Cuba's Cineteca Nacional, Enrique Urbieta and the entire staff graciously provided assistance and guidance and screened rare materials for me. Fellow Cuba observers, interested beyond the passing vogue, have provided leads to relevant information about the island. I wish to thank my film festival partner Denis de la Roca for his constant support; thanks also to Ann Louise Bardach, Luis Clemens, Hiram Enriquez, Jairo Marin, Tiffany Roberts, Esther Whitfield, and Walter Lipman.

During the past few years, Patrice Petro's generous support has made a crucial difference in providing a broader context for my work. Leslie Mitchner at Rutgers University Press warmly embraced the project and provided expert feedback. Marilyn Campbell, Paula Friedman, and Rachel Friedman have been helpful and kind throughout the editorial process. I am extremely thankful to Julianne Burton-Carvajal for her candid response to earlier drafts of the manuscript and for always providing strong encouragement and affection. My appreciation too to Maria Gordon for her brilliant nature, tireless support, and loyal friendship in helping me bring the manuscript into shape, and to my always cheerful colleague Peter Bloom for helping me reenter the process of rewriting with a little less suffering. Longtime colleagues Ana M. López, Marvin D'Lugo, Kathleen Newman, Catherine Benamou, Gilberto Blasini, Laura Podalsky, Yeidy Rivero, Tamara Falicov, and Ariana Hernandez-Reguant have consistently supported the work and invited me to teach or present earlier versions of chapters at conferences and seminars. James Hay shared his lucid comments, recipes, and cookbooks over years of exquisite meals.

For the past six years, at the University of California, Santa Barbara, I have found a welcoming home of brilliant colleagues who have expanded the context for my thinking and provided a supportive working atmosphere. Kathryn Carnahan, Joe Palladino, Victoria Duncan, Flora Furlong, Melany Miners, Keith Boynton, and Dana Welch have always helped me do what's right for the book. Bhaskar Sarkar's wonderfully curious mind, enthusiasm, and friendship has spurred many conversations and provocative diversions; Lisa Parks has been a friend, a mentor, and an ardent supporter of the work—and of making time for the rest of life. Bishnupriya Gosh was a sharp reader of early versions, Janet Walker a constant champion. Thanks as well to Jennifer Holt, Constance Penley, Melinda Szaloky, Greg Siegel, Chuck Wolfe, Edward Branigan, Anna Everett, Dick Hebdige, Cynthia Felando, Anna Brusutti, and Dana Driskell—the best group of faculty colleagues one would want to have. Dean of Humanities and Fine Arts David Marshall consistently provided assistance throughout the writing process.

Vibeke Sorensen and Heitor Capuzzo embraced my work over the years, adding boundless imagination and creativity. An expanding network of colleagues provided intellectual sustenance and cheer: Carl Gutierrez-Jones, Maria Herrera-Sobek, Francisco Lomeli, Leo Cabranes-Grant, Swati Chattopadhyay, Victor Fuentes, Sara Poot-Herrera, Lisa Hajar, José Rabasa, Michael Solomon, Cecilia Cornejo, Luis Ulloa, Henry Jenkins, David Thornburn, Lucia Saks, Jennifer Earl, Bruce Bimber, Rita Riley, and Lisa Jevbratt. Graduate students Nicole Starosielsky, Veronica Córdoba, Patricia Bermudez, Ilana Luna, Noah Zweig, Sarah Harris, and Jason Crawford contributed to this project with their ideas and questions.

During the project's early stage, as my doctoral dissertation at the University of Southern California (USC), my advisors Marsha Kinder, David James, Nora Hamilton, Tara McPherson, and Doe Mayer provided confidence in my work as well as provocative commentary. I benefited immensely from the rich environment of graduate learning and from professors Lynn Spiegel, Michael Renov, Rick Jewell, Todd Boyd, Frantisek Daniel, Phillip Rosen, and John Belton, as well as from the support of Elizabeth Daley, dean of USC's School of Cinematic Arts. I am grateful for having learned the basics of multimedia authoring from the talented crew of the Labyrinth Project at USC: Kristy Kang, Rosemary Comella, and Charles Tashiro. Colleagues at the Media Institute of the University of Bergen, Norway—Alvaro Ramirez, Kate Goodnow, and Randi

Heimvik—welcomed me on many occasions to teach, and provided a warm working space for the first writing of the manuscript.

My family's oceanic support knows no bounds. My mother, Emma Zapata, is the best example of perseverance, strength, and partnership in learning and laughing. Marisa Venegas, my dazzling sister and soulmate, is my most valued sounding board and editorial advisor. With Ana Zapata, I learned how economic theory and monetary policies affect our day-to-day existence. José Ainsa's help and support in our lives is profound, and he has reminded us that the world is often not what we often imagine it to be. Alvaro Venegas, my brother, is my extended lifeline; his talent, love, and humor are absolutely essential. Ena Lucía, Roberto Antonio, Ena Baez, and Roberto Zapata extend the long reach of our family where the love is finally grounded.

There is a world of friends whose cheer and companionship have made possible the writing of this book: Elsa Atilano, Tony and Viola Balbinot, Reid Burns, Claudia Calviño, José Manuel Calviño, Karla and Loipa Calviño, Alfredo Calviño, Patricia Coronado, Patsy Hicks, Steve Hicks, Patricia Martin, Alejandro Pelayo, Teresa Ponte, Robert Robin, Kofi Taha, Gary Taubes, Victor Ugalde, and David Veloz. Roger S. Christiansen, through his confidence and his unflagging spirit, made a difficult process more enjoyable by undertaking the adventures with me. Finally, I wish to thank Cedar Sherbert, careful and thoughtful listener, reader, and companion of books, films, and life.

ACRONYMS

AIR   Asociación Interamericana de Radiodifusión (Interamerican Broadcasting Association)

ALBA   Alianza Bolivariana para las Américas (Bolivarian Alliance for the Americas)

APC   Association of Progressive Computing

CENIAI   Centro Nacional de Intercambio de Información (National Center for Automated Exchange of Information)

CEDISAC/   Empresa de Tecnologías de la Información y Servicios Tele-
CITMATEL   maticos (Information Technology and Advanced Telematic Services Company)

CMEA   Council for Mutual Economic Assistance

CENSAI   Centro Nacional de Superación y Adiestramiento en Informáticas (National Center for Teaching and Self-Advancement in Informatics)

CIGB net   Red del Centro de Ingeniería Genética y Biotecnología (Network for the Center for Genetic Engineering and Biotechnology)

CUBACEL   Unidad de Negocios Móvil de ETECSA (Mobil Telephone Company from ETECSA)

CUC   Peso Cubano Convertible (Cuban Convertible Peso)

EICTV   Escuela Internacional de Cine y Televisión, San Antonio de los Baños (International School of Film and Television in San Antonio de los Baños)

ETECSA   Empresa de Telecomunicaciones de Cuba S.A. (Cuban Telecommunications Company)

GET   Grupo Electronico del Turismo (Electronic Tourism Group)

IBI	Intergovernmental Office of Informatics
ICAIC	Instituto Cubano de Arte e Industria Cinematográfica (Cuban Institute of Film Art and Industry)
ICRT	Instituto Cubano de Radio y Televisión (Cuban Institute of Radio and Television)
INFOCOM	Red de Datos de Mensajeria Pública de Cuba (Internet Service Provider in Cuba)
INFOMED	Red Telemática de Salud en Cuba (Network of the Medical Sector in Cuba)
ISPAJAE	Instituto Superior Politécnico José Antonio Echeverría (High Polytechnic Institute José Antonio Echeverría)
ISA	Instituto Superior de Arte (High Institute of the Arts)
IUJ	International Union of Journalists
NAFTA	North American Free Trade Agreement
NGO	Nongovernmental organization
NIC	Network Information Center
UCI	Universidad de Ciencias Informáticas (University of Information Sciences)
UNDP	United Nations Development Program
UNEAC	Unión de Escritores y Artistas Cubanos (Cuban Union of Writers and Artists)
UNESCO	United Nations Educational, Scientific, and Cultural Organization
UPEC	Unión de Periodistas de Cuba (Cuban Union of Journalists)
USAID	United States Aid in Development

DIGITAL DILEMMAS

INTRODUCTION

Until 2001, the Russian government operated the largest radar base in the Western Hemisphere, located in the Cuban village of Lourdes, a few kilometers south of Havana. Set amid palm trees and tropical fields, the site at first glance appeared to be one of the island's rural residential neighborhoods of anonymous, post-1959 high-rise apartment buildings. However, a military zone designation and an enormous dish antenna signaled that this was no typical communal housing sector. Rather, the base had been "Radio-Electronic Station/Cuba," where Russians conducted telephone espionage monitoring U.S. military and commercial movements, and also communicated with Soviet nuclear submarines.[1] Established in 1964, two years after the Cuban Missile Crisis, this base became a strategic location for both the Soviets and the Cubans, with Cuba's intelligence agents sharing valuable information with the Russians. Despite a drastic change in Soviet economic agreements with Cuba in 1991, the Lourdes base remained open, a remnant of the Cold War, housing some fifteen hundred Russian personnel, for another decade. Data gathered about American operations continued to bring Cuba a measure of national security during these years.

In October 2001, thirty-nine years after the founding of the Lourdes radar base, and under the specter of September 11, Russian president Vladimir Putin announced the base's closure, with rent owing to Cuba of 200 million dollars. The money was never paid. What had happened was that President Putin, looking to the United States for economic alliance, instead had found pressure from the Bush administration, and, to the dismay of Russian generals, agreed to schedule the immediate dismantling of the base without consulting the Cuban government. In a diplomatic coup, the United States had taken advantage of the "War on Terrorism" to force the Russian president's hand over Cuba.

In a move reminiscent of past transformations of spaces and their uses,[2] the 28-square-mile secret compound was converted by 2002 into the high-tech University of Information Sciences (UCI), housing fifteen thousand students, faculty, and staff. Cuba has invested heavily to transform the Cold War listening post into a center for the education of software programmers and engineers to be inserted into the worldwide informatics labor force.[3] In doing so, the Cuban government has mobilized human, technological, and economic resources to foster a new Cuban economic direction. If the Lourdes base, with its extensive system of satellites, embedded Cuba within a Cold War network of spies, military infrastructure, and invention, UCI shows the state repositioning communication and information within a chain of education, production, consumption, and finance linked to global networks of labor and economics.[4] That it does this in the model of an "elite" campus, under the centralized tutelage of the state, is evidence of ideological traces lingering from the compound's original purpose of espionage. Cuba thus uses digital technology to redirect the country away from an essentially defensive orientation and into an offensive economic strategy. This is one of the Cuban government's choices as it works to resolve its digital dilemmas. The political and social uses the government confronts in the process raise serious questions about digital development far beyond the island.

In this book, I analyze the impact of the Internet and digital media on media policies, procedures, and practices in Cuba, as well as their broader social effects and implications. I seek to understand institutional and human networks evolving out of contested public and private interests through new technologies, and the artistic and personal terrain these technologies help to construct. And indeed, I find that a mix of openness and restriction stemming from government policies, beginning in the 1990s, reveals a process of shifting institutional relations heavily influenced by the role of information technologies. The theoretical framework thus strikes a balance between a view of the state in determining the development and deployment of media technology and its uses and users, and an investigation, prompted by the exhaustion of an ideological paradigm, into the way individual challenges have imposed limits on such development/deployment in the context of globalization. Locating the social uses of, and motivations for, the appropriation of media technology by governments and individuals serves, I argue, to correct views of technology as progress; rather, focusing on intentionality reveals a complex set of forces that normalize, renew, regulate, and reform. The present volume grows out of a mid-1990s project in which I set out to examine how Cuban media would be influenced by global changes. Would the turn to greater global participation cause anxiety or reassurance? What types of cultural networks would be created, and by whom? What type of infrastructures had Cuba's relationship with the USSR left behind? Throughout this book, I seek to establish the interrelations among developments of media technologies past and present through a study of different sites of media use. I provide a discussion of technological development that combines the role of state and private activities in evolving definitions of democracy, information science education, exile politics, tourism, cinema, and digital social networks. I formulate each chapter to work as an access point that underscores the multiple strands of an emerging media geography, interconnected by government policies, responses to these policies, and private initiatives. By focusing on the linkages of media developments, I also argue that a reading of overlapping media infrastructures can nuance established chronologies with complex associations. By concentrating on the rising factor of media technology, I sharpen the focus and avoid easy categorization of ideological practices, technological development, and economic strategies. My research here probes official rhetoric produced by the Cuban state about the value of the Internet, investigates the communication of opponents and supporters, and examines what influences the activities of media users and producers.

UCI represents the nuanced nature of dilemmas viewed in terms of a paradoxical aspect of the Cuban state. UCI forms part of an investment in education and culture that produces the type of "soft power" for the state that political scientist Joseph S. Nye maintains can make a nation attractive to others.[5] In a nation where Internet access has been limited and guarded by the government, a select number of students are equipped with the latest hardware and software in classrooms and dormitories, putting these tools to use under what amounts to a new social contract between the state and the individual. The internal network involved, connecting upward of seven thousand computers, and itself connected to a megagigabyte fiber-optic backbone, is the largest on the island. Yet UCI still fits the model of development that Fidel Castro imagined for the beleaguered post–Cold War Cuban economy. Part educational institution, part software factory, UCI not only trains students but also focuses on authoring code for the open software economy. The expected reach of the products is national and regional in scope.

"What they [Cubans] have achieved in medicine," asserts historian and political commentator Tariq Ali, "is about to be replicated in information technology."[6] Thanks to their high security clearance, newly trained network specialists and administrators enjoy high social status and the knowledge of how to participate in the global economy. They are young, skilled, and "on the inside" of strategic awareness. On the radar-base-turned-high-tech-classroom, students serve the state's latest economic strategy and fulfill both their and the state's social needs and desires through the acquisition of knowledge and training in digital systems. In Cuban argot, hardware has even become a verb: to *hardweriar*, often encountered as the participle *hardweriando*. "Hardwearing" substitutes the association of hardware with, the military, with control, and with proprietary technology with its concepts of recycling, rerouting, restructuring, repurposing, and rewiring, concepts that use components as singular objects—motherboard, power source, or processor—ready for assemblage. The term *hardweriando* also shows the influence of hip-hop rhyming on attitudes about technology, as skillful users appropriate the activity to other forms of being (such as *habaneando*—being in the city). Specialists with access to a broadband connection and the ability to download entertainment (television shows, movies, or music), software, or sensitive data from state networks and the Internet create new possibilities for the circulation of content and goods among friends, among enemies, or in the barely visible consumer market. The state's selected practitioners can also travel in real personal zones forbidden by that very state, carrying contraband to satisfy popular demand for the products of advanced technology. Nonetheless, graduates still carry out the state's plan for technological literacy across the island; only a small percentage has jumped ship to swim in more lucrative private waters. Such an outcome ironically appears to demonstrate the resilience of Cuban socialism to market forces against which the state guards so vigilantly. But the same outcome may also serve as vindication for the government's contention that its restrictive actions are necessary for the pursuit of social aims for technological development.

The transformation of the radar base into UCI stands in contrast to the U.S. national security response to the terrorist attack on the World Trade Center towers. At a time of terror wars and "axes of evil," the inauguration of

UCI stood for the creation of a new economic, social, and ideological infrastructure that carried a risk of empowering political opposition and of major security lapses. Despite increased aggression by the George W. Bush administration (often delivered by Jonathan D. Farrar, the administration's appointed representative in Havana) and the Cuban government's crackdown on independent journalists in 2003, UCI graduated its first two classes by 2007.[7] The governing bodies of an incipient post-Castro society have set a delicate balance between shoring up the revolutionary project and undermining its system of power. Presented with a cornucopia of digital options, Cuba's bold, astute, and ambitious students have so far made the gamble worthwhile—as when three UCI students won top international research awards from the Institute of Electrical and Electronics Engineers (IEEE) in October 2007.[8]

The powerful convergence of forces—media, knowledge, and history—at the beginning of the twenty-first century requires evaluation of individual and social experience in the increasingly complex context of media networks, digital tools, political aspirations, and personal practices in a variety of social and political settings. In *Digital Dilemmas*, I reflect on the implications of technology for the body politic and for the individual, as seen through the lens of a society that grapples with powerful forces in bold experiments potentially illuminating alternative possibilities for media and society everywhere.

Cuba's digital landscape can be viewed as overlapping zones of expression and experience made prominent by living and working with digital technologies and with constraints upon these technologies. The zones form a complex structure involving individuals, commerce, and the state. The resulting geography reveals the movement of capital, the power of stakeholders, and the spaces of intimacy. It is a map of interrelated consciousness, of a digital culture that depends, perhaps more than in many other developing economies, on local histories and characteristics, and that responds to transnational exchanges and relays. Cuba amply demonstrates how people use digital technology to sense the world, build creative social experiences that reshape virtual contours, and produce new infrastructures.

Although opposing ideologies prescribe much of what can be said about Cuba, I attempt in *Digital Dilemmas* to strike a balance. In it, I do not fantasize about the potential of electronic technology to overthrow the Castro regime, nor do I celebrate technological invention as a tool of externally contrived advancement or development, uprooted from history or location. Instead,

I examine digital technology as based on a set of social and technological relations—among government, institutions, and individuals—that affect the way we inhabit the world. I make clear that innovation, appropriation, and invention respond to past and present neocolonial structures, social needs, elusive political utopias, and globalization.

In chapter I, I plot Cuba's uneven technological development, both in industry and media, and the historical relationships that grew up around cybernetics. A genealogy of the infrastructures of commercial radio and television in prerevolutionary Cuba (infrastructures connected first to U.S. media and later to Mexican interests) reveals traces interrelated with the nationalized media industries after 1959, when the ideological paradigm redirected media practices from commercial to state-centered. In this survey of the infrastructures, I show that technology and the way it contributes to the social imagination is best understood as acting through the geopolitical location of power relations, since frameworks of regulation and cultural identification exert influence at the global, regional, and national levels. Staging such connections, I seek in this chapter to reaffirm how Cuba, and particularly its political culture, can be considered outside the outdated but persistent binary thinking that defines the island in terms of Cold War geopolitics and concepts of democracy. The example of UCI underscores this last point: Cold War remnants have been repurposed for their strategic potential in a new century; Soviet technological investment, whether in the form of a radio electronic base or of Cuban investment for developing a computer industry, brings together the residue of technological forces. But observers, too, must go beyond the entrenched logic and polarizing views of the twentieth century; approaches to digital technology in Cuba invite a reappraisal of political dynamics and particularly of the meaning of democracy.

Significance of the Cuban Case

Cubans often argue defensively that their country, in its shortcomings and pitfalls, resembles other less-than-affluent countries. Yet Cuba is remarkable in many ways, and it offers a case study in how new private and public selves, aided by digital media, can evolve from the ruins of both capitalist and socialist schemes.

After 1989, as the Soviet Union crumbled, considerable skepticism arose about the survival of Cuba's revolutionary socialist project. Almost two decades later, economist Bert Hoffman found that "Cuba poses the question of the relationship between economic and political change in an exceptional way."[9] Given the experience of other socialist countries, where governments fell as they opened to market economies, Cuba indeed stands out. Hoffman's explanation is that national independence "in the face of an overwhelming hegemonic power is the trump card not of the opposition but of the socialist government."[10] The idea of national autonomy partly drives the ideology of the Cuban political regime; this was especially só as it helped develop the necessary economic conditions and political leverage to survive the shocks of the 1990s. In a 1993 interview granted to Italy's *La Stampa*, Fidel Castro considered what the crumbling of the Soviet bloc meant for Cuba: "The [U.S.] embargo is still in force, but the support is gone! . . . Nevertheless, we have never doubted that we should follow our own path. We have proved that we are not a satellite, but a star that shines thanks to its own energy."[11] This recourse to national pride, even while scarcity and uncertainty whittled away at some of the prized achievements of Cuban socialism, has proven effective at fueling resilience. But conversely it expands the incongruence between lived experience and the leadership's heroic rhetoric. As an impetuous young Cuban woman articulates in Aram Vidal Alejandro's documentary *De generación* (2006), neither capitalism nor socialism seems to hold any great promise for her generation. Disenchantment with ideology may lead to lucid solutions or it may lead to a revaluation of the notions of revolution and socialism in a context no longer defined by oppositional Cold War debates.

Numerous factors define Cuba's unique contours. An intellectual and political legacy of decolonization before and after the 1959 revolution informs the nationalist project. As socialist experiment, it has broken with Stalinist Marxist doctrine to present an alternative paradigm of governance in the Caribbean. It represents a notion of democracy found problematic by many holding Western views, but one that has created greater levels of social equality than has any other economic approach in Latin America. This has been so even though, for more than four decades, under the charismatic paternalism of Fidel Castro, Cuba also endured the longest economic embargo against any nation in history.

The story of Cuba's digital dilemmas began during the 1990s, against the background of three interrelated historical strands. All three shaped Cuban culture around information technologies: the catastrophic economic downturn, a time of peacetime struggle (named euphemistically by the Cuban government the "Special Period in Times of Peace") that created conditions of special significance for the appropriation and direction of technological development; a well-established "embargo culture" that has long contributed important ideas and tensions to Cuba's relation to the United States and the Cold War; and a renewal of socialism intended to generate new social meanings absorbed, distributed, and explored by and with digital media. Faced with the sudden end of Russian subsidies and support, Cuba's response in the Special Period drew on digital technology to help plot its survival course by targeting industries to exploit. The nature of that response led Cuba into political and cultural dilemmas. Although the government has invested heavily in updating telecommunications infrastructure, the official line on open Internet access reverts to limiting the space of expression to a small sphere of participants, fomenting discord rather than acceptance.

The issue is more complex than crude censorship. The aforementioned investment in the development of Internet technology, practitioners, and participation in world forums for Internet development means that the new contradictions are defining policies and uses of the technology. The initial steps taken by Cuba to connect to the Internet came at a critical time of turmoil concurrent with the worst economic and political crisis since the revolution. As Cuba debated nationalist positions during the Special Period, the state had carefully to acknowledge that the Internet should constitute a high priority in the shaping of the country's future. In remarks at a UNESCO conference in 1999, Fidel Castro characterized the Internet as part of a larger strategy to benefit Cuba. "Internet? Yes, we can use it—to tell the 80 percent of Americans online that they have to stop and realize that Earth is on the edge of an abyss. . . . In the revolution we used our loudspeakers as much as our weapons."[12] The contrast raises interesting questions about political culture and the nature of a new culture of democracy.

Technology, Development Legacies, and Media Studies

A study of the adoption and dispersal of digital media technologies must consider the importance of the intellectual frameworks that define technological development and the policies that pertain to it. Technological development is embedded in systems of knowledge and specific historical, cultural, and political processes. Scholars such as Armand Mattelart have identified the historical ideas that saw in worldwide interconnection the realization of a rationalist project: "From road and rail to information highways," Mattelart argues, "this belief has been revived with each technological generation, yet networks have never ceased to be at the center of struggles for control of the world."[13] In the battle against world communism and in programs of development organized by the global North for the global South, communication became synonymous with modernization. Development agendas prominent after World War II positioned modern technology as a solution to all manner of social and economic problems. Importing technology and know-how, it was assumed, would produce parity or, at the very least, alleviate the harshness of poverty. In 1995, half a century after the introduction of *development* as a cultural system to remedy the world's inequalities, Colombian sociologist Arturo Escobar presented a study that began to question this "dream of development" as posited and overwhelmingly accepted by governments in both North and South. Escobar found that, on the contrary, "the discourse and strategy of development produced its opposite: massive underdevelopment and impoverishment, untold exploitation and oppression."[14] Development as a discourse of power—of the North over the South—postulated a move toward high levels of industrialization, technical capacity, and growth of material production for areas of the world deemed backward and poor; in the view of such development schemes, technology was meant to jump-start poorer nations.

As a "satellite" member of the former Soviet Union, Cuba found its technological development influenced equally by Soviet development policies, by command economy strategies, and by a critique of modernity. In this way, technology became imbued with utopian properties, but also formed a mode of resistance to the economic model of capitalism. "By questioning the economic and international communication order," Mattelart proposes, "the new historical subject [in the 1970s] constituted by the third world revealed the numerous manifestations of unequal exchange."[15] Worldwide interconnectivity seen, as in Cuba, in light of a complex historical lineage of discourses, government policies, agreements, and systems injects media technologies with more deliberate and wider-reaching political and social intent than when interconnectivity is seen mainly as a vehicle for development. Media technology as a prioritized subject for national governments and commercial institutions as they guide and define policies, regulation, and economic viability becomes an important element for the governance of populations—for what Michel Foucault has called "governmentality."[16]

Too often, studies about technological development in less affluent nations take a functionalist perspective, arguing that technology, as a tool of development, would end inefficiency and food shortages, stimulate production, and diminish poverty. Technology thus appears as an inevitable agent of so-called progress. This perspective obscures the social needs, political aspirations, and economic imperatives that demand much more tailored, multifaceted development. In his 1974 study of television as a cultural technology, British cultural theorist Raymond Williams provides useful direction and questions about the evolution of technologies as social forms. A demonstrated social need, he contends, does not necessarily find or produce the right technology, because such technology does not necessarily exist within the realm of conditions or knowledge required for its production: "The key question, about technological response to a need, is less a question about the need itself than about its place in an existing social formation."[17] The social formation corresponds to the priorities of dominant groups and social interests; thus, to ask how institutions and individuals have used and responded to networked computing and other digital forms of media at a critical period of transition in Cuba can reveal key relations among social forces. On a larger scale, the interaction of social formations creates interdependent conditions such as economic crisis, political change, and the intensification of external global forces; together, these conditions cycle back on social formations, helping to determine the practical and ideological needs and priorities that bring about particular forms of technology. Williams's perspective frees the analysis of media technologies from the assumption that a technology should acquire an essential, natural, or ideal form; instead, such a perspective assists in understanding technological development as idiosyncratic, its evolution and appropriation occurring as a result of specific historical forces and geopolitical location.

Other postulates for technological development privilege dominant economic players. In the case of Cuba, this dominance is seen in the role of North American interests in technological innovation, which historically regard Latin America as a growth market for the computer industry or as a source of cheap labor for producing or recycling electronic goods; the continuance of such scenarios relies on a system of global exchange that perpetuates unequal power relations. Studies that deliver paradigms of dependence provide a glimpse of the unequal global flows of technology, but do not perform in-depth analysis of how advanced technologies come to shape national policies, or become a driving force behind informal, even illicit, arrangements, such as piracy, that influence formal governance practices, or become new organizational paradigms.

Steeped in the language of modernity, projects of technological development proclaim prosperity and wellbeing, and embrace misleading prophecies of a resultant peaceful and democratic world. All nations possess histories of technological appropriation that reveal scientific and political priorities, social attitudes, and economic opportunity and failure; these contribute to the diverse ways that people and nations experience technology. Yet utopian visions of technology exert tremendous power in the commercial, military, and social aspects of the Internet and deserve particular scrutiny given the existence of wide social inequalities. The new millennium did not find the entire planet connected, as Vint Cerf had once predicted, but there is a rush in developing nations to find innovative ways of providing connectivity, telephone lines, cell phones, and computers. Only recently has this drive turned from improving connection in dominant nations to advancing capacity in the poorer, producing countries.

Utopian visions of technology divert attention from concrete infrastructures and represent a biased discourse about digital media networks (a discourse heard in elite circles around the world) that tends to project what occurs in the United States or Europe onto digital development everywhere else.[18] This is true even of well-intentioned analyses of the growth, development, and uses of the Internet. Not all national and international governing bodies agree on policy, regulation, or the path of future development of the Internet. Not all users work, play, create, or communicate under similar cultural equations or economic circumstances. The analytical gap between tendentious utopian thought and carefully examined social realities allows the development of the Internet in Latin America to be seen as a matter of advancing "free commerce" and "development" when in fact different political paradigms are actually bringing about, in Latin American nations, alternative needs and strategies for the development of technology.

In the case of Cuba, state-centered control emphasizes a social characteristic and purpose defined by the political, economic, and social transformation that began in the Special Period. The investment in high-tech education evident at UCI shows an interest in creating producers of multiple and unforeseen systems and contents. These new Web participants, like their counterparts in other locations, will, according to Tim Berners-Lee, director of the World Wide Web Consortium, "produce environments in which our

Gramley Library
Salem College
Winston-Salem. NC 27108

students and their students will be doing things . . . we cannot imagine."[19] Further, as technology analyst Nicholas Carr maintains, hardware, unlike software, has the potential to "produce power over our intellectual life and the life of the mind."[20] The ecology growing up around digital technology in places like Cuba offers a much richer source of study than do national contexts that automatically confer superiority on more commercially and speedily propagated models.

In Cuba, the political and cultural debate surrounding the Internet and related new media focuses on the perceived potential for economic and cultural development, for a greater level of global democracy, and for decentralizing hierarchies of expression; indeed, popular debates decry limited access to information networks. Cuba's historical relationship with the United States was decisive in promoting technological development earlier than in other Latin American countries, albeit through a dependent model; the ongoing U.S. economic embargo since 1961, however, contributes to a near-total social, political, and cultural isolation that has profoundly hindered Cuba's technical advancement. U.S. policy has also restricted other countries' trade with Cuba, as was made evident in the Helms-Burton Act of 1996; as a result, the island suffers an information blockade that motivates official and unofficial uses of the Internet to bypass the constraints. The Internet in Cuba brings benefits to the government like such circumvention of sanctions, but it also brings a considerable measure of political friction, defying stereotypical images of a repressed populace. However, the government determines and manages system capacity through centralized access, raising troubling issues of personal freedom.

Any view that the Internet anywhere is control-free is a fantasy, as media scholar Wendy Chun reminds us in her book *Control and Freedom.* The fantasy of such freedom nevertheless helps to shape the development process.[21] This is true despite increasing controls on Internet infrastructures throughout the world, heightened commercialization, and increasing regulatory pressures that run contrary to the notion of worldwide connectivity, presumed to require decentralization and openness.

In chapter 2, I analyze Cuban political culture and social imagination, examining how the revolutionary–nationalist project and ideology have shaped approaches to culture and political participation. In this chapter, I argue that Cuba's state-centered democratic principles (equality, community, solidarity) underlie the centralized organization of access to the Internet.

Cuba's connection to the Internet follows the model of the early years of development of ARPANET (eventually Internet). In those years, access was primitively limited to a community of scientific and academic users and was basically research oriented; it was not until the Internet became a proven commercial outlet that access became more widespread. The question thus arises whether Cuba aims for national connectivity and, if so, whether it can achieve this without recourse to commerce. Cuba's experience in this regard helps us explore the limits and possibilities of centralized planning, the nature of democracy in communication, and the need to construct viable social avenues for new developments in technology.

At the time of this writing, approximately 1.4 million researchers, professionals, and artists, out of slightly over eleven million Cubans, are officially counted as Internet users.[22] Although representing still a small percentage of the nation's population, this figure represents an increase of 865,000 users since the year 2003. It is important to bear in mind the context: in Cuba, even the minimal act of browsing on the Web is limited and requires separate security clearance. Personal access is routed through official institutions such as government entities, approved economic ventures, and cultural institutions. At the same time, in 2009 the government promised to continue increasing access and liberalizing controls as it expanded legal mechanisms to create greater access while maintaining national security.

The charged political atmosphere generated by the U.S. embargo and ongoing aggression poses a challenge to an adequate understanding of the cultural and political investment in the Internet in Cuba. Popular reports in the Western press decry the heavy hand of state restrictions, violations of human rights, and lack of individual access to the Internet. Yet confining analysis to totalitarian Cuban practices obscures the tensions generated by phenomenal changes in the social fabric. Censorship is real, but the typical discourse about limited access in Cuba tends to reduce the individual to a consumer free or not free to consume information, ideas, and goods. An enlarged view of an individual's role in society does not nullify the debate, but it leads to larger questions. How can the Cuban state continue to exercise its historic soft power through policies of generous social investment while it also actively restricts not only Internet use, but also the mobility of citizens, the press, and oppositional parties? To what extent are claims of self-determination expressed in the policies of Internet development? Do the benefits of technological advancement evident in the Internet outweigh calls for openness and political plurality espoused by both supportive and dissenting groups? And, finally, how important is the expression of resistance to what are perceived as normal paths of technological development? Responses to these political and human predicaments are not simple. The tensions produced in encounters between people and their governing structures create social and political identities, identities that are now mediated by digital tools. Examining these tools, their uses and users, can shed light on political and social dimensions.

Both government and individual users understand that the technology presents an unstoppable social force with a potential yet to be fully realized. While the groundwork is being laid for broader (and faster) access, the current restrictions have created an underground market of pirated connections leading the government into the unsavory business of cracking down on "illegal users." Some journalists claim that an illegal connection to the Internet in Cuba is easily attainable.[23] The topic, though, remains veiled in taboo because of the restrictions, official penalties, economic limitations, lack of information, and negative external press coverage that continues to view Cuba through myopic Cold War spectacles. Still, Cuban officials willingly provide information about their network architecture and policies, as seen, for example, in reports published over the years and by international press organizations in the United States.

The problem remains one of perspective, for Cuba's strategy seems doomed to be forever examined mainly as a policy of exclusion, a perspective driven by superficial correlation of freedom with connectivity. For instance, an article by Patrick Symmes in the February 1998 issue of *Wired* focused on censorship and on the backwardness of the Cuban system, yet provided a level of detail and sources that suggested the reporter had broad access for his investigation. Under the guise of hacker solidarity, the author mixed fact and fiction in an attempt to discredit the very sources that helped him. His perspective also betrayed a prejudice against a system that operated differently than the one in which he usually participated.

Symmes argues, "If the Internet is ever allowed to flourish on the island, it should foster a decentralized flow of information that would help democratize the centrally planned, closely controlled society."[24] According to Symmes's argument, then, a decentralized flow of information is naturally conducive to democracy; this is true, given the instrumental definition that the latter term has acquired. However, decentralization does not guarantee the free flow and exchange of information, or ensure expression by citizens of their personal views. Decentralizing the provision of technologies for communication would certainly produce a different relationship between individual citizens and the Cuban State, and that shift could be beneficial in producing new types of expressive potential. However, democratic societies do not rest on the decentralization of technology, and, though a centralized system is cumbersome, restrictive, and inefficient in most instances, global media conglomerates are on the rise: centralized power of communications exists also in the hands of private, mobile enterprises. Big brother watches and listens in societies of many different political stripes.[25]

Just as the historical and political context guides technological development, the creative and personal expression of individuals in society and in their government policies provides important insight into technological appropriation. Personal expression helps to mold the relationships among human experience, everyday life, and mechanisms of governance. Since the mid-1990s, a handful of official Cuban entities like InfoMed (the medical network) and Cubaweb (the tourist network) have produced virtual identities for the Cuban government through expert but simple graphical Web interfaces. At that time, these efforts, encoded in hypertext structure, announced enthusiastically that the Cuban nation was undoubtedly a participant in the development of digital media. Monitoring how the Cuban government and Cubans on and off the island have constructed national, oppositional, intimate, and artistic identities on the Web—in blogs, social networks, digital art, and cinema—and how they migrate to a variety of screens across the globe is necessary for a full understanding of personal and political issues.

The role of media in shaping public discourse in Cuba has been well documented by others. In prerevolutionary Cuba, radio, film, and television were key to developing a tourist consumer economy and social, personal transactions with American culture.[26] The artist and the entrepreneur were crucial in bringing technology into the society, and this became manifest again during the Special Period, when, amid extreme scarcity, digital tools began to be made available sporadically and added to the experience of everyday life. Films and television shows, going beyond entertainment and forms of cultural mediation, are a constant reminder that consumption is a dynamic process of interactions and sometime secret practices. After 2000, television shows on Cubavision and Tele Rebelde, the Cuban national networks, began to insert the use of the Internet into programs (like the political talk show

Mesa Redonda) even while the medium's general use by the population was still off in the future.

Strategies of expression on the Internet extend arenas of argument and confrontation. From early in Cuba's connection to the Web, the conflict between Cuba and Miami featured on competing domains; for instance, Cubaweb.cu, hosted in Cuba, provides basic tourist information and links, and Cubaweb.com from Miami was a clearinghouse of information about doing business in a post-Castro Cuba, until going off-line in 1998. The intense political and ideological dynamic between Cuba and its largest and closest exile community has resolved, that is, in favor of the nation-state at least at the level of domain name. Mapping the competition for identity expressed through technological means can help to illuminate significant power relations as well as give direction to more comprehensive surveys.

Locating Technology in Scarcity

Historical and cultural specificity notably marks the process through which technology emerges as a cultural and political force. The Special Period finally gave the lie to official state rhetoric since the 1960s that requisite sacrifices by Cuban citizens were only temporary. Lasting throughout the 1990s and into the early 2000s, the Special Period was characterized by varying levels of scarcity and uncertainty, as well as by continuing familiar international acts of aggression like the tightening of the U.S. embargo (in place since 1961). The dismantling of Soviet communism signaled the forthcoming end of the Cold War, with its binary political framing of international relations for half a century. Eastern European, Balkan, even Soviet states moved decidedly away from communist-style regimes, embarking on a path toward post-socialist market cultures, albeit with trepidation on the part of governments and individuals about prospects in the twenty-first century. Despite these momentous transformations, Cuba–United States diplomatic relations remained intractable, save for the work of activists, academics, and family members of all political persuasions and on every side of the conflict, who were ready to expand any opening in the stalemate. The entrenched conflict, which remains locked into the language, culture, and politics of the Cold War, considerably exacerbated conditions of scarcity in Cuba during the 1990s.

The Special Period resulted from immediate repercussions of the loss of trade preferences and economic backing from the former Soviet Union. These losses, occurring simultaneously with the spread of transnational capital and global markets, along with an intensification of the U.S. embargo, brought utter devastation to Cuba in the early 1990s. While the circulation of the U.S. dollar had been made illegal since the 1959, and the need for hard currency in the ensuing decades mitigated by preferential trade with the Council for Mutual Economic Assistance (CMEA), the government authorized its use in 1993 (and ended its circulation in 2004) in order to inject hard currency into a failing economy. In *Cuban Currency: The Dollar and the 'Special Period' Fiction*, Esther Whitfield has argued that the depenalization of the U.S. dollar "was the farthest reaching reform measure introduced in the special period."[27] The search for dollars transformed attitudes toward capital and its social impact, as well as its use as a central theme in much contemporary popular culture. Reforms also altered the path of economic development by creating a new plan for foreign investment, and passed a series of legal and economic reforms to promote economic growth through trade agreements with countries outside Eastern Europe. In his July 26, 1993, address Castro candidly expressed both misgivings and resolve: "Who would have thought that we, so doctrinaire, we who fought foreign investment, would one day view foreign investment as an urgent need?"[28] Gasoline, food, and electricity were rationed. Even with these measures, food supplies dwindled, and industry and transportation came nearly to a standstill.

What occurred in Cuba was fundamentally different from economic decline in other underdeveloped countries. The grim situation was not relegated to a portion of the population; it affected everyone, and influenced the system of governance. The new shortages compounded old problems with devastating impact. Citizens were allowed to create subsistence ventures like small home restaurants. Energy conservation, longer lines for goods and services, and more sacrifices on the part of the general population were key to surviving the hardships.

The state relied more than ever on socially oriented production such as medical research to generate *divisas* (hard currency). Individuals craved more entertainment at home to offset the darkness of city streets. The need for temporary adoption of economic and political measures of the Special Period loomed in the background of a new lexicon of products, markets, and characteristics; it shaped the adoption of Internet technology by Cuba in intriguing and controversial ways.

The scale of collapse and uncertainty in the Special Period led official state institutions to define the legal parameters of the Internet as part of the state's survival strategy. The new model retained centralized access but introduced decentralized relays of information, aligned with Cuba's new imperative to form closer economic links with other nations. The Internet became a new means of circumventing sanctions in a time of persistent shortages and provided possibilities for national self-determination and advancement. The state officially justified its nationalist-protectionist slant in its descriptions of the Internet, citing the continued assault, literal and figurative, by the anti-Cuba lobby in the U.S. Congress and the ever-present economic embargo.

The extent of material scarcity placed technological investment within a system of ranked priorities. This was especially true in the early 1990s, when prolonged shortages, whether of food or electricity, produced unpredictable responses from the population. Scarcity itself was, although experienced by everyone, not experienced equally, since it varied with access to hard currency; some Cubans could afford the purchase of staple goods, while others had to depend on rations. Shortages only added to the burden of problems generated by inefficiencies or bureaucratic malfunctions that predated the Special Period. After all, in an environment with centrally directed policy, costly technological investment must be sporadic and geared toward catching up with the fast pace of innovation; technology is both a luxury and a necessity, and shoring up the national infrastructure must be prioritized to provide basic services. Cuban citizens had—and still have—limited disposable income to invest in luxury items like computers and cell phones. Over the long decade of the 1990s, computers became necessary in medical and educational institutions, cultural agencies, hotels, research centers, and some private homes. As a result of international donations and official purchases, they formed a nascent computer user community within the networked global infrastructure. Infrastructural limitations, electric and economic, as well as concerns about national security drove the Cuban leadership to establish prohibitions on the purchase of electronic components.

Indeed, scarcity formed the justification, though not a convincing explanation, to restrictions on the purchase of computers, cell phones, DVD players, and other items. When restrictions were lifted in 2008 (under Raúl Castro), droves of consumers rushed to designated retail outlets with cash in hand. The new customers obviously deemed their purchases essential, since their retail preferences could not be explained by theories of disposable income while difficult conditions still marked their daily lives.

Infrastructural limitations are part and parcel of any developing nation, but Cubans and the Cuban state had (and have) also to contend with premiums charged by third-party suppliers and the difficult access to goods resulting from the U.S. embargo. The resulting restrictions by the state on Cubans have increased the tension inherent in choices of direction for digital technology. Raúl Castro's move to remove "unnecessary" prohibitions early in his government may have begun an experiment testing Cuba's socialist strategies and the country's democratic parameters.

Economic Restructuring

Changes in economic policy, including new openness toward foreign investment, coincide with the development of the Cuban Internet infrastructure. A process of economic "rectification" beginning in 1986 changed the nation's economic course and intensified its goals. The demise of the former Soviet trading bloc forced Cuba to focus on foreign exchange. Until then, the country had relied on credits from Soviet-bloc partners that allowed the Cuban government to maintain unrealistically low prices for utilities, rents, and telephones and to receive preferential pricing for sugar and other products. Exports went primarily to Soviet-bloc countries, with food, industrial supplies, and oil imported from the Soviets. In 1986, citing poor economic conditions, Cuba suspended foreign debt payments to the USSR, and has since received few loans; only in the mid-2000s has investment from Russia begun again. Given Cuba's substantial outstanding debt to Russia, the two nations have signed several agreements that use debt repayment as a point of negotiation.

In chapter 3, I cover how tourism and social ideology form concrete expressions of the digital arising from Cuba's negotiation of state and private enterprise. Cuba responded to its debt crisis with a redoubling of efforts to develop tourism, and done so in a manner that has made that industry a site of advanced information technology. I also consider possible connections between earlier developments in technology and new investments in technological artifacts like the Internet. Centralized control of digital education has characterized the state's strategic approach during the post-Soviet period of transformation and economic and political reforms. Although joint ventures have been permitted since 1982, for many years a foreign partner could not hold more than 49 percent of controlling interest. As amended in 1992, the Cuban constitution recognized a variety of property relations, including foreign investments, Cuban corporations, and joint ventures; in 1995, the foreign investment law was amended to permit foreign firms to hold up to 100 percent ownership of a company in certain designated and prioritized sectors of the economy. The companies are guaranteed that they can repatriate profits in hard currency. Foreign investors may also acquire and develop real estate, but not in the name of Cuban nationals.[29] Foreign investment is not permitted in the areas of health, education, and the armed forces. The strategy has paid off, with the number of companies investing in Cuba increasing every year. In December 1999, the chief economic ministers reported that Cuba's domestic product grew by 6.2 percent, the second highest rate since before the catastrophic early 1990s.[30] The benefits of economic growth and new partnerships, however, have brought new challenges for Cuban citizens, as the prices of previously subsidized services like utilities and telephone have increased to reflect real costs. Economic growth since 1999 has fluctuated between 3 and 5 percent, consistent with the rate in other Latin America countries.[31]

Beginning in 2000, Venezuela surpassed Spain to become Cuba's largest economic partner, as President Hugo Chavez and Fidel Castro signed a series of economic agreements designed to foster cooperation between the two nations. The agreements would be extended to include Bolivia later in 2005, following the election of Evo Morales as president. Under the leadership of Brazilian president Lula da Silva, the three countries crafted the Bolivarian Alliance for the Americas (ALBA), a network of trade focused on the southern hemisphere. Indeed, Cuban economists are engaged in a dynamic process of transforming the economy with multination partnerships.[32] By 2007, Venezuela had become the largest exporter to Cuba (28.1 percent), followed respectively by China (12.7), Spain (9.9 percent), Canada (5.6 percent), the United States (4.9 percent), and Brazil (4.6 percent).[33] In the tourism sector alone, "Cuba holds an average of 80 percent of assets."[34] U.S. investment in Cuba is made possible under a revision to the U.S. embargo—the Trade Sanctions Reform and Export Enhancement Act of 2000—legalizing the sale of medicine and food to Cuba for humanitarian reasons. Cuba is not, however, extended credit, and must pay for these goods in hard currency.[35]

In 1993, the government's drastic option of adopting a two-currency system saw the circulation of the Cuban peso alongside that of the U.S. dollar. This desperate measure helped rebuild the value of the domestic currency and the economy, while it figured symbolically as a betrayal of the leadership's old politics. By 2004, the U.S. dollar was replaced by the Cuban Convertible

Peso (CUC), its conversion mandatory for visitors in Cuba. The dual monetary economy operates in the pricing of services and goods available to the Cuban population. Some telephone lines, satellite television services, and Internet accounts are priced only in CUC. This system undermines the Cuban peso, since most desirable goods and services can be obtained only with CUC. The value of the peso is further weakened by a robust black market—where goods are available for hard and Cuban currency—and inflated consumer prices driven by a tourist economy and the U.S. embargo.

By the late 1990s, Cuba's economy became further embedded in the global commodities market as Cuba created free-trade zones to increase and diversify the nature of foreign investment on the island.[36] These trade zones, unlike other foreign partnerships, remain under the control of the foreign investor, with Cuba providing a low-cost and skilled labor force. The emphasis is on increasing production, exports, and domestic jobs while trying to eke out a competitive space against the free-trade zones already operating in the Caribbean and Latin America.[37] This economic approach is not without its dangers, since the Cuban labor unions stand to lose bargaining power and, ironically, may not be able to rely on the state for support.

In 1997, the Fidel Castro government instituted taxation on citizens and businesses for the first time, with higher tax brackets for the latter. According to the government, these measures were necessary to prevent the "illicit enrichment" of those whose private commercial enterprises might allow them to earn hard currency and amass small fortunes.[38] In other words, the state hoped taxation would prevent the re-creation of class divisions that the revolution fought to liquidate. However, disparities in income levels increased, the result of unequal access to dollars and remittances arriving from family members abroad. As sociologist Susan Eckstein observes, "Whereas in the predollarized economy the ratio between the highest and lowest salary had been five to one, as of the 1990s, some Cubans attained several hundred times more income than others."[39] Here the Cuban state demonstrates an ideological principle disassociated from reality, since the divide has become palpable.

To maintain the perception of political consistency, free-trade zones, tax laws, tourism, and other efforts to win foreign investment have become politically defined as necessary for the survival of the Cuban Revolution. The predictable downside of economic disparity for the population has made prostitution more visible and a recurrent survival strategy, and fostered economic migration and a demonstrable growth of illegal markets; affecting black Cubans more significantly than whites, the shocking economic situation brought the issue of racism again to the foreground. According to the revolutionary government, the negative effects were unavoidable to maintain the advances gained since 1959. Since Fidel Castro turned over the reigns of governance to his brother Raul in 2007, the most aggressive reforms continue to be economic.

The bleak economic situation of the Special Period led a new wave of Cubans into exile in the early 1990s, exacting an emotional toll on families, who nevertheless found necessary the contributions of remittances from their members living and earning abroad. Facility of communication with loved ones abroad remained a crucial issue for many individuals. In addition, the severity of the economic crisis and the surrealism of survival practices created by it contributed to a series of public protests (known as *habanazo*), which opened the way for the *balsero* (rafter) crisis in 1994.[40] The disturbances indicated that there was a limit to how much the population was willing to sacrifice for an unspecified time and without concrete results. It became necessary then for Fidel Castro to reinforce his longstanding influence with the people of Cuba. In the United States, the *balsero* crisis led to a change in the immigration status of Cubans and the implementation of a policy colloquially known as "dry foot, wet foot." This policy holds that a Cuban refugee who lands on U.S. soil by any means is eligible to apply for political asylum within a year, while those refugees picked up at sea are repatriated to Cuba. The policy would be duly tested in 2000 during a binational custody drama, the Elián Gonzalez case (discussed here in chapter 5).[41] This change in immigration policy conditioned expectations about the possibility of leaving the country, and also increased the remittances entering the Cuban economy from family members outside the country. By 1998, remittances in one year had reached $800 million dollars. However, viewing the remittance allowance to Cuban families in Cuba as a way to prop up the Castro regime, the George W. Bush administration reduced the monthly remittance limit. The economic and emotional value of family remittances was taken up again in the 2008 U.S. presidential campaign by Barack Obama, who subsequently made good on his promise to, once in office, lift restrictions on family visits and on the amount of family remittances to Cuban nationals.

The socially negative consequences of post-Soviet economic changes presented serious concerns for the Cuban regime, especially as it implemented them while investing in Internet infrastructure. The heightened tensions of the 1990s ensured politicization of the governance of the network, which was formed under a grouping of government ministries.[42] To avoid wholly private enterprise as an engine of economic gains, the state would turn only to socially oriented information networks and to tourism. The calculation of social gains and losses weighed with economic benefits did lead Cuba out of the Special Period, although problems with shortages have continued, and the quality of life remains precarious for the majority of the population.

The process of rebuilding involved not only infrastructure but also material structures to help restore Havana and the country for tourism and a new business culture. By 2007, the impact of foreign investment, especially in tourism, had become visible in the form of new hotels and continued restoration of the old city center in Havana, including the renovation of the historic chamber of commerce, to make room for the modern offices of foreign companies. But joint ventures brought new problems in construction and urban planning, producing what urban planner Mario Coyula regrets are "disruptive new buildings that neither fit the city's valuable urban context nor incorporate good contemporary architecture."[43] Coyula, the director of the Group for the Integrated Development of Havana, seeks to build different forms of productive international partnerships, such as the Neighborhood Transformation Workshops to improve "living conditions in historically dilapidated districts . . . and deal with rehabilitation of substandard housing, health and environmental campaigns, cultural expressions, assessment of needs, and leadership training."[44] The group aims to break down large metropolitan problems into manageable tasks, while rolling back setbacks driven by technocratic policies that, since the mid-1960s, had turned against architecture as an integrated social endeavor.[45] Coyula's approach to sustainable architectural projects, it may be imagined, might provide a model for future, less centralized, management of digital Cuban sites and networks.

By creating job opportunities through foreign enterprise—albeit at the cost of economic ills, class differentiation, and corruption—the Cuban state appears to provide the necessary conditions for survival of the population, as well as the means to move out of the pervasive Cuban economic crisis. By continuing to pursue a socialist agenda, the state also maintains a form of democracy. Despite the unrelenting attacks from the United States, it still attempts to enact principles of equality through complicated legal structures.[46] The Cuban government's efforts to balance past and present difficulties against the successes of the revolution create continuity and maintain relative social order. They have also created a climate likely to favor further investment in digital technology for social as well and economic purposes as the state responds to internal as well as external concerns.

Raúl Castro's economic reforms, introduced early in 2008, foster the development of a domestic consumer market. Allowing Cubans to be guests in Cuban hotels—for the first time since the early 1990s—to purchase the tools of a networked and wireless society, and to expand their earning potential aligns with the movement of consumers who, as Jorge Dominguez observed in 1993, were "already engaged in a transition to a market economy, albeit one that remains illegal to a substantial extent."[47] All of the reforms, along with creative and emergent forms of criminality, provide juicy content for police dramas on local television, dramas that moralize about the evils of corruption and illicit enrichment. Personal restrictions may have been lifted, but tourism and social information networks remain important economic drivers, each politically quite distinct from the other. Keeping the enterprise of social information networks ahead of private ones defines the political economy of the Cuban nation to date, a political economy to which its government still seems committed.

Embargo Culture

Sanctions by the United States against the government of Fidel Castro began in 1961 and were expanded in 1962 to include all trade with Cuba except unsubsidized sale of food and medicine. The Kennedy administration in 1963 prohibited travel to Cuba by U.S. citizens and made illegal any commercial transaction with Cuba, a policy that has persisted for nearly half a century. Bills introduced in the U.S. Senate to eliminate specific aspects of the policy have made no progress, due to an entrenched ideological position on Cuba through the last ten U.S. administrations.

Economic hardship resulting from strict sanctions and the reactive redirection of the economy to trade with the Soviet Union has affected all aspects of Cuban life and has dictated the way Cubans consume both essential and so-called luxury goods. Life under sanctions has colored the experience of many generations. It has conditioned attitudes toward material goods, ways of living and waiting, and modes of thinking. It creates especially, as Dominguez concludes, the long-term political effect of "the need . . . to place ever more power in the hands of government."[48] Direct pressure on the government adds to this effect: the constant threat of sabotage has produced a psychology tending to reinforce the centrality and power of Fidel Castro's revolutionary leadership. On this reading of the evolution of the centralized character of the Cuban government, Dominguez is persuasive: "The need to mobilize people to work where they were needed so that the country could become economically self-sufficient placed the entire economy and society on quasi–war status . . . the United States did not bring Cuba to its knees; it brought about political centralization in Cuba and alliance with the Soviet Union."[49] U.S. administrations, however, appear blind to such explanations, unable to reflect on the possibility that their forty-plus years of economic embargo of Cuba may have contributed to the very centralization of government that they find so objectionable. Recognition of a pyrrhic strategy would surely lead to its end, but cannot occur while political benefits accrue from blindness, benefits that serve interests of power if not of government.

The strategy of self-discipline and preparedness for potential catastrophe, invasion, or the lifting of the U.S. embargo has created an experience of postponement in daily life and in the actions of a government accustomed to reacting to constraints and shortages. Complete disaster is delayed and pride in genuine national accomplishment often translates into the stubborn hope that better days will come. Such hope is continuously reiterated in the rhetorical guise of staunch nationalism and anti-imperialism (fig. 1). The continued wait for life without restrictions, for the lifting of the embargo, and even for a post-Castro government suspends substantive political and economic processes, forcing decisions instead to approaches to impending decline. A culture of deferral obscures policy failures. Evading the embargo and its consequences becomes part of quotidian existence for Cubans on and off the island, producing stillborn reforms and adherence by the state to a stale rhetoric of revolution that perpetuates a defensive response to accusations of illegitimacy. The April 2008 congress of the Unión de Escritores y Artistas Cubanos (UNEAC) presented an example of this conundrum. Even though artist-delegates to the congress tabled a number of probing questions about institutional reforms, debated the role of the institution in forming open cultural practice, confronted censorship in the media, and so on, their interviews for the national media after the conference only conveyed praise for the Cuban Revolution and revolutionary behavior. Stock answers indicated a reticence about speaking openly or critiquing internal processes.[50] Plain speaking outside formal venues of debate, they seemed to feel, could

——————— I. "Anti-imperialistas," billboard in Havana, Cuba ———————

signal a national lack of will and prompt "triumphalist" moves by the United States. This kind of thinking prevails; a united front persists as a shell of self-protection and pride.

Embargo culture also results in widespread politicization, a process that includes digital technology and its acquisition. The main embargo issue for technological development centers on who owns and controls the infrastructure; it reveals the ideological constraints of infrastructure.

The trade constraints of the embargo have helped to determine the political scenario for the Internet, as well as individual social and cultural responses to the uses of digital technology. The pattern of technological development in Cuba since the demise of the Soviet Union includes uneven but necessary multinational cooperation. As for the rest of Cuba's international business and investment since the 1990s, limited partnerships, insidious opposition, and occasional solidarity come from the United States, Europe, and Latin America. Cuba-friendly nongovernmental organizations (NGOs) lie behind computer donations, and, through USAID, the U.S. government provides economic support for groups that oppose the Cuban government.

Built-in delay applies to economic partnership with groups in the United States who anxiously wait for lifting of the embargo. Publicly traded, the Miami-based Herzfeld Caribbean Basin Investment Fund plans for the post-Castro era by raising capital for eventual investment in Cuba.[51] Closer to the heart of one entrenched conflict over expropriated properties, digital tools developed by Terrafly.com, a private company in Miami, are intended to produce an "interactive archive that would document the current architecture of Havana, but which would also allow users to register claims to their former homes."[52]

In *Digital Dilemmas* I attempt to move away from frustratingly simplistic views about democracy and its relationship to media in Cuba, views long promulgated principally by news media and politicians. This does not mean discounting the weight, pain, and suffering caused by restrictions imposed by the Cuban government. But it does acknowledge that the government, admittedly sometimes in acts of grandiosity, has been compelled to react to external pressures of aggression, financial hardship, political sanctions, and political stalemate, and that the resulting emotional, psychic, and material world is particular to a culture of embargo.

Socialism as "Eternal Ideology" and Essential History

Official political ideology formulated during the Special Period redefined Cuban socialism independent of its Soviet ties. It re-legitimized the revolutionary project and justified the harsh economic measures imposed to salvage it. Early government Internet portals responded similarly as Cuba emerged onto a digital global environment. Touting connectivity for business, medical service networks, tourism, new legal codes, and introductory country information, the new Web presence revealed an independent socialist nation-state. The content reinforced the underlying state network architecture and its modest forms of e-government. Cuban socialism began to look different. The legalization of foreign investment further expanded the new global-outreach model of Cuban socialism—what Cuban cultural critic Desiderio Navarro calls "market socialism"—and exacerbated unintentional divides between foreigner and national, and between technocrat and average citizen. Sustained challenges to state policies from political activists inside and outside Cuba led the state to reaffirm its socialist character through a constitutional amendment in 2002 that declared socialism in Cuba to be irrevocable. Cuba made it official that it would never return to capitalism, and opposed the privatization schemes and market essentialism of neoliberalism.

Although revolutionary Cuba with its single party structure and political leadership appears as a monolithic political project, the Cuban Revolution's character is, and has been, a dynamic process of opening and narrowing political culture. The changes in monetary policy and the mixed capital system characterizing life in the Special Period showed an evolution of political expression: socialism would be rescued from near-oblivion or at least from destruction by the same "dark forces" that had signaled its demise in the former Soviet Union. The incipient process of renewal took place amid a rupture of ideas initiated in the 1980s in response to conservative political interpretations of Marxism begun in the 1970s. Political debates occasioned by the dynamic forces at work during this period and aided by the use of Internet technology exposed the competing layers making this process of redefinition possible.

Going beyond the structural changes begun in this period and contributing to new relationships to capital and to foreign nations, the shift in power from Fidel Castro to his brother Raúl changes the dialogue about the future in immediate ways. Adhering to the political project of the revolution as defined by his older brother, Raúl Castro nonetheless began "pragmatic" and bold moves to improve relations with the United States and expand the economic infrastructure to put more money in the hands of Cubans. Three devastating hurricanes in the summer of 2008 exacerbated the need to move forward in rebuilding infrastructure and expanding domestic production.

More obvious changes had begun to occur at the ideological level a few years earlier, as the state "battled ideas" through a sloganeering campaign in early 2000 intended to maintain unity and focus on the survival of socialism. Newly orchestrated national campaigns—the Elián Gonzalez custody battle and the Cuban Five case (discussed in chapter 5)—required massive participation, but, occurring in the context of ideological failures, they created further distance between state goals and individual concerns. Political directives that in the 1970s promoted a one-dimensional approach to Cuba's important political referents, Marx and Lenin, gave way, in the final decade of the twentieth century, to a reconsideration of Marxism in the cultural intellectual sector. Post-Soviet Cuban nationalism thus has continued to emphasize Cuba's roots in the ideas of independence leaders José Martí (1853–1895) and Father Felix Varela (1788–1853), as well as a renewed interest in Italian political theorist Antonio Gramsci.[53] More than any other Cuban leader, José Martí is considered the father of Cuban independence struggles and antiracist, anticolonial, and anti-imperialist ideology. Jorge Luis Acanda, a professor of philosophy at the University of Havana, interprets the renewed interest in, and acceptance of, Gramsci not as a replacement for Marxism but as an index of opening in the Cuban political and ideological sphere, a return perhaps to the multivocal spirit of the 1960s.

Political alternatives within Cuba, like the Varela Project led by Oswaldo Payá[54]—inspired by Father Varela's independence movement in the nine- teenth century—advocate personal freedoms, particularly freedom of expression.[55] Founded in 2002, the Varela Project's challenges to the Cuban state have also fomented crisis within Cuba's Catholic Church.[56] Calls for political and ideological liberalization thus confront core entities of power in the nation and are considered by Cuban analysts to be behind the con- stitutional amendment of 2002.[57] In this environment, media users in Cuba are thus confronted with a socialism rewired away from Marx and Lenin, still anchored to the territory of the state but linked within emergent media practices that emphasize de-territoriality, mobility, and decentralized media strategies.

The redirection of Cuban socialism after 1991 is best understood through the historical tensions informing the formation of a socialist project. Marx- ism remains resilient in the face of challenges facilitated by revolutionary modern media technology.

The contradictions of Marxism in Cuba originate not in the revolution itself, but in the early part of the twentieth century. The revolution, how- ever, invigorated the debates; the conflicts were exemplified by the schism between revolutionary Cuba and the Communist Parties throughout the hemisphere and the USSR. The new Cuban leadership felt that the region's Communist Parties were "corrupted and weakened by their allegiance not only to the Soviet Union but to its unconditional defense, accustomed to wheeling and dealing with government elites, and supported by constituen- cies with a vested interest in the status quo."[58] Thus, Cuba's revolutionaries felt that the traditional Communist Parties refused to "accept the armed struggle, the socialist nature of the revolution, the need to abandon old alli- ances and adopt a truly hemispheric strategy."[59] The revolution in this way represented a major break with the Soviet model. It was, even in the words of the often critical Mexican political scientist Jorge Castañeda, "freer, more democratic, disorderly, tropical, and spontaneous, as well as being intellectually more diverse and politically more liberal."[60] This freer tendency and the legacy of José Martí were the catalysts for an internationalist vision as Cuba supported revolutionary initiatives throughout Latin America, a stance that the Soviet Union opposed.

The debates of the mid-1960s between those who lent support to a more subjective application of Marxism in Cuba and those, the orthodox ideologues, who prescribed undiluted Marx-from-the-manuals, positioned Gramsci at the center of philosophical inquiries. Cuba was attempting to reinvent society from its own historical logic; Gramsci's notion of subjectivity was particularly influential and gained acceptance, especially in Cuba's cultural sector, where historical reassessment invaded all aspects of artistic production.[61] By 1971, however, conservative views—assisted by economic failures and increased U.S. interventionist policy against Latin American socialist governments—won out, setting Cuba on a stringent path of exclusionary policies that became known as the *quinquenio gris* or fifteen-year gray period.[62] The Cuban leadership looked more toward the Soviet Union, which demanded Soviet-style order and discipline as a condition to aid. Cuba would have to wait until 1985–1986 for a distancing from Soviet policies, and until the fall of the Berlin Wall for new oxygen that would result in a more moderate political position on Marxism and a reinvigoration of the country's nationalism. These ideological reversals underscore the dynamism of the Left in Cuba and identify the contradictory forces behind a culture of prohibitions that would eventually also define the limits and parameters of media use. Renewal of ideological projects required, as ever, recognition of potential conflicts to reassert the value of staying the socialist course.

In the 1990s, Gramsci was once again published in Cuba, and taught in philosophy departments. Currently, the intellectual trend is accented by the legacy of Martí's nationalist thought, as well as Fidel Castro's.[63] Because the Internet remains mostly the province of Cuban institutions privileged as vehicles of the nation's current, still evolving, political project, the present theoretical tendency as applied to much-needed technological development revives an ideology rooted in a Cuban revolutionary nationalism, itself based on Pan-American Martí-influenced ideals. The reality of and since the 1990s exhibits overlapping concerns: a socioeconomic model rooted in Marxism but incorporating changes that brought about social differences; the discrediting of Marxism; and a lack of ideological initiative, due in part to years of empty ideological dogma. Since Marxism-Leninism no longer drove the educational curriculum, a diversity of discourse as well as a reinterpretation of Marxism ensued in the 1990s. Manuel Calviño, a professor of psychology at the University of Havana, passionately expresses the flexibility of direction inherent in Marx:

> Marxism continues to give us many reasons to opt for growth, for development, for an emancipatory project that strengthens our hope as irrevocable anticipation of happiness. The only thing we need is for our compromises not to blind our creativity, for our truths and convictions not to become unquestionable dogmas, for our anxieties about the new not to be curtailed by the ghosts of the old. Marxism is by essence the appropriation and regeneration of the new. Contrary to it is anything that implies a resistance to change, paranoia about new things, a dogmatic confusion between ideological contamination and critical intercultural transposition.[64]

Of course, there is not a homogeneous Cuban consciousness, but the prevailing ideological consensus remains "nationalist and anti-imperialist."[65] Acanda's call in the late 1990s for an opening of the field of debate to a broader intellectual community reverberated in responses from the cultural field as conservative ideologues came face to face with more moderate protagonists in the early 2000s. The opening built on the space already provided by journals such as *Criterios, Gaceta de Cuba, Temas, Encuentro de la Cultura Cubana,* and others—all available online—that presented a challenge to the torpor, that of a single political view, remaining in the Cuban media. For the younger generation with little or no first-hand experience with the victorious energy of earlier years, identification with socialism branded by Cold War history and associated to daily life is quite difficult. Official media are slow to recognize that this generation is more aware of the world and more apt to search out information from relatives and friends abroad, from magazines, and, clandestinely or not, from the Internet.

In the arts, according to Cuban scholar Margarita Mateo Palmer, changes emerging in the Special Period favored "openness and questioning, dialogue that invited reflection about the peculiar historical conjecture of the nation."[66] Debates about the appropriation of concepts such as postmodernism "irrupted in the Cuban cultural sphere like a mocking spirit complicating important national debates and confrontations" that contributed to understanding the transformation taking place within Cuban political and cultural life.[67] Irony and mockery seemed appropriate responses to the disjunction produced by discussing theories associated to postindustrial capitalism when farmers in Cuba, faced with fuel and fertilizer shortages, were forced to readopt animal labor for toiling on the land. Such dizzying circumstances alongside the push to develop an Internet infrastructure provided both politically conservative responses and creative and daring solutions and debates.

For Cuban intellectuals, discussing the potential benefits of global media networks seemed far away, even while the Cuban leadership promoted the role of such media to pull Cuba out of the death knell of socialism. Yet in the face of limits of access to the Internet, important intellectual debates took place, through email, concerning the lack of reflection and memory about the turbulent political events of the 1970s. Navarro maintains that the unprecedented debates of early 2007 make clear the failure of existing spaces of public expression as well as the possibility of creating new spheres of representation to supplant them.[68]

Literature, cinema, and the plastic arts, Navarro states, took up topics previously omitted, such as "homosexuality, gender problems, emigration, frustration and disenchantment, and a crisis of values."[69] I discuss, in chapter 4, how new media have the potential to catalyze social change—in particular through the cinema. Historically, Cuban cinema has played a crucial role in mediating between the revolution and the Cuban people. The cinema became a key cultural institution addressing social conflicts and challenges of the revolutionary undertaking, and promoting cinematic arts through experimentation, cultural activity, and industrial promotion. Headed by filmmakers and writers rather than by technocrats, the new institution—the Instituto Cubano de Arte e Industria Cinematográfica (ICAIC), created in 1959 by the revolutionary leadership—reflected the vision and concerns of its founders; ICAIC escaped being an instrument of the state through the insistence and lucidity of its members. Yet, even as Cuban cinema has been a place where Cubans "recognize themselves," the ICAIC too would experience periods of conservative policies. The key difference, until the early 1990s, would be that filmmakers in the ICAIC leadership articulated and navigated internal conflicts, maintaining a healthy climate of critique and debate. I do not, in chapter 4, intend to recount the rich history of the cinema in Cuba and its key role in the New Latin American Cinema movement, but to note in this history specific analytical strands connecting past and present endeavors. I do review the utopian views of filmmakers as expressed in such examples as "For an Imperfect Cinema," by Cuban filmmaker-theorist Julio García Espinosa, to show how the discourse of media use in Cuba has adapted to the digital age. Converging artistic energies, and the questioning of taboos through low-cost digital technologies of production, also expanded filmmakers' exploration beyond the official centers of production. Film culture thus has become emblematic of the transformation of media and its production, revealing that the digital dispersal of production beyond a state-centered organization contributes to creating, as Navarro suggests, a multiplicity of debates.

In chapter 5, I further explore how digital technology helps organize communities around the territorial longings of exiles, contested political views, and new forms of citizenship. I ask what these digital environments are, where can they be found, what they tell us about ways of living and learning that develop despite controls on information and activity. I ask how new networks of culture help people adapt to changes triggered by globalization, as well as what new forms of knowing, language, and art arise out of digital worlds. Digital media networks displace the notion of national unity, or of a singular focus of ideas onto viscerally fragmented conceptions of society as a whole, adding another dimension to the digital dilemmas. The fragile "nation" rubric seems to operate only "on and off" in personal Web sites, blogs, Internet video sites, and the expanding electronic genres. Examined together, these networks reveal the tensions imposed on technological use between state initiatives and personal investment.

Cuba's history and socialist ideology engages with ideas of cultural dependency and policies of self-determination to make the discourse of technology for the state about the state. Thus, debate about digital technologies in Cuba carries extra weight during a unique transition to a global system of relations and greater exposure of Cuba to international political currents. So far, however, Cuba's new alliances and digital expansion show little sign of challenging its socialist determination.

Research Considerations

The processes of globalization increase the necessity to evaluate emerging relations of technologies across cultural, economic, scientific, personal, official, popular, academic, and artistic fields. To disentangle the complexity of influences on Cuba's changing mediascape, I interviewed officials of the National Center for Automated Exchange of Information (CENIAI, the government agency charged by the Ministry of Science with developing the Internet connection) as well as directors of electronic information in the tourism sector, the telecommunications and telephone industries, and medical networks. Helpful information came also from my meetings with radio producers, with those persons involved in digitizing the Cuban press, with the director of information for the *Prensa Latina* news agency, with the director of a multimedia Cuban firm (CEDISAC/CITMATEL), and with media theorists, researchers, and the director of UNESCO in Cuba, as well as with administrators at the center for information for UNESCO in the Caribbean, the oldest in the Americas. Interviews also included filmmakers, television producers, educators, Web programmers, and graphic artists. I also studied press materials, official speeches, official and unofficial Web sites, and other publications about the topic of information technologies in Cuba. Outside of Cuba, I have spoken with historians, filmmakers, and designers of personal Web sites whose Web activity focuses on Cuba.

Without such a survey, I would risk tracing a research path, in *Digital Dilemmas*, with a view only across the boundaries toward Cuba's digital landscape. Walking through this landscape, however, with institutional representatives, critics, artists, and, above all, everyday users uncovers the contours of a nascent topography and the character and actions of the elements that shape it. In the resulting book I thus draw the map of the research journey and seek to discover and assess the major longlasting, life-shaping structures created by the powerful currents of digital technologies.

To reflect on the development of digital technologies in Cuba is to chronicle a difficult, multifaceted, managed transformation that intersects life and society at all levels. Discussion enlivened by the heightened tensions and emotions of "old" and "new" requires periodic analytical assessment that keeps pace with technological innovation and social and political change. For this reason, this volume focuses on the political and social tensions infusing the issues at stake as Cuba adopts and deploys digital technologies. *Digital Dilemmas* not only explores the key perspectives in play, but imagines what possibilities exist for the application of new technologies loaded with history and incidentally and strategically located and appropriated in a post-Castro Cuba.

1

INVENTING, RECYCLING, AND DEPLOYING TECHNOLOGIES

Science has eliminated distances. . . . In a short time, man will be able to see what is happening in any place in the world without leaving his own house.
—Gabriel García Marquez, *One Hundred Years of Solitude* (1970)

"We need magicians!" Arnaldo Coro, Cuban communication expert, radio host, and cofounder of Radio Habana Cuba,[1] knew what it took for early Cuban Internet users to eliminate distance. His frank admission in a personal interview applies in many parts of the Cuban "house," where numerous obstacles block Internet connection, even as the officially sanctioned educational and technical areas flourish. Navigating through an uncertain infrastructure, experienced and new users alike can never forget that they live in an "underdeveloped country."[2] Because access to technological gadgets is either unaffordable or unavailable, desire or the drive of necessity to acquire and master modern media science defines adaptability. Implicit in Coro's statement is the sense that it takes a large dose of creativity to acquire technological expertise in the face of Cuba's complex material conditions. This creativity manifests itself in an idiosyncratic integration of old and new that is typical in all technological fields in Cuba and contributes to the character of the country.

A long-time amateur radio operator and a science editor for Radio Habana Cuba, Coro has for decades been a radio spokesperson for low-cost solutions to Cuba's myriad infrastructural problems. From promoting solar electricity to consulting on the digitization of the Cuban press, Coro enthusiastically teaches and shares ideas with an international community of listeners. Maneuvering Cuba's initial connection to the Internet required skill, ingenuity, and low-tech solutions. Coro practiced Cuban-style magic, establishing several e-mail accounts through his work sites to provide backup against the failures caused by unreliable telephone lines and slow connection speeds. Unix programming helped him work his way around even the worst computer crashes. His studio equipment piped digital signals through old speakers from who-knows-what-country, and parts officially requisitioned for old soundboards would be unofficially transformed into computer housings. Celebrating Cuban ingenuity, he offered a surreal allegory, "A country that invented the repatriated chicken can make anything work!"[3]

Coro was referring to the extended life and purpose given to food on the national airline during the Special Period. The daily Havana–Mexico City flights left Havana early in the morning with the exact number of dinners for a full round trip. When the flights weren't full, the crew would save the returning chicken dinners, which, as Coro pointed out, by law should have been discarded. In the eyes of the bureaucracy, unused meals did not meet certain criteria for food destined for Cuba. A creative crew realized they could bypass one set of regulations by classifying the chickens as "repatriated"; thus the chickens might be allowed to return to Cuba, through a different set of laws, laws equally divorced from realities. Arriving back in Cuba, the repatriated chickens were distributed among the crew. If someone had a birthday party, a wedding, or visiting guests, they received a special allocation of repatriated bird. Other birds were reserved for airport security personnel. These Cuban homing chickens helped alleviate some of the food scarcity on the island, in the same informal, clandestine fashion employed by Coro as a computer engineer faced with externally imposed restrictions. This kind of "resolving," today of fetishistic proportions, is a legendary element of Cuban life, but one with deep significance. Understanding the specificities of underdevelopment and undersupplied needs helps in reading the ways that technology is used in societies, how it can become a "repatriated chicken" retrieved from official routes to serve unofficial and independent necessities.

In this chapter, I chart the expansion of digital technologies, including the Internet, with regard to the development of previous media infrastructures. Consistently uneven, but always subject to political control, patterns emerged showing ideology and pragmatism in inventive combination. A survey, for example, of post-1959 nationalized media industries shows traces of the prerevolutionary commercial radio and television that operated before the ideological paradigm redirected media practices from commercial to state-centered. The current cultural and political geography of media and technology, and of their social and political uses in Cuba, emerged from a revolutionary imagination, just as these media were and still are used to construct this imagination. From this perspective, media trajectories that are usually considered separate are seen as connected in ways that reinforce the national and remake the local while meeting specific social needs for technologies. In this chapter, I explore how the Cuban model of alignment of telecommunications with national and political interests affects their personal appropriation and influences individual expression and interaction.

Early Media Developments

Discussion of the development of the Internet in Cuba needs to be set in the context of the island's early technological culture and the singularity of its relationships to the United States and the former USSR. The history of technological experimentation in Cuba dates back to the turn of the twentieth century, when the island was a fertile testing ground for new technologies. The island's importance as a world sugar producer had underscored the importance of developing an infrastructure for the relay of information to serve its Cuban and U.S. investors. As a result of the island's close economic relationship to Wall Street, patents and systems were often tested there prior to implementation in the United States. So strong were telecommunications ties between Cuba and the United States in 1900 that the first overseas telephone call was made from Key West, Florida, to Havana. Half a century earlier, an Italian named Antonio Meuci allegedly directed the first electronic transmission of a human voice, while doing research in Havana. The newspaper *Granma*, the official newspaper of the Cuban Communist Party, in 1999 lauded his experimentation as a contribution to the development of the telephone.[4]

Telegraph lines established the first viable telecommunications link between the Caribbean and the United States, an advance emblematic of colonial politics. In his classic study of the role of sugar in the development of Cuba, Manuel Moreno Fraginals points to the central place of information in the growth of a local economy:

> From 1840 on, telegraph lines, uniting the principal Cuban sugar-
> producing zones, were installed by American technicians with

American material and capital. Without much ado, the telegraph complex of the island was then linked with the American telegraph complex by underwater cable, inaugurated on 9 September 1867. . . . The modern telegraph system, uniting European markets to each other, American markets to each other, and later, through underwater cables, England to the Continent (1851), Cuba to the U.S.A. (1867), and the U.S.A. to Europe, contributed much to the revolution of commercial practices.[5]

During the first half of the twentieth century, Cuba, despite its previous battles for independence, became a proximate yet exotic neocolony of the United States. Not only did it serve the personal and business interests of major U.S. industrialists (and later, in the 1950s, of the Mafia), but it became an offshore site where technological innovations and products were often tested before broader distribution in Latin America. This strategy also helped U.S. industrialists plan and test distribution practices. Such a situation, seemingly advantageous although one of dependence for Cuba, heightened development in radio and television communications. As television scholar Yeidy Rivero makes clear, between 1950 and 1953 Cuba was one of the programming leaders, in these media, in Latin America.[6]

Out of its dependent relationship (orchestrated through the Platt Amendment, 1901–1934, which gave the United States the right to intervene in Cuban events), Cuba became, for all practical purposes, a territory of the United States. The close relations between the countries, and their ties to the sugar industry, spurred the early experimentation with radio by Frank H. Jones, an American who had gone to work in the Cuban sugar industry. Cuban American entrepreneur Manuel Alvarez documents in a personal history that, in 1912, Jones installed and operated a 2000W spark CW (continuous wave) transmitter, and later, in 1922, he operated an experimental radio station from a sugar-cane mill.[7]

But the first commercial broadcast radio station, PWX, was not inaugurated until 1922. PWX was owned by the Cuban Telephone Company, which in turn was owned by International Telephone and Telegraph Corporation (IT&T); the inaugural transmission was a speech in English by then-president Alfredo Zayas, broadcast also by WBAY in New York. The prominence of baseball in Cuba factored into the popularity of radio, and Alvarez claims that the World Series in baseball was listened to in Cuba more than in any other Latin

American country. At the time, broadcasters who could afford the service would provide a delayed broadcast of the games in Spanish with local-color commentary. After Word War II, the national commercial networks became established throughout the island, and "by 1958, 1 out of every 5 inhabitants had a radio receiver."[8]

Entrepreneurial bonds emerged between Cuban business leaders and the two largest radio networks in the United States, NBC and CBS, in similar fashion to those between other Latin American countries and the United States. Cubans Goar Mestre and Abel Mestre, his brother, radio and television entrepreneurs and owners of CMQ, the largest network in Cuba, were backed by investment from the NBC network, then the broadcast division of equipment manufacturer RCA.[9] In 1945, after World War II, the United States formalized its relationship with Latin American broadcasters by creating AIR (Asociación Interamericana de Radiodifusión, or Interamerican Broadcasting Association), which encouraged the expansion of U.S. networks. According to John Sinclair, who has studied the development of television in Latin America, AIR's first congress, with Goar Mestre as its first president, "resolved to concentrate on the establishment of television." From then on, AIR lobbied "national governments to ensure that television was introduced on a commercial, American model, rather than a European, state-operated basis.[10] Sinclair argues that the type of development that occurred was due not only to U.S. imposition of its interests in Cuba (and in the rest of Latin America), but also to the powerful interests of Cuba's ruling entrepreneurial class, whose aspirations and determination accelerated the commercial pace. Major and minor media tycoons competed fiercely for what they perceived would be tremendous advertising revenues from American corporations doing business on the island.[11] The competition among local entrepreneurs would be portrayed as intense in a 1958 article in *Variety*, the main Hollywood trade publication: "The feud between Barletta and Mestre is one of the more celebrated Hatfield-McCoys of the island. . . . Just how an American tele-operator, unversed in the mores of the stormy Cuban political and competitive situations, can make out in such an atmosphere remains to be seen."[12]

The significance of Mestre in Cuba's broadcasting history goes beyond his leadership at AIR. Mestre was one of the first exporters of radio programming to the Latin American region, helping to establish the radio soap opera (which originated in Cuba and is the predecessor of the *telenovela*) as a powerful commercial genre. After the revolution, Mestre went into exile, continuing his career in broadcasting from Argentina, where, in partnership with CBS, he founded one of the first privately owned television channels. He later invested with Time-Life in a Venezuelan network, which was also plowing money into Brazil.

After 1959, the move toward nationalization of private industries in Cuba galvanized a technical and artistic Cuban diaspora throughout Latin America, helping to foment other nascent industries throughout the hemisphere. Cuban writers were instrumental in the deployment of the televised soap operas, first as a Pan-American genre and then as a transnational one.[13] By 1960, the Castro government had nationalized the Cuban networks and created Televisora Nacional, Cuba's state-owned network, out of Mestre's CMQ and the other networks.

It was another entrepreneur, Gaspar Pumarejo, who first introduced television in Cuba, in 1950, after the leading broadcasting networks were already established in the United States. By 1954, Cuba figured as the fourth largest television market in the world, and a leader and innovator in programming.[14] Although reported statistics differ slightly, both Michael Salwen and Alvarez say that, by the time Castro came to power, there were about twenty-seven television stations operating in the country: three national networks, and seven independent local stations in Havana and the Camagüey province. "One of them was a full color television station, Telecolor, Channel 12 in Havana," according to Alvarez.[15] Pumarejo was responsible for bringing color television to Cuba, making the island the first market outside the United States for this new technology (and the third market overall), with the island's initial color transmission on February 24, 1958. Telecolor installed its transmitter atop the Havana Hilton Hotel; its programming was dedicated mainly to news and films.[16] At this time, too, NBC and CBS in New York did sporadic broadcasts in color; however, color television broadcasting did not fully emerge anywhere until 1964, five years after the revolution in Cuba.

Until Castro came to power, the strength of the Cuban consumer market had made it a prime target for American programming. Cuba had become "the first nation in the world to extend television to its entire, if rather compact, national territory,"[17] and this had necessitated a certain level of technological infrastructure capable of relaying television signals throughout the island. The prerevolutionary goal had been to create a broader base of consumers, since Cuba had fine-tuned American consumerism. According to Alvarez, a favorable exchange rate for businesses, along with the close proximity of Florida (Key West was only forty-five minutes away by plane) to the island, facilitated entrepreneurial interactions.[18] Despite Cuba's pioneering introduction of color television, however, once the revolutionary government took over, the expense of maintaining the transmission infrastructure was perceived as extravagant, and color television was not reintroduced until 1976.[19]

Statistical reports indicate that, by 1958, one out of eighteen homes in Cuba had a television set.[20] Although this suggests a relatively high television density for the era, it is not clear how this figure divided between the capital city and the regional centers. After 1959, recognizing television (rather than film) to be *the* mass medium for its purpose, the revolution made it a priority that television sets be available to a broad national constituency. The new government would thus take advantage of the advanced development of television and its capacity to reach a yet unrealized number of viewers. To this end, sets were imported from the Soviet Union. Later, in the 1970s and 1980s, the government created regional *telecentros*, television centers that created programming reflecting regional as well as national interests. The regional *telecentros* currently receive a daily time slot to transmit their programming on the national networks.

Thus, though the emergence of television in Cuba was underwritten by American consumer interests, leading to its initial adherence to the commercial American model, the revolutionary government in 1959 turned the commercial medium to political advantage, implementing a quite different model. Since then, the state has controlled all aspects of television programming, ironically proving to its dissatisfied viewers that state bureaucrats should not be a part of decision making in programming.[21] Regardless of quality issues, television allowed the new revolutionary government to transmit a new consciousness, central to which was delivering Fidel Castro's speeches to the people.

The postrevolutionary broadcasting model centralized all decision making and production capacity. It also served as a training ground for individuals who would end up in the ranks of the national film culture. Within a noncommercial model, the content of programs included national and regional news, variety and music shows, telenovelas, educational and children's programs, documentary segments, special interest programs, and dance. The decidedly ideological and paternalistic character of most programming has subsequently been the source of much criticism and debate.

Recognizing the limited quality of programming and the ideological requirements and greater openness of a new era, by April 2008, the Unión de Escritores y Artistas Cubanos (UNEAC) congress called for broad reforms.

At the end of the twentieth century, Cuban television expanded by adding two more national channels (for a total of four) focused on culture and education, as part of a government attempt to increase and diversify the sorts of cultural programming available to Cuban viewers. Added to this national system is the Television Serrana network and the city channel Canal Habana. Expanded focus on education furthers the Cuban government's aim to use television to achieve greater emphasis on the distribution of Cuban and international culture as determined by a programming committee.

Historical Framework for Cuban Computing

Prerevolutionary Cuban entrepreneurs advanced television transmission and networks, always connected to evolving U.S. networks and media infrastructures. Early computing in Cuba also advanced alongside computer developments in the United States, and with the same imbalance of power. According to Armand Mattelart, data processing systems were installed in Latin America at almost the same time as in producing countries, a characteristic, he suggests, deriving from the internal logic of the capitalist system.[22] In other words, contiguous development was key to achieving a global expansion of the system; the main conduits of this technological transfer were, of course, the large transnational enterprises with interests in the vast, productive natural resources of Latin America.

In 1969, reflecting on the effect of territorial proximity on development of information technology in prerevolutionary Cuba, leading Cuban communications scholar Enrique Gonzalez-Manet chronicled an example in the newspaper *Granma*. In the late 1950s, two first-generation U.S. computers were secretly installed in Cuba.[23] The fast development of integrated circuits, which by the mid-1950s were manufactured out of silicon, coupled with the significant drop in prices of semiconductors, increased the computers' production and capacity. Gonzalez-Manet found that, until the existence of the pair of computers came to light, most people believed that the only electronic computer in Cuba had been a Universal Automatic Computer (UNIVAC) 120, obtained by American interests in the 1950s to compute gambling pay-outs in horse racing. Mafia organizations running the casinos used the machine to have automatic control over "premiums" and to ensure stable profit margins.[24] The two other machines in Cuba were used to control processes and computations at a refinery, in experiments performed by Americans employed by Esso, a division of the Exxon Mobil Corporation. Such experiments, Gonzalez-Manet notes, were carried out under strict secrecy, with the operating costs charged to Esso's Cuban affiliate in Havana. After Cuba nationalized petroleum and other industries in 1960, the only remnant of the two U.S. computers was the associated, complex web of telecommunications cabling.

The Electronic Numerical Integrator and Calculator (ENIAC), the most well known of what are sometimes called the first-generation, post-analog computers, had been developed in the United States in 1946 by a team at the University of Pennsylvania. Industrial- and postindustrial-age computing machines were used for decoding in Word War II. Sociologist Manuel Castells has documented in detail the early advantage of U.S. researchers and manufacturers in the area of information technology.[25] ENIAC took up an entire gymnasium, and the electric consumption required could dim the lights of a city. But a smaller commercial version, UNIVAC-1, produced in 1951 by Remington Rand, was used to successfully process the 1950 U.S. Census. The first computer in Latin America was installed in the 1950s in the Venezuelan offices of the Creole Petroleum Corporation and, according to Mattelart, "became a launching pad for computer development" in that nation. In Peru, Occidental Petroleum "installed the most advanced system of communication, so as to be linked to the world network of information."[26]

Markets and the National Interest

Global expansion of markets, it must be noted, combines with national interests to advance local development that serves the interests of an elite class. This is why technological advancement per se does not achieve a new social consciousness, and why the revolutionary government of Cuba would drive technological development adhering to a differentiated socialist-styled progress as the anchor of the new society.

In Cuba, the emergence of computers is the story of how Cold War adversaries (Russia and the United States) played an influential role in the island's technological development throughout the first half of the twentieth century, and how Cuba in turn appropriated information technology for its own historical need to reinvent itself in the second half of the century. This also meant a shift in relations over technology, as motives swerved from the strictly commercial and profit-driven to state-owned centralized interests. According to telecommunications specialist Coro, the communications infrastructure had been in the hands of American companies, and its post-revolutionary development was thus guided by new historical conditions.[27] In 1921, American Telephone and Telegraph (AT&T) laid the underwater cable between the United States and Cuba, replacing it in 1950; in 1966, the cable was exempted from the 1962 trade embargo for humanitarian reasons. But ongoing political conflicts between the two nations have continually affected the way in which AT&T has been able to carry out operations. This has created an ironic situation where current e-mail communication between Cuba and the United States flows regularly but, as a retaliatory measure against unfavorable policies toward Cuba, the Cuban government can at times curtail the number of lines available for telephone service to the United States and interrupt telephone communication.[28] In some respects, the state of United States–Cuba telecommunications reveals the fragility of geopolitical boundaries erected by transnational communications corporations. For Cubans, however, it shows the government's willingness to sacrifice individual benefit for the good of the state. Consent of the population to subordinate private for public good, a cornerstone of socialist policies and ideology, has waned over the decades, in response to increasing personal frustrations. Telecommunications services have increased and improved since the beginning of the Special Period, but so has their cost. The increasing mobility of Cubans during this period, resulting from economic opportunity or exile, has also meant that telecommunications will play a pivotal role in the future of Cuban lives and personal ambitions.

The suspension of trade between the United States and Cuba subsequent to the revolution meant that machines of all types would be purchased from France and, more regularly, from the Soviet Union and other Eastern European nations. The telephone system, for example, was constructed from equipment acquired from multiple sources. Coro confirms that having so many sources was one of the biggest obstacles to better operation of the system, since the admixture of components built to different specifications and supplied by such a variety of countries—the United States (originally), France, Canada, Scandinavia, East Germany, and Hungary—made interoperability and maintenance difficult.[29] Digitization of the telephone system, modernizing telecommunications operations, had to contend with the material reality of Cuba's complex political history.

In 1964, Cuba's relationship with Eastern Europe was further solidified through the purchase of equipment from Poland and the training of specialists in East Germany and the Soviet Union. Commenting on the island's early computer developments, political analyst Larry Press notes that, during the 1970s, "Cuba embarked on a program to develop its own second-generation minicomputers at the Central Institute for Digital Research."[30] This program began the use of computers in planning and in increasing resource efficiency. The Cuban government aimed to produce microcomputers to help in transport, agricultural machinery development, labor efficiency, equipment and building design, and communications. Bilateral agreements with the USSR supported the nascent industry, and the first computers were assembled in 1978, comprising mainframe, mini-, and microcomputers.[31] Modernization was at the heart of development approaches not only by earlier capitalist tycoons but also by the state-centered new revolutionary government. In the 1970s, the national emphasis of technological production and education rejected prior paradigms of development, evolving in a pronounced conservative turn toward instrumentalism in scientific development. How these technological advances were to contribute to the creation of a new society coincided with the Soviet government's "scientific and technological revolution" from the 1960s onward, which promoted investments in technological modernization. A less repressive but still restrictive Soviet ideological climate overlapped with the Cuban leadership's closer adherence to Soviet ideas. By then, cybernetics in the Soviet Union had "ceased to be a bourgeois science, mathematical models were introduced in economics, . . . and, most significantly, the Academy of Sciences received strong material support and considerable bureaucratic autonomy to take care of its own affairs, including exercising its own ideological controls."[32]

By 1965, Castells observes, rather than continue to develop an endogenous computer industry, the USSR adopted, first, IBM computing systems and, later, Japanese models. "Instead of developing their own design and production line, Soviet electronic R&D centers and factories (all under the Ministry of Defense) engaged in smuggling of computers from the West, proceeding to reverse engineering and to reproduce each model, adapting them to Soviet military specifications."[33] The Soviet information technology revolution of the 1970s rested on copying computers and operating systems from the West, a move that in turn prevented the Soviets from keeping up with or developing advancements. Such paradoxical development is substantiated by the logic of the Cold War: according to Castells, Soviet scientists and the military approved this strategy because they feared that development in the new area of information technologies, isolated from advancements in the West, was too "uncertain" to convince Soviet intelligence to invest in its exploration.[34]

Gonzalez-Manet chronicled the emphasis on information technology in 1969 in a three-part feature series that ran in *Granma;* in it, he considered and explained the development of cybernetics and what it meant for Cuba. Typical of the Marxist ideology of the era informing scientific and technological development was his suggestion that, "given the things that Cuba was doing, it could situate itself as an example of the enormous endeavors in the area of productivity."[35] It was necessary, he wrote, to incorporate "cybernetic technology both in directing the economy and in production, at its various levels, and in helping the development of scientific and technological research."[36] Cybernetics was perceived as a "science of salvation," a way to build communism.[37] Contemporary Cuba uses similar slogans to salvage its forty-plus-year socialist trajectory; only, today the slogans are not linked to the reigning ideology of the Soviet Union.

Technological development, whether in computers or in industrial design, is thus linked to the process of building a communist nation, and in this way has become the subject of the idea of progress. The revolutionary leadership in the 1960s understood that Cuba was positioned favorably for the integration of advances in technology, not in the dependent model perpetuated in any developing country, but rather as a force to escape underdevelopment. The audacious spirit of the era intertwined development with financial support and preferential trade status from the Soviet Union, a situation that, although different from Cuba's previous neocolonial relationship with the United States, was risky. The Soviets traded economic support for a foothold on what Russian documentary filmmaker Roman Karmen once dubbed the "island of freedom" ninety miles off the coast of the Soviets' Cold War enemy. The Lourdes Radar Base was the crowning jewel of electronic surveillance within a larger Soviet network called Dozor. Cuba's relationship with the Soviets was fittingly tested during the 1962 Missile Crisis, when Cuban territory, in the eyes of the U.S. government, became synonymous with nuclear weapons. It was at the high point of negotiations between Soviet President Nikita Khrushchev and U.S. President John F. Kennedy that the Soviets' ultimate strategy was revealed: in return for the USSR removing its nuclear missiles from Cuba, the United States agreed not to invade the island. However, Castro had not only not been consulted on this agreement—he found out about it after it was signed. This undermining of Castro showed just what little leverage Cuba could exercise in political conflicts between the two superpowers, and to what degree economic sustainability would be tied to the whims of Cold War ideologues.

Having overthrown the pre-1959 power structure and ended the privileged position held by the United States in Cuba, the nation set out on a course where the newly legitimated republic could chart its own development strategies in a society no longer tied to the neocolonial structures considered responsible for poverty on the island. Gonzalez-Manet affirms: "To apply science and technology at their highest levels one has to overcome underdevelopment . . . and for this task one must first have a revolution."[38] In the early years of utopian enthusiasm, the Cuban government, and indeed the people of Cuba, believed they were well underway to defeating underdevelopment. Almost overnight, the rupture in the historical process had transformed social, political, economic, and cultural relations on the island, and a new process had to be constructed. This new orientation toward development included efforts to acquire or create the necessary tools to jump-start the building of the revolutionary nation.

As has been discussed, the view of technology as a force that shapes a modern nation is not particular to Cuba, finding echoes in all discourses on modernization, and tied to theories of development that emerged in the postwar period, when the concept became used to account for differences in industrial achievement worldwide. Cuba's historical situation, however, must mean that technology alone cannot lead the country out of underdevelopment. Key Cuban discourses on nationhood—those that propose the creation of a new society—point to the necessity of first altering the society in which the technology is introduced. Gonzalez-Manet's reading of technology to chart a path out of neocolonization, given the already successful revolution, positioned such discourse within the movements and rhythms of the process of building communism in the Caribbean.

Gonzalez-Manet's tone reflected the patriotic fervor of the era. Through the media, the ten-million-ton sugar harvest campaign in 1970, the highest projected harvest ever, acted on the social consciousness, becoming a symbolic way of achieving an arbitrary goal—and its failure created huge economic problems. The notion of beating the odds was always a rallying cry for Fidel Castro and for the Communist Party leadership, as is evident in speeches after the U.S. embargo was imposed, in which the Cuban government positioned itself as the survivor of aggressions from the United States and of the inhumanity of the embargo. In the Cuba of 1969, technological advances were factored into the aim of achieving the largest sugar harvest ever as a concrete and symbolic manifestation of the will and spirit of the new nation. That the ten-million-ton harvest target was not achieved did not subdue state rhetoric. The decline in credibility of this type of economic planning would be addressed by "rectification" campaigns in the following years. The hyperbolic nature of political rhetoric, however, continued to detract from real advances made by Cuba. The state today continues to insist that successful but narrowly prioritized development—for example, in the medical and biotechnology fields—indicates success for the state and therefore for all Cubans; however, such claims can only ring hollow to a populace continually asked to sacrifice with no sign that state successes improve daily quality of life.

By 1978, the Centro Nacional de Superación y Adiestramiento en Informáticas (National Center for Training and Advancement in Informatics—CENSAI) began training the first crop of what would become, in over two decades, some sixty thousand computer science specialists. CENSAI's first decade was devoted to training experts to make efficient use of the national computers, indicating a commitment to some form of future self-sufficiency and the possibility of establishing a domestic industry. Using "Made in Cuba" first-generation computers, the newly trained specialists were assigned to the prioritized sectors of information and health, business and defense—sectors that always influenced the introduction of new technologies in postrevolutionary Cuba, defining the relationship between technology and the state.[39] CENSAI also provided technical support for the nascent Joven Club de Computación (Youth Computing Clubs), as well as for vocational work with children from the Palacio Central de Pioneros (Central Palace for Pioneers), and aided in the creation of a methodology for curriculum planning for very young children. Training in informatics and computers was also instituted at the University of Havana, the Instituto Superior Politécnico José Antonio Echeverría (ISPAJAE), and the University of Las Villas in Santa Clara.[40] The computing clubs, which have received support since their inception in 1987, are the means by which all youths receive instruction in basic computing. Clubs, institutions, and individuals in the social sciences, culture, health, education, and other fields were connected through a network called TinoRed, which operated as a non-profit, nongovernmental association.

In the context of Cuba's close relations with the USSR during the 1970s, a period in part of Marxism-by-the-book, and given the political ramifications of this relationship, the Cuban government made timely investment in computer technology. That decade saw increasing innovation in microelectronics in many countries, as American entrepreneurship sealed its lead in the field of computing; new information technologies were diffused widely during the period, although many of the discoveries on which they were based had been made in prior decades. In 1964, IBM, despite its early reservations about entering the personal computer business, came to dominate the computer industry. Then, in 1971, the invention of the microprocessor, which allowed chip-based computing, revolutionized the computer industry.[41] For Cuba, of course, such development and innovation in technology and social investment in human development were (and are) driven by priorities historically determined by governments in power.

As a result of investment to create a small hardware industry during the 1970s and 1980s, Press observed, Cuba "produced a variety of products that were used domestically and exported to Council for Mutual Economic Assistance (CMEA) countries."[42] Press explains that about three hundred microcomputers "as well as thousands of asynchronous terminals," were made, part of a modest microcomputer industry that assembled thousands of Intel-based PCs from imported components. He argues that the Cuban domestic economy was not large or sophisticated enough to justify an indigenous hardware industry, which could account for how Cuba became "an outlier of the partially integrated CMEA computer industries, building subsystems from imported components and with guaranteed exports to the CMEA countries."[43] Two plants near Havana that built printed circuit boards (PCB) and asynchronous terminals were affected severely by the economic decline. It seems logical, given Cuba's previous export arrangements, that the government would have attempted to position itself again to secure export contracts within a greater global economy. Doing so, however, would require substantial investment in production and training capabilities, and the collapse of communism in Europe affected the Cuban manufacturing sector particularly severely; thus it has been a slow process of rebuilding to operate at previous levels. According to Press, the PCB factory "had purchased manufacturing equipment from several European and Asian suppliers, [and] the electronics assembly plant had started construction of a new manufacturing facility that was to be the tallest building in the plant compound."[44] The accelerated pace of global developments in information technologies since 1991, when Cuba was hardest hit economically, indicates that the nation's competitive edge could indeed lie in developing a highly trained high-tech labor force (as India has done), and in making inroads into software production, rather than in non-niche technology and expertise. This strategy extends the approach of the PCB factory, since the strategy develops internal production to help integrate Cuba into global economic development. Ideally, domestic production would permeate all levels of society, not just those of the scientific, manufacturing, or business sectors.

The changing relationships among centers of technology—Cuba, the United States, and the former Soviet Union—supported, in numerous ways, revolutionary change in Cuba. Early contact with U.S. industrialists, however defined by the power imbalance, and the technological advancements such contact brought about, contributed to the revolutionary government's perception of technological development as an effective means for consolidating the revolution. Traces of technological engagement with U.S. industry and media networks, although such engagement did not register immediate results in the economy or production system in postrevolutionary Cuba, could be seen in the importance given to training in microelectronics during the 1970s, and in the move to invest in a national microcomputer industry. Although there was an almost complete exodus of the entrepreneurial class after the revolution—the class that drove development of technological transfers and experiments—there remained remnants of technological achievement, remnants that were appropriated by the government and invested with different social and economic categories. The closer relationship with the Soviets during the 1960s and 1970s prompted Cuba to make technology the engine for realizing a socialist model of development—in actuality, continuing an established historical trend in Cuba, where physical proximity to the centers of innovation, even through an undesirable neocolonial relationship with the United States, fueled the transformation of society, from plantation to consumerist economy, and then from socialism to what some wryly call "market-Leninism."

The revolution's accomplishments in education, biomedical engineering, and scientific development have been underwritten by the Cuban state as viable avenues to becoming economically independent and socially responsible.

They have also continued to earn significant soft power for the Cuban nation. Such endeavors lay the foundation for future economic growth, centered on a highly trained work force. However, social investment in future telecom engineers creates a second edge to the sword of professional development, in the potential for "brain drain." Severe economic circumstances erode citizens' willingness to make daily sacrifices asked of them by the government. One method used by the Cuban state since the mid-1990s to end the outward flow of trained people was the slight liberalization of the private sector, allowing mixed ownership of enterprises between state and foreign investors, combined with a less intrusive presence in the commercial firms created by the government to streamline services. This tactic, in the face of an unrelenting environment of restrictions, does not guarantee an end to the labor exodus, as young Cubans may still find themselves restricted by jobs that fail to nurture creative and intellectual development.

Cuban Internet Infrastructure

By the end of the millennium, the working structure of connectivity in Cuba had gone through several changes that reflected the complexity entailed in opening up to global information networks. As the first computer networks were designed to connect with Soviet research partnerships, the early character of computing was embedded in the logic of a "technological revolution." The redirection of networking partnerships when they occurred also changed the characteristics of networking infrastructure. First and foremost were the contributing factors in the economy. Second were the competing interests within both Cuba and the United States that politicized decision making about Internet connectivity. Although it was obvious that Cuba could use new Internet technology to help mitigate immediate shortages, it was also clear that the Internet would provide a new way to propagate antigovernment attitudes. The decision to establish an official connection was reached with trepidation, but also with a formal statement to favor directed development and access.[45] The initial phase, as Nelson P. Valdés has observed, was to connect institutions rather than individuals, but the Cuban government promised that there would be a gradual opening to individuals once the country's technological infrastructure was shored up.[46]

   The tension between centralizing Internet operability and needing to decentralize institutional management fluctuated in response to internal and external pressure. Not only would strict adherence to centralized planning not automatically lead to more democratic structures and greater public access, but decentralization in the context of a commercial network infrastructure would equally disappoint, as was evident in many democratic nations. The area of greatest interest, in terms of democratic use of media technologies, lay, and lies, with the Cuban people and their thoroughly decentralized and increasingly global efforts to use technology for their own benefit. These tensions would be replicated in the eventual design and implementation of the policies that enacted access to the Internet.

Prioritizing is a byproduct of central command economies, and is the means by which the Cuban government directs its internal investments and distributes institutional support. The creation of priorities cannot hide neglected interests, as ranking importance distracts from and disguises overlooked concerns. Cuban state priorities tend to belie conditions of underdevelopment and scarcity of economic resources that elsewhere might serve as priorities directing development strategies. In the late 1980s and 1990s, connection to the Internet offered ways of reaffirming a socialist agenda, and of moving out of isolation and overcoming the information embargo.

Electronic mail networks with the USSR had been established since 1981, and a satellite connection in 1983 gave Cuba access to close to fifty computer databases, primarily scientific databases and those related to economic planning. Valdés notes that, until 1988, "computer networking among Cuban institutions was almost nonexistent."[47] This changed with the dissolution of the USSR and the prioritization in 1993 of information technologies as part of a central mechanism for Cuba's economic development. Also significant is the effect of the increase in domestic networking on relations within institutions. These changes in relations in turn affected the culture of information, reconcentrating it domestically; the meeting of necessity with technological innovation thus allowed Cuba to apply information technology to several short- and long-term problems. The role of the United Nations through UNESCO (United Nations Education, Science and Cultural Organization) and the UN Development Program (UNDP) is significant, as it helped to guide Cuba's Internet policy. Given Cuba's political isolation, the United Nations has served as a supportive forum for voting against the restrictions of the U.S. embargo and as a platform for Cuba to air its complaints. By 1990, the UNDP began fomenting connectivity throughout the developing world, funding the start-up costs for such networks as CENIAI and the medical network InfoMed.

In 1997 UNESCO's Executive Council drafted a resolution concerning the problems that face developing nations with respect to information technologies. The motion approves continued funding initiatives, and supports policies that help provide access, resources, and training of personnel to explore and maintain new economic markets made viable through information technologies. The magnitude of the investment in developing nations, and the task of carrying out such a plan (particularly in Africa, the least connected continent) in even the task of laying telephonic cable, accounts for UNESCO'S policy to "focus on community programs and the strengthening of development sectors like education, prior to the wiring of each individual home."[48] Cuba's focus on access to the Internet through institutions in the sciences, tourism, and education is in line with this UN policy.

Cuban connectivity is also aligned with the strategies of other Latin American countries, their efforts to share insights and successes, and their struggle to establish common ground for future networking. Prior to full Internet connectivity, Cuba maintained a "gopher" server in Uruguay with generic information.[49] In 1991, Cuba sent a representative to the international forum on the Internet in Brazil, where plans were discussed to create a Latin American high-speed backbone to facilitate connectivity in the region. Jesús Martinez, an automated systems engineer and the first director of the Centro Nacional de Intercambio de Información (National Center for Automated Exchange of Information), or CENIAI, established personal links with network leaders in Peru and Venezuela, because pan-American regional cooperation is key in fortifying commercial domestic markets as well as in expanding trade possibilities (for example, Cuba maintains distributors in fifty countries for the biomedical products it advertises on the CIGBnet Web site, since the restrictions of the U.S. embargo would otherwise prevent it from shipping or selling to many of its customers).[50]

CENIAI became the central node through which Cuban networks routed their international connection. In 1989, Cuba made its first non-Soviet email link, with Peacenet in Canada. According to Press, "twice a week WEB/NIRV, an Association for Progressive Computing (APC) affiliate in Toronto, Canada, called CENIAI and exchanged international traffic."[51] Although fragile, a dial-up connection through Canada's Web networks in 1991 covered the cost of the telephone connection and allowed weekly contact.[52] Martinez suggests that this connection, however inefficient, often proved the best way to communicate with people on the island.[53]

By 1992, Cuba had established several email networks within the country, connecting medical, scientific, and cultural institutions. In 1993, the number of UUCP (Unix-to-Unix Copy Programs) nodes increased from three to twenty. CENIAI, TinoRed, CIGBnet, and InfoMed were Cuba's four networks with international dial-up; Internet connections were later reorganized to connect directly through CENIAI. A report by Larry Press and Joel Snyder in 1992 found that CENIAI enjoyed "freedom from regulation or control by the Cuban Ministry of Communication" despite its position within the centralized government structure.[54]

In 1994, following government approval, CENIAI took the first steps to secure authorization for Internet connection with Sprint International, a commercial communication company. CENIAI held a working conference in 1995 to continue discussions among high-ranking government officials, U.S. information scientists, and potential Internet Service Providers (ISPs) about the viable means and strategies to develop information technologies in emergent economies such as Cuba's. The conference took concrete steps toward the goals of training specialists and identifying international institutional contacts to increase cooperation.

Finally, on June 14, 1996, the Interministerial Commission was designated by Decree 209 to "regulate access to and management of all Internet information, to supervise the development and functioning of national networks, to monitor technological change and its use, and to supervise security procedures."[55] The commission included representatives from five ministries: Science, Technology and the Environment (issuer of licenses and accounts for information); Communications (operator of the telecommunications hardware and structures used by the networks); Justice (responsible for legal framework and legislation); Interior (establisher of technical security policies); and Revolutionary Armed Forces (guardian of national security, ensuring it would not be weakened by the Internet). Decree 209 expressed "the need for the country to establish laws for connecting [to the Internet] and regulations that guarantee a harmonious development [of the Internet] as well as the interests of national security and defense."[56] The decree set the legal framework for Internet operation, defining regulations to protect national security. The deliberations of the commission finally led to Cuba's 1996 connection to the Internet through CENIAI. Plans to install a fiber-optic cable infrastructure and digitize all telephone service were laid in 1998, reaching the eastern province of Guantanamo in 2004.[57] Acknowledging the need for greater managerial flexibility of a global information-based economy, the head of CENIAI was allowed a certain amount of autonomy because the agency was a commercial enterprise and oversaw the modernization of operations.

What had grown into a disarticulated group of networks in the late 1980s (CENIAI, TinoRed, Red David, InfoMed, CIGBnet) was reorganized in 1993 in response to increased network capacity and the need for efficient traffic routing. This in turn was a response to debates among interested groups about the pros and cons of more open communication with the West. The resulting network architecture conceptualized the national network infrastructure in light of operability, capacity, and potential threats to national security and how best to control them. The centralized structure made CENIAI a central hub of organization, communication, and support for the sciences.[58] Restructuring pooled scarce resources maximized available bandwidth and provided a service that restricted access to authorized individuals. The inability of the government to fully fund the needed technology led CENIAI to operate in a dollar economy, subject to new managerial styles that fit within global markets and influenced the focus of its services. CENIAI representatives also formed part of international Internet governing and research bodies. The reorganization designed to provide structure to the previously unorganized e-mail networks established service contracts with other Cuban institutions, rates for connecting, technical support, training, Web design, and other assistance for its institutional and commercial customers. The Network Information Center (NIC) was established in 1995 to manage the .cu domain under which most accounts are registered in Cuba.[59]

CENIAI would become part of the Information Technology and Advanced Telematic Services Company (CITMATEL, the Empresa de Tecnologías de la Información y Servicios Telemáticos), incorporated in 1999, as the government firm to commercialize information services and generate revenue.[60] The reorganization of Cuba's computing networks serviced the new business clients as well as the existing computer user community in the country's scientific, cultural, and academic organizations. In effect, the network structure facilitated interinstitutional relations.

Internet connectivity in Cuba is intended to encourage research, business, and tourism, and to improve communications, all within a "national interest" model. According to the newspaper *Trabajadores*, the connection must provide truthful and ethical information.[61] *Granma* adds, in an article, "the politics of access must focus on the interests of Cuba . . . prioritizing access for the judicial system and institutions that have the most relevance for the life and development of the nation."[62] Evident in this view of priorities is the premise that a nation is the sum of its institutions, and individuals express their needs and desires through those institutions. The individual citizen does not figure as a priority per se, but as a benefactor of national priorities and projects enacted by the institutions.

The question of centralization or decentralization of Internet infrastructure becomes evident again in institutional changes. In 2001, a Ministry of Information and Communication was created, charged with advancing Internet development. The ministry took over from the Interministerial Commission, which had overseen development since 1996. The new ministry has, since, actively promoted international forums that promote a global culture of information. However, it has done so without making any significant changes to the overall policy of Decree 209. While national policy is decreed by law from the Council of the State, Internet regulation and oversight has been divided up among the ministries charged with maintaining centralized state control. The actual working structure, though, has been both centralized and decentralized. Connection (application and oversight) was approved through CENIAI, while other government-sanctioned ISPs connect networks, have their own direct Internet connection, and provide e-mail and Web services. The IT infrastructure will continue to evolve, reflecting legal and administrativge challenges brought about as users expand the system and the state reorganizes its institutional and commercial interests. Meanwhile, digitization of telephone service has improved service and expanded the number of telephone lines. Expanded service also means more public services such as public phone booths and Internet cafes, but like mobile telephone service, these services come only at a premium. This combination of centralized and decentralized services reveals a pragmatic approach that partially solves the political dilemmas created by the use of the Internet, but also extends them, as it stretches the capacity of the citizenry.

In 1993, Cuba was designated by UNESCO's Intergovernmental Program on Informatics as a regional coordinating center in the fight against computer viruses. The Laboratorio Latinoamericano para la protección contra los Virus Informáticos (Latin American Laboratory for Protection against Information Viruses) had been established by UNESCO with the mandate of detecting new viruses in member countries, and of exchanging information to counteract virus damage.[63] That Cuba continues to play this designated role indicates recognition of its credibility and integrity in the field, a quality demonstrated in recent years by its investment in UCI, with an enrollment of several thousand students, and by its efforts against copyright violations.

Cuba has encouraged a cyberculture of international research and cooperation, hosting international conferences on digital and information technologies since 1988. The first Informática meeting was an endeavor of the Intergovernmental Office of Informatics (IBI) and "various Iberoamerican institutions, universities, and research centers."[64] Twenty-eight nations sent nearly 200 foreign delegates to the island. Out of almost 900 Cuban participants, more than 150 presented research, gathered from a multitude of social sectors; this participation revealed the breadth of efforts to discuss joint approaches, problems, and solutions. Subsequently held biannually, the cyberconferences have served Cuba's plan to become a software development center by facilitating international exchange among academics, engineers, developers, and distributors. The conferences also give the government an opportunity to show off its support for information technology.

A government priority since the Special Period has been to make the country a software development site so as to prepare economically and politically for the results of having new economic and social groupings. Developing a particular sector of the economy allows a degree of competitiveness in territories defined by trading blocs—for example, the Caribbean. Sites such as India have successfully created economic advantages by developing a highly trained informatics economy and workforce; Cuba has taken steps toward the same end. One such step, its commitment to educating software engineers, redoubled with the creation of UCI.[65]

To create a national software industry, Cuba must find areas where its software products can compete without interference from software giants. Cuba's educational and scientific software products circulate in schools and top research facilities. Rather than reinvent leading commercial software applications, native software is developed with Cuban domestic specificity in mind. New systems designed for tourism and science are created for Cuba's isolated, resource-deprived situation. In the late 1990s, software applications were developed that made managerial systems more efficient, saving money and time for hotels, banks, ports, news agencies, and other institutions. The new tools are also used in computation, communications, design, systems management, medicine, multimedia presentations, and general services to run the new business sector. During the 1990s, the state focused educational assistance on applications, for all ages, in mathematics, statistics, and medicine, a focus that still contributes to the state's overall commitment to education. A decade after connection to the Internet, a beta version of Cuban search engine dosportres.cu was presented at the Informática 2007 conference. Concerns about the U.S. embargo and the information blockade, raised at the initial conference, continue to guide efforts to create an alternate image of Cuba in the global imagination. The place of media technologies in art and culture forms another constant on the Informática agenda, focusing on tools for creativity, art education, research, and cultural dissemination.[66] As conceptual artist Nam June Paik stressed in the late 1960s, artistic use of digital technology helps "to humanize the technology and the electronic medium."[67] This is true in Cuba even though access is limited.

When possible, Cuba displays its software development plans and products so as to establish national brand identity, become a global player, and continue to provide institutional welfare for its citizens.

Three principal motives—financial, infrastructural, and political—lie behind the centralized design of the Cuban Internet. Payable in convertible currency, telecommunications in general and connectivity in particular are expensive for Cuban residents and tourists. Given the obstacles resulting from the U.S. embargo, Cuba's use of the Internet to generate hard currency has yet to mature. The logic of centralization seeks to limit Internet growth to better control its direction and development, given political and technical limits on the nation's available bandwidth. Domestic telephone infrastructure remains a problem, despite its receipt of the first foreign investment (from Italy) allowed in postrevolutionary Cuba, when, in 1992, the state relaxed some restrictions. Further foreign and domestic investment projected for communications infrastructure should alleviate connection scarcity as well as structural problems, but the pace of improvements tends to be slow. Centralization of the Internet theoretically organizes users through specific locations (work, public entities), to make the system efficient within resource constraints. For now, by connecting through institutions, borrowing access codes, or reselling computer components, Cuban users have in fact fostered an informal economy of the Internet (see chapter 5), an economy that must be resourceful and inventive, given the penalties, including large fines and jail time, for illegal use.

Centralization as a tool to control Internet use is not unexpected in a country with limited freedom of the press and general control by the state over information. Restrictions will become harder to maintain as the user community becomes more adept and the Internet more pervasive. Expansion takes place as electronic technology is absorbed into more forms of working, writing, and communicating. This growth is concurrent with, and truncated by, the high cost of services. E-mail, Web hosting, and other services have been available through several government-run ISPs, but at tariffs payable in hard currency (CUC) and too high in relation to the average Cuban salary to be easily affordable. Further, the need for many structural installations under the management of different agencies has led to several projects becoming ensnared in bureaucratic tangles. This acts as another factor prompting many creative Cubans to bypass obstacles by dialing in to "borrowed" connections from home. Restrictions and limitations directing Cubans to specific government-authorized spaces to access information technologies have prompted individual responses defiantly creating decentralized and quite disunited, if often shared, individual spaces.

The New Face of News Service and Medicine

Milagro (miracle) was the effusive term used by Jorge Barata, chief of information for the Cuban-based Prensa Latina—Latin America's second largest news service, cofounded by Gabriel García Marquez in the 1960s—to describe the entry of the service into the Internet, a strategy which saved the company. With reduced financial subsidies from the state, Prensa Latina had become unable to do business effectively. The cost of telegraphic service was prohibitive, as was the cost of maintaining correspondents in other nations. At first, in 1991, Prensa Latina reduced the number of journalists in its foreign offices from forty to eighteen. Hurricane Andrew in 1992 had left the telephone service in shambles. For some time after the hurricane, calls to Cuba from the United States took an unexpected detour through Italy. Without twenty-four-hour telephone access, the agency could barely maintain its service; journalists reduced to calling in information to the central office three times a day could not compete in the provision of up-to-the-minute news. Therefore, in 1995, (before Cuba's 1996 official connection to the Internet), Prensa Latina contracted with New York Transfer, a news collective in New York City, to distribute twice-daily news updates through the collective's server and Web site.[68] Given the problematic telephone connection, the strategy was fraught with peril; the limited service facilitated by the Transfer Web site could not make Prensa competitive against the immediacy and resources of other news services around the world. The agency could nevertheless use the Internet for its survival. For Prensa Latina, possessing Web real estate was key to providing information about Cuba at a crucial time when a socialist news agency might appear to some as out of step with history. The goal to carve out a virtual news presence that insisted on Cuban socialism despite the collapse of the USSR would later become the driving force behind the Cuban government's strategy in its National Information Project.

For Prensa Latina, financial difficulties formed only half of a bleak picture. With the fall of Communism, the news agency faced the challenge of redefining its image for a new market where a news service based in socialist Cuba could be considered irrelevant. The agency reconsidered its global image and its services, and found ways to use its trained technical staff, albeit with outdated equipment, to modernize its presentation on the New York Transfer Web site. By 2006, Prensa Latina had acquired its own domain and service in Cuba and developed a Web presence with advanced subscription news service providing access to a number of electronic services, including several linked to Cuba's prioritized sectors of medicine, tourism, and international business. Select links to alternative news sources began to offer a pan-American and increasingly global political and cultural profile, highlighting topics such as the U.S. war in Iraq, torture, and terrorism.[69] The result has become an information paradigm that defies the commercial and political orientation of global media empires (such as Rupert Murdoch's News Corporation).

At the end of the 1990s, the situation of Prensa Latina was representative of how historical change and economic hardship conditioned technological needs for which only a tenuous infrastructure existed. To look around the Prensa Latina press room in 1995 and see "miracles" carried out with scores of outdated computers recalls the spirit of José Arcadio Buendía and the gadgets of Melquíades the Gypsy in *One Hundred Years of Solitude.* The Prensa example illustrates that technology may be decreed outdated by manufacturers but not by the functions it can serve.

The Prensa Latina news agency is, moreover, an example of how Cuban state enterprises have been redefined as commercial enterprises, taking on the task of funding their operations (in hard currency), and improving services and facilities to compete in a broader market and at a profit. In addition to providing the news service, Prensa Latina has diversified and now, in collaboration with Cuban new-media firms, co-produces DVDs and CD-ROMs, among other educational and informational products, for sale online.

Prensa's reinvention took place in the context of the larger process of the remaking of Cuban institutions to serve both public interest and commercial sustainability. The difficult, even treacherous, nature of this challenge has become evident in the way Cuban businesses function. In the case of Prensa Latina, which works in an international framework, the focus is to become more competitive in a global media market so as to raise capital and generate revenue. Production is reoriented to serve foreign markets, and interests are realigned to meet the needs of the tourist and business sector. This highlights a move to exporting services, rather than fostering domestic consumption (a service filled by a limited number of news outlets); such a move crucially affects all aspects of production, particularly on the Internet, and creates a vicious circle for Cuba's economy. As digital technology is deployed as a tool for survival in a globalized market, it becomes an example of the result of diversion by the Cuban government of individual initiative to benefit state institutions. The perpetuation of scarcity and dilapidated infrastructure in Cuba in the modern, digital era in turn perpetuates a society where the everyday information world beyond the island becomes, for those living in Cuba, a world of information "miracles."

Predictably, the scientific–medical community benefits directly from the Internet and has been helpful in expanding the information culture on the island. InfoMed, the medical sector's intranet, began in 1994 with a grant from the United Nations Development Program. A team of specialists designed the network using infrastructure already in place for the exchange of medical information. Given the Cuban state's historical prioritization of the medical sector, this existing system, however limited, facilitated construction of a more sophisticated network. InfoMed not only provides information and e-mail access to people in the health sector, but also hosts a multitude of home-grown databases, chat rooms, and a regional subnetwork linking health care facilities throughout the island. Although many of the hospitals are online, principal medical facilities have priority.

InfoMed created a new service while following a conceptual design rooted in what Cuba's health care professionals perceived as their mission: to expand information within the health-care community, educate, and advance international medical cooperation.[70] The highly trained medical practitioners on the island have thus contributed to the rapid creation of an information culture in the field of medicine. Their goal is not only to provide cutting-edge medical information, but also to educate medical practitioners about the new electronic tools and its new ways of searching for information. InfoMed also provides a social space for discussion and sharing of information. Because not all medical professionals have the security clearance to access the World Wide Web, access is also provided through UNIX systems, as well as by trained staffers who download information that is later circulated among interested parties.[71] Since 1998, cooperation among the Ministry of Communications, the bioengineering sector, the telecommunications firm ETECSA, and InfoMed has brought telemedicine capabilities to central locations on the island and to sites of distance learning.[72] InfoMed is also partnered with a US-based nongovernmental organization, USA-Cuba InfoMed, dedicated to the support of public health development in the Third World and the Republic of Cuba.[73]

InfoMed's progressive-minded leaders sees their function as defined by flexible organizational parameters that benefit medical research and public health, adapting their approach to meet their objectives—a far cry from technocratic control. This community-based model is tailor-made for places with limited resources and restricted on-line access. Its success is due not only to its prioritization by the state, but also to its careful attention to the needs of the professionals whom it serves. The scope of this group has expanded, increasing reciprocation of international research information to InfoMed through the Internet, because the Cuban government promotes medicine on an internationalist basis. Since the 1990s, Cuban health-care workers have been first in rapid-deployment operations to assist in natural disasters occurring from Central America to Africa and the Balkans, and have served repeatedly in educational missions in Venezuela.[74]

Despite the successes of InfoMed and the global reaches of a revamped foreign trade sector based on tourism, instances in which media technologies play a key role, incongruities persist. The international opportunities associated with trade and science lead to selection of these areas for development while the arts lag behind. Analogous disparities also occur in countries such as the United States, albeit for different reasons. Cuba's doctors are as highly regarded as their counterparts in the West, yet, for the urban population, the condition of medical facilities, access to prescription and over-the-counter medicines and medical supplies, and so forth, all negatively affected by the economic downturn of the 1990s, have yet to fully recover. The situation is such that a number of solidarity projects supply medicines and computer hardware through international donations in support of the growing InfoMed network. Technology serving one particular sector, that is, cannot alone resolve a basic scarcity of resources.

Old Tricks in a New Era

Beyond the official way that the Cuban government promotes the creation of informatics experts in the fields of education and the sciences, technology has been redirected for other social uses. The same Cuban expert who celebrates the repatriated chicken is a long-time short-wave radio amateur who values the importance of information networks for skilled professionals in under-developed societies. He would be *hardweriando* when building a computer at home out of components from varied sources. A friend or relative traveling to the island would bring a motherboard or a modem to be added to a standard computer box and electrical core. Coro would then give the assembled, fully functioning, if completely nonstandard, computer to a doctor in the neighborhood. Installed with a basic Unix system, the homemade computer in one case allowed the doctor to log on to InfoMed, the Cuban medical network, from home. Crude as it was, the improvised system helped solve a problem caused by a fuel shortage during the Special Period, a problem that prevented the doctor from accessing the shared network at his clinic. For the doctor, this still-analogue access transformed the way he worked and researched, and added to the social and professional networks facilitating both activities. At least temporarily, the doctor's professional need was met through a web of personal relations that yielded expertise, equipment, and access.

As Coro notes, it is crucial to realize the "social importance of technology utilized for human development."[75] Paradoxically, the Cuban state would agree. The gap between the visions of social benefit framed in Party rhetoric by the state and its limited, inadequate material provisions creates a fascinating interstitial territory. The resultant adaptive, flexible space is created by Cuban citizens, whose frustrations are shaped not only by a sense of unmet individual needs but also by a desire for more than personal consumption; remarkably, the insistence on a command economy over the decades of the Cuban socialist project has built communities of people willing to risk state sanctions in order to fulfill aims consistent with those of the state by means made illicit by the state.

With four decades of economic embargo, Cuba is ripe for leapfrogging technological and other development. The embargo, as a fundamental barrier, and then the aftermath of the withdrawal of Soviet support form significant obstacles to projects such as the timely installation of a fully modernized communications infrastructure. Although Cuba's geography facilitates the cross-island branching of fiber-optic cable, the execution of the project depends on foreign capital. In 2005, Cuba had 7.5 telephones per one thousand inhabitants, double the number in the early 1990s but still barely half that of the world average of 12.1.[76] According to Valdés, "on July 26, 1996, Radio Habana Cuba announced a plan to increase telephone lines from five hundred thousand to a million, with a goal of 20 telephones per one hundred urban inhabitants and ten per one hundred rural inhabitants."[77] Linking the announcement to July 26—the commemoration of the revolution—typifies the Party's exploitation of official days of celebration for hailing accomplishments. Since the announcement, a small number of digital lines have been made available—for customers who can pay in dollars. The government thus continues to attempt to garner support for the revolutionary vision notwithstanding the severe constraints and everyday sacrifices it asks of the Cuban people. Telecommunication scarcities may slowly be mitigated as the state draws in new investment and develops greater access to cellular technology. Raúl Castro's 2008 relaxation of consumer restrictions, including those on the purchase of cell phones, to some degree lets the government off the hook, at least temporarily, in terms of responsibility for telecommunications infrastructure. The lack of public provision in this field and in computing nevertheless means Cubans will have to continue to rely on their ability to work "magic" to establish claims on the virtual world for their own or their neighbor's good.

Hesitant approaches in the arts sectors and audacious ones in medicine illustrate the gamut of state prioritization of technological development in relative importance to the national project. In nonprioritized areas, progress is slow and uneven. In the fall of 1998, I asked a filmmaker how the Instituto Cubano de Arte e Industria Cinematográfica, or ICAIC (Cuban Institute of Film Art and Industry) was benefiting from the new Internet connection. The lukewarm response, while disappointing, was understandable, since the ICAIC was busy rebuilding its infrastructure and leadership ranks.[78] Some established filmmakers had not made a film in ten years, and in 1996 the ICAIC was unable to complete any feature films. A year later, however, a Web site was launched, and, though its development has been slow, the Cubacine. cu portal of the ICAIC features information covering the island's expanding audiovisual culture.

Although Cuba has made significant changes since 1991 with regard to economic policy, tax laws, employment, etc., the Party leadership reiterates that these changes are in line with a socialist agenda. The government rejects wholeheartedly the assumed market benefits of neoliberal platforms seen during the 1990s in Latin American countries such as Mexico and Argentina, pointing to the worsening of the already huge disparity between rich and poor. Cuba faces increased economic disparities at home as a negative consequence of its own economic reforms produced by the influx of foreign capital and the concentration of the economy on tourism. Its resolute stance against neoliberalism nonetheless finds support in the UNESCO 2005 Human Development Report, focused on international cooperation, which stated, "One-fifth of humanity live in countries where many people think nothing of spending $2 a day on a cappuccino. Another fifth of humanity survive on less than $1 a day and live in countries where children die for want of a simple anti-mosquito bednet."[79]

The Cuban government has acted quickly to establish partnerships when other Latin American nations have elected leaders friendly to Cuban socialism. Economic agreements to foster cooperation with Venezuela followed the 1999 election of Hugo Chávez as president, and also extended to the members of the Bolivarian Alliance for the Americas (ALBA) in South America.[80]

New trade agreements, the opening to global markets, and alternative theoretical positions have had an impact on the cultural landscape of Cuba at the beginning of the twenty-first century. However, the information provided on state Web sites does not question single-party rule, as the Communist Party remains the sole political party listed under the government portal. Participation by NGOs remains limited. Since they are often linked to U.S. financial support, not all are allowed access to e-mail, making it difficult for individual groups and potential partners to form a base from which to operate. The Internet has become much more publicly visible in the new century, albeit mainly on an official level. It has become a topic of discussion on television, a revenue-generating business, a political tool, and a form of subversion. These are signs of an emerging cyberculture where state and citizen have variable input. National service for Cubans entrusts them with firearms, but the state has yet to arm its people with full access to information and communication. Raúl Castro has so far limited relaxation of restrictions, but he has lifted enough to stir excitement in Cuba and elsewhere that a resolution of the scarcities preventing widespread entry by Cubans into the digital world may be pending. Until official debate about the subject produces action, however, Cubans will surely continue to pick the digital locks, perhaps increasingly for personal gain rather than common good, as global cybercultures creep under the Cuban door carrying new forms of social expression.

2

MEDIA TECHNOLOGIES AND "CUBAN DEMOCRACY"

One of the essential advantages of this new technology [the Internet] is that it is the proper means through which we can reveal to the world, on a more even field of struggle than that of other mass media, the realities of our country and of the Revolution. Therefore, in addition to its being a strategic necessity for the country, it is also an important challenge not only technologically, but also economically and politically.

—Carlos Lage Dávila, vice president of the Cuban State Council, 1996

Search for "Cuban students" on YouTube, and you'll find numerous versions of a public meeting held at UCI that turned into an international media story.[1] Six months prior to elections for the Cuban National Assembly in January 2008, Raúl Castro launched a national debate on Cuban society, inviting Cuban citizens to critique the state of the nation. The call appears to have prompted over a million written responses from a national population of just over eleven million. The open forum at UCI between students and Ricardo Alarcón de Quesada, president of the National Assembly of Popular Power, was videotaped and the video anonymously provided to the BBC in Havana. Uploaded to YouTube, the four-minute video (a longer version was eventually also uploaded to the Internet) made provocative headlines: "Videos Hint at Public Discontent in Cuba," "Students Challenge Regime in Rare Video," "People in Cuba Are Becoming More Vocal in Their Calls for Change."[2] International news sources, including CNN, covered the story, and the video ran on various Web sites. Among the students seen in the video, Eliécer Ávila would become the unwitting online celebrity for his tough questions about Cuban inequities and travel restrictions—why, for example, could he not visit the place in Bolivia where Che Guevara died? Most surprising was Alarcon's evasive reply and the anachronistic worldview it embodied: if six billion people traveled at once, he lectured, imagine the resulting gridlock of people. The video clip, copied onto flash drives and distributed hand-to-hand around the country, took about two weeks to reach international audiences. From Ávila's point of view, the type of personal freedoms he desired in no way contradicted the purpose and ideology of the revolution. Other online videos of the conversation between the students and Alarcón reveal similar concerns, agreements, disagreements, and exchanges of personal anecdotes.

The political volley that followed on the Internet developed the story in several directions: potential changes to result from the new leadership of Raúl Castro; media manipulation; matters of truth; ongoing repression; examples of authoritarianism; and examples of openness by the Cuban regime. At the core of discussions about the exchange lies an understanding that media is malleable, digital, and difficult for a single agency to control. Taken together, the semiotic analysis reached surprising levels. Participants in the on- and offline analysis of the Alarcón–student exchange reviewed the body language of students and other audience members for signs of nervousness, assessed clothing for symbolism (Avila's tee-shirt bearing the @ sign was thought to be an emblem of anarchy), and attached importance to the order in which students presented their claims. While this live, political event continued the entrenched pro- versus anti-Cuba debate, it also multiplied the connections between media spaces on and off the island in its widespread, multimedia distribution, from video and Web to television and newspapers.

However low the percentage of Cubans officially connected to the Internet, the Internet is clearly connected to Cuban society, even as the government attempts to manage its visibility. Wherever and however they log on, users increase the role of media technology within political and private life. Awareness by the regime that this would occur can be seen in predictions such as that by Carlos Lage, vice president of the Cuban Council, who said in 1996 that deployment of the Internet in Cuba would bring political challenges. The heated 2008 exchange between students and politician, along with the students' impassioned responses, surely represent such a challenge, but one whose forms lend unexpected complexity.

Beyond (and because of) the assertions of repression or censorship, the students' views reiterate that Cuban society has moved on from its earlier revolutionary character, as reflected in the shift in how people talk about their freedoms, expectations, and futures. Young people tend to articulate their claims to the revolution differently from their leaders, even as they use language from the earlier campaigns, such as "solidarity," "revolution," and "manipulation."

"Problems debated in the 1960s—responsibility and revolution," Jean Franco contends, "have altogether disappeared from view, giving way to discussions of democracy and civil society."[3] These issues leave Cuba's formative modern history behind, and relate instead to immediate sentiments about contemporary lives at the edge of global pressures.

As noted in chapter 1, in Cuba, digital media technology is officially cast as an instrument of the state in the pursuit of public benefit, encouraging personal expertise and use for the common good. Setting the Alarcón–student forum in Cuba's high-tech university emphasizes the symbolic social role assigned to media technology. Repeated, unchanging claims from external critics that the policy strategy is authoritarian in nature produces the usual response from Cuban leaders and bureaucrats about Cuba's rights to self-determination. Constructive criticism needs to recognize the complicated currents flowing through Cuba and exemplified in popular and state deployments of media technology. Examination of such deployment reveals a measure of validity to the position of both critics and state, locked in stalemate. Such an engagement addresses the alternative notions of democracy each represents.

The Alarcón–student exchange evokes a general question about media—the weight of the broadcast event on society—and focuses on digital media and the creation of new spaces of democratic expression. The present chapter, however, examines also media technologies in Cuba from the perspective of the political and social democratization process that presently infuses the nation, challenging denial by critics that any such process is at work in late-Castro-era Cuba. It also looks at how the processes involved become constrained by attempts to "impose democracy" from the outside through approaches that associate democracy with a particular form of the state and representation. It is worth recognizing that Cuban society is built on democratic values of equality, community, and participation as defined and limited within a Martí-inspired and Marxist-Leninist ideology.[4] The revolutionary government has long implemented centralized cultural policy strategies to facilitate the transformation of Cuban culture, and contemporary practices continue this historical approach to the needs of society. Fear of the characteristics of networked digital technology (decentralized networks, one-to-one and many-to-many communication, and so on) prompts a centralized command of the Internet. External reporting by U.S. telecommunication researchers on Cuba typically centers on this centralization, ignoring the historical values that inform the government's social ideals. Such analysis limits the interpretation of democracy to structures of power strictly associated with free-market models. In the case of Cuba, the state's values may steer the course of the ideological project, but the ideological project unfolds as differently as in response to foreign attacks and a politics of embargo. Unfettered, nonauthoritarian access to media and its technologies can only come about when a state does not feel attacked.

Defining Cuban Democracy

As the end of the Castro era approaches, exiles, Miami hardliners, USAID projects, and American businesspeople prepare to export what they consider true democracy. Just as firmly, the Cuban state stands guard over its democratic achievements, sovereignty, and vision of the future. Increasingly significant, however, are larger concepts of democracy underlying various models of globalization and the role of media technologies within them. As the island attempts to leverage its international future, its government's legitimacy continues to be questioned by an external opposition reluctant to acknowledge the country's changes. None of the government's likely new partners will be fixed on the Cold War paradigm that preoccupies the United States in its policy toward Cuba. Pragmatic relations, even when couched in idealistic terms, will determine the nature and degree of engagement with the island. This is true also of nongovernmental groups in the United States that advocate for an end to the embargo. Still, the pervasive discussion about Cuba is focused on electoral democracy. Paying attention to processes of democratization less visible through the electoral lens may reveal, however, a dynamic process as people respond to the shift in power.

As the locus of aspirations, adaptations, ingenuity, protest, creative expression, and spirituality, culture plays a significant role in processes of democracy. Exactly how Cuba is democratic will not be determined by state openness, but rather by all the forces contributing to the people's survival.

However, assessment of Cuba's political system needs to go beyond, for example, standards set by the World Bank to enable the operation of corporate trade. "Global democracy"[5] needs to account for each point of intersection in what Anna Tsing calls the "chain link" view of globalization, avoiding the hyperexploitation of those "working at the edges of legality."[6] Media technologies convey ideas of global democracy and expose whether or not they are enacted. Cuba already faces the challenge of entrenched views that consider state institutions undemocratic; in working toward its aim of full global legitimacy, the Cuban government confronts historical limitations not detected in the heat of external scrutiny. A cessation of the hostility frequently entailed in the international focus on Cuba would likely assist the development of a more open society.

A more realistic understanding of the Cuban state could begin with a greater recognition of the historical process that shapes the way the government creates its political model. Cuba exhibits a complex evolution of systems of governance—from colonial–extractive to neocolonial capitalist, to socialist, and to hybrid. Interacting with various forms of economic models, democracy in present-day Cuba, as in many capitalist countries (including Indonesia and the United States), is not coherent. Rather, it mirrors proliferating global challenges resulting from new models of economic production, social participation, and war. The understanding of democracy needs to shift away from strict institutional and political considerations—particularly since the implementation of democratic principles in earnest remains elusive throughout most of the world—to include the role of social movements and culture in general in public and private spheres.[7] To respond to challenges posed by increasingly mobile populations dispersed from their cultural origins, as well as by limited natural resources, shifting patterns of global labor, and the global hegemony of privatized capital, approaches to democracy must address individual and collective well-being, not rights alone, and not only within but also beyond the confines of the nation-state. Such an understanding of democratic standards unmasks the duplicitous nature of proscriptive projects where democracy itself is a buzzword cum policy, a duplicitous nature evident in U.S. legislation such as the Cuban Liberty and Democratic Solidarity Act of 1996 (the Helms-Burton Act) intensifying the U.S. embargo. President Bill Clinton clearly stated his administration's goal in such terms in a 1997 report to the US Congress: "Promotion of democracy abroad is one of the primary foreign policy objectives of my Administration."[8] According to the restrictive Helms-Burton Act (discussed below), Cuba must not only answer the call for electoral reform, but its government cannot be considered "democratic" until no individual named Castro is head of government and the economy is fully opened to private enterprise. Beyond such ad hoc considerations under its selective interpretation of democracy, the U.S. government reveals an unreasonable stance over Cuba in its designation of countries to anoint. It suggests deeply rooted political conflicts often dramatically played out through exile politics in the United States.[9] This position differs from that in which the United States engages in free trade agreements with the government of Mexico, communist China, and Vietnam. Despite repeated electoral controversies and charges of government corruption, at no time has the United States broken diplomatic relations with Mexico. China's single-party rule also appears less problematic than Cuba's, as it openly embraces an open market economy.

The advocacy of democracy defined in the context of market economics has become the typical means to pressure governments deemed unfriendly to U.S. interests. As an incentive to achieve desired transformations in a nation committed to defying the model of private, individualistic capitalism, the goal of "freedom" is promoted as an aim to be attained through consumerism, dissidence, and a private media model. In this way, media channels become arms in a battle to impose external, Western notions of democracy in place of homegrown processes already occurring and ripe for cultivation.

Issues like the environment, trade, human rights, and terrorism increasingly demand transnational solutions, and, as media connections go global, defining democracy is no simple task. A definition by political scientists Dietrich Rueschemeyer, Evelyn H. Stephens, and John D. Stephens in their 1992 book *Capitalist Development and Democracy* suggests that the concept of democracy "entails, first, regular, free and fair elections of representatives with universal and equal suffrage, second, responsibility of the state apparatus to the elected parliament (possibly complemented by direct election of the head of the executive), and third, the freedoms of expression and association as well as the protection of individual rights against arbitrary state action."[10] The first two components of this definition—universal suffrage and responsibility of the state apparatus to the elected parliament—are traditionally considered the essence of democracy. The third dimension of civil rights does not in itself constitute democratic ideals, but is a necessary condition for the creation of a stable democracy as contained within and limiting the power of the state.

With a view toward global democracy and away from the central role of democracy confined to the nation-state, British political theorist David Held stresses not national institutions but, instead, shared principles as a basis for the "protection and nurturing of each person's equal significance in the moral realm of humanity." These principles include equal worth and dignity, active agency, personal responsibility and accountability, consent, collective decision making about public matters through voting procedures, inclusiveness and subsidiarity, avoidance of serious harm, and sustainability.[11]

The definitions both of Ruechmeyer et al. and of Held take into consideration the weight of external influence on the accountability of state power. But Ruechmeyer and his joint authors see democracy territorially bound within the nation-state, where the negotiation of power lies at the core. Democracy in this way is tied to power relations between classes, to the impact of transnational power on the structure and strength of the state, and to the interrelation between the state and civil society. The focus of this approach is to examine the forces that, in relation to the state, predict a democratic outcome. In the case of Cuba, the balance of domestic power is distorted by the punitive U.S. embargo and by hostile relations with the exiled Cuban community. Neither Cuba nor the United States are acting democratically, in Held's terms, because neither upholds the principles he outlines within their own states, nor do they act to share those principles universally to guarantee safety and respect within the greater community of humanity. Held's ideas grant human beings equal rights across competing ideologies, accounting as well for non-nation-based territories and for stateless peoples.

The latter expansion of the philosophical terrain of democracy potentially ends the circularity of debate about Cuba and its authoritarian tendencies. It would recognize the negative influence of the embargo culture that plagues the greater evolution of democratic practices and even lessens the prospects of regime change. Held's wider concept underpins French economist Daniel Cohen's notion of interconnected "levers" that move together toward global democracy. In acknowledging that shared dignity encompasses the ability to make choices, Cohen agrees with economist Amartya Sen's statement that such dignity "is itself an essential step of human liberty."[12] A Cuba regime free from paranoia about U.S. aggression, and therefore free to play a full global role, might well act to bring about much-increased personal liberties and individual freedoms. Cubans will demand a relaxation of media restrictions to expand the personal and social benefits of digital technology, thus transforming the vital function of Cuban networks; however, the first necessary step on this road would be democracy (re)defined both globally and locally.

Contemporary debates often treat democracy as absent from Cuba. In establishing an alternative role for culture, however, postrevolutionary Cuba successfully made "culture at all levels accessible to the entire population" and embarked on an ambitious literacy campaign.[13] These culturally and socially democratic projects redressed a legacy of cultural policies favoring mostly U.S. cultural industries. For over a century, the United States forcefully and repeatedly articulated programs for "achieving democracy in Cuba"—in manners ranging from extraterritorial legislation (say, the Platt Amendment that became U.S. law from 1901 to 1934) to forceful action (Bay of Pigs invasion, 1961) and even position papers by special interest groups (like the International Committee for Democracy in Cuba, 2003). This U.S. intent to mold Cuban political culture has remained remarkably consistent, whatever the U.S. regime in power. The capitalist, antisocialist U.S. strategic approach during the Special Period was typified by the U.S. Cuban Democracy Act of 1992 (CDA) and the Helms-Burton Act of 1996; both legislative measures tied democracy to telecommunications media in a plan made effective with the cooperation of third parties and successful only if used to benefit U.S. interests. Through the Helms-Burton Act, the United States gives financial assistance to nongovernment groups in Cuba in the hope of fomenting opposition.

Tactics designed to support the export of U.S. political and economic ideology have remained basically unchanged. Prescriptive programs for democracy in Cuba seem to downplay ongoing debates on Cuban soil, working mostly with independent, hostile groups. As a sovereign nation, the Cuban government decries this type of foreign interference in its domestic politics. State-sponsored campaigns to generate debate, especially during the Raúl Castro presidency, are attempting to work through the challenges confronting the development of civil society with fewer prohibitions. Prominent Cuban literary journals, such as *Criterios* and *Temas*, address controversies, connect Cuban scholars with globally critical issues, and provide a space for the renovation of ideas. Media technologies open up new social, economic, and political opportunities for Cubans by advancing the speed of communication, expanding its scope, and increasing its forms. The juncture of digital media technologies with a society in transition presents important components of globalization limited by extant conditions.

Imposing "Democracy"

Ironically, the potential for increased democratization of Cuba realized through social improvements is restricted by the U.S. embargo, which blocks Cuba's economic, trade, and communications development. Media have been used in attempts to bring about the end of the Castro regime ever since the early 1960s, when "Radio Swan" in Florida served as base of communications for planning the Bay of Pigs invasion. In the early 1980s, the U.S. government revised its policies concerning United States–Cuba communications, fearing, after the Nicaraguan socialist victory, that communism might spread to Central America. Propelled by these fears, the 1983 Radio Broadcasting to Cuba Act (P.L. 98–111) established Radio Martí and was followed in 1990 by Public Law 101–246, which created TV Martí. Both stations came under the Voice of America network. Funded by the U.S. government, both Radio Martí and TV Martí, have from their inception, broadcast news programming with an emphasis on criticism of the Castro government. TV Martí produces some hours of original programming, interspersed with political commentary meant to offer listeners in Cuba news deemed missing from Cuban media, and thus an alternative ideology. The broadcast spectrum for these stations has been defined strategically, but unsuccessfully for signals to penetrate the island's blocking maneuvers. Radio Martí and TV Martí also broadcast on the Internet. Opposing sides, it should be noted, both claim Martí, the romantic poet and independence leader, as their ideological mentor, one as a proto-socialist, the other as a modern democrat.[14] In 1992, following the demise of the former Soviet Union, Senator Robert G. Torricelli from New Jersey wrote the Cuban Democracy Act, which, in addition to tightening restrictions, authorized telecommunication connections and information exchange between the United States and Cuba—but only to increase the potential for regime change. The Helms-Burton Act amended the Cuban Democracy Act by prohibiting investment in Cuba's domestic communications infrastructure.[15] Ushered in by Republican senators Jesse Helms and Dan Burton during Clinton's presidency, the act penalizes any foreign company doing business with Cuba by preventing it subsequently from doing business in the United States, and threatened litigation for property claims made illegal by the act. According to the U.S. State Department Web site on United States–Cuba relations, "The legislation, among other provisions, codified the U.S. trade embargo into law and imposed additional sanctions on the Cuban regime."[16] Lifting the embargo would previously have been a matter of presidential decree; with the passage of Helms-Burton, it became subject to an act of the U.S. Congress.

The Helms-Burton bid to undermine the government of Fidel Castro has been repeatedly denounced throughout the world as a violation of international trade agreements. Canada, Mexico, and Spain have been particularly vocal in denouncing Helms-Burton, and have forged ahead in cementing economic relations with Cuba, at a time when countries in the southern hemisphere are showing increasing independence from the United States.[17] The European Parliament threatened to file an international lawsuit with NATO if the United States enforced the law. Helms-Burton has also backfired: twice, the U.S. government sent "warning letters" to the Sol Meliã Group, one of Spain's largest investors in hotel and construction projects in Cuba, stating that an inquiry into its business holdings in Cuba would determine if they were in violation of Articles III and IV of Helms-Burton. Sol Meliã's executives were also to be denied visas to the United States, where they operated two hotels (in Florida). Satisfied with the status, profits, and potential for expansion in Cuba, the Meliã Group said that it would rather close its hotels in the United States.[18] Repeatedly, from its inception in 1996 and through the Clinton administration, enforcement of Title III of the Helms-Burton legislation (which targeted foreign firms investing in American expropriated properties in Cuba) was suspended due to rising international pressure from the European Union, the Organization of American States, and powerful Canadian investors. The George W. Bush administration maintained the same policy and, in 2004, implemented further restrictive travel and economic constraints for tourists and visiting family members. Within the first six months of his presidency, in 2009, Barack Obama announced to the U.S. Congress his action to suspend, for six months beginning August 1, 2009, such action under Title III of Helms-Burton; he had first shelved travel and remittance restrictions on Cuban family members.

During Bush's presidency, funding for Radio Martí continued alongside the legislative strategy embodied by Helms-Burton. The U.S. Broadcasting Board of Governors (BBG) and the Office of the Inspector General mandated an independent panel of experts to conduct a review (1997–1998) of Radio

Martí's journalistic practices, program content, and adherence to Voice of America standards. The BBG was responding to mounting allegations of problems at Radio Martí, allegations that proved well founded and implicated top management. The 1999 report called for a revision of oversight policies, for implementation by the International Media Center at Florida International University (FIU). FIU oversaw the programming review for the panel of experts, and carried out training of journalists to improve the quality of reporting. Professional survey research contracted by the BBG showed dramatically reduced audience share, which in 2001 fell 5 percent, from 9 percent in 2000 and 71 percent in 1992.[19] A Cuba Working Group review of U.S. policy toward Cuba recommended termination of the ineffective transmissions.[20] Negative results notwithstanding, the BBG's 2005 annual report conveyed a positive outlook for the success of the policy, and complimented its unfounded optimism with a recommendation for a funding increase. Indeed, former U.S. Secretary of State Condoleezza Rice, a member of the BBG Board, was quoted in the report: "Radio Martí's truthful broadcasts are among the most effective U.S. weapons in the war of ideas." She also made clear her support for the airborne transmissions of TV Martí.[21]

The intensification of Radio and TV Martí broadcasting has failed to yield immediate results, and show the types of confrontations generated by efforts to impose programs of democratization. Under the ongoing pressures of legislation and the bombardment of U.S. propaganda, Cuba resists, selectively blocking external access. Cuba easily locates and blocks the signals coming from the blimp, tethered at Cudjoe Key, that is hoisted when TV Martí broadcasts. Slow signals headed to Cuba thus encounter atmospheric politics while occasionally subversive and unobstructed submarine fiber optics pulse below. The new strategy of broadcasting for longer hours sends the TV Martí signal via satellite from AeroMartí, a transmitter on a Gulfstream jet; this too has failed to garner the expected audience, leading a 2007 report from the Center for International Policy to conclude that the broadcasts "have little or no audience and are largely irrelevant to Cubans on the island."[22] Meanwhile, episodes of *Desperate Housewives*, *House*, *CSI*, and *Lost* (tacitly permitted by the Cuban state, and broadcast, oddly, on Cuba's educational channel) find a warm welcome from Cuban audiences, who have always been avid fans of American television and film.[23] And the Cuban government resists the spread of the intended satellite footprint created by the incoming frequencies (as media scholar Lisa Parks proposes in *Cultures in Orbit*, satellite footprints shape the impact of television signals and help to redefine cultural territory).[24]

Official U.S. efforts to force its concept of democracy on Cuba have persisted in large part due to power wielded by Cuban exiles holding senior positions in the U.S. government, among them U.S. Representatives Lincoln and Mario Díaz-Balart from Florida. The power base of these politicians in turn resides in Miami, and includes such diverse elements among the Cuban exile community as vocal, hard-line, anti-Castro conservatives and more moderate groups (see chapter 5). Mutually reinforcing, the U.S. government and the exile community perpetuate a partial view, one that serves their individual interests, of the Cuban state as an authoritarian threat. Human rights violations by the Cuban government emerge as a common topic, the subject of numerous homegrown Web sites, and much Radio Martí and TV Martí programming. Web sites used to stage conflicts over civil liberties are harder than radio or television to block, demonstrating the greater capacity of modern media technologies to successfully propagate divergent points of view.

In the hands of well-resourced nongovernmental organizations, media combined with an organized presence within Cuba play a more powerful role in presenting the picture of Cuba as an undemocratic state. A growing network of NGOs (in 1994, 2,200 were registered with the Cuban government) defines the political contours of the ideological tug-of-war among accounts on Cuban networks, accounts held by cultural institutions like Casa de las Américas and Centro Memorial Martin Luther King, media networks such as Radio-Habana-Cuba, and religious entities like Consejo de Iglesias de Cuba. Gillian Gunn, who conducted a study of Cuban NGOs and analyzed their relationship to the government, asks "Are Cuban NGOs government puppets or seeds of civil society?" and concludes that "the answer is ideologically and intellectually unsatisfying. They are both, though the latter characteristic is very gradually growing."[25]

As seeds of emerging civil society, NGOs can receive significant funding from U.S. federal agencies, such as USAID, for "democracy assistance." Official findings from USAID note that its Cuba program "provided a wide range of democracy-related assistance from 1996–2006. Citizens in Havana said that this assistance provided moral support and enhanced their ability to continue their pro-democracy work."[26] Cuban grantees received humanitarian and material assistance that include shortwave radios, DVD players, cameras, office equipment, and supplies. Using Cold War rhetoric, the Cuban government repeatedly produces evidence that NGOs are funded by the CIA (or USAID, etc.) and support counterrevolutionary activity on the island.[27] Because NGOs do receive funding from the U.S. government, spread anti-Castro propaganda, and foster antigovernment activities, the socially constructive functioning of any and all US-related NGOs is obstructed by official suspicion.

Even without intent to support dissent, the supply of media equipment by NGOs mirrors the constant drive by U.S. organizations to push for greater connectivity. Just as the latter ignores the reality of a boundary-ridden Internet, the hope of outcomes to force deep political change underestimates the strength of the Cuban construction of media technologies around social rather than individual use. Collective connectivity permitted through worksites and social spaces like the youth "computing clubs," and even through illegal routes, is already having an impact on the way technology is used. This social, collective access, although still incipient, coincides with the energy produced by the initial reforms of Raúl Castro's government. Only time will define how users render the technology useful to them and how much government direction will have shaped its characteristics. NGOs with a broad focus, like the Centro Memorial Martin Luther King, sponsor cultural programs, scholars, journalists, and libraries, leading to burgeoning assistance for participatory cultural institutions supported by the Cuban government but separate from it. On the other hand, technology observers like Christopher R. Kedzie, who focus on *individual* access in relation to interconnectivity, do not see the potential of popular culture to mediate democratic participation.

Given an official political line stringently upheld in the face of constant threat, the state is unlikely to allow unfettered private media access to flourish until secure measures are in place. Computer networks and media access provide only part of the solution. Answers lie both in acknowledgment of the democratic dimension of the Cuban revolution and in a relaxation of the Cuban state to permit the dangerous freedoms that come with open networks and societies—changes clearly difficult for Cuba.

In summary, Cuba actually demonstrates forms of democracy that are undervalued in the assessment of openness and are therefore ignored, producing an intractable conflict and confounding debate that has ensued for five decades. By imposing fixed political ideas, external agents inadvertently prolong Cuba's own political fixity, which includes a rigid framework for deployment of media technologies that is both personally restrictive and socially generous.

State, Media, and Democracy

The state responds to accusations of authoritarian control by justifying its own version of democracy, a position evident in its development of global information networks. Emerging during a period of tremendous uncertainty, the Internet has enlivened the political challenges alluded to by Carlos Lage. There, groups deemed dissident carve out an independent space of transmission outside the central contours of power, connecting like-minded users and coalitions under a universal rights paradigm. Restricted access to media portals has become the red flag signaling Cuban authoritarianism in the digital age, and has been perceived as a flagrant obstacle to democracy, yet Cuba's support of technological literacy and its cultivation of expertise in digital media place the evolution of technology in the hands of individuals. The state defines the framework for application of the skills learned, but no bounds can be placed on the inventiveness and innovation allowed in the prescribed public service arenas, an inventiveness that lets Cuban people circumvent difficulties.

Recognizing the importance of the Cuban government's emphasis on educated participation in technology, Lage pointed out, in his plenary speech for the Informática 2000 conference, a major inadequacy of privatized technology in the face of global inequities. Using the same language as Cuba's critics, he exhorted, "Without democratic access to technological development, all predictions of a new global economy based on informatics and communications will only be available for a minority and will continue to be an unreachable dream for the majority of humanity."[28] The Cuban vice president echoed Cohen's description of a system of "economic levers" that further the wealth of a nation beyond human labor, with education and machines serving as the first two levers augmented by a "third, more mysterious lever called 'global efficiency,' which includes technological progress and the organizational efficiency of businesses."[29] Lage challenges the international community to meet democratic expectations in the twenty-first century by opposing prominent models of economic privatization and work to achieve Cohen's "global efficiency." From this perspective, more democratic advancement and application of media technologies would see less virtual monopoly by companies like Microsoft and more internationally standardized but indigenously developed technology of the kind encouraged by the Cuban state. Beyond the creation of software and technology, where does the threshold of democratic access lie? Judging democracy from media practices, or by degree of social function (for example, the extent of public health programs) may provide insights into nontraditional democratic processes. Even though there are no clear-cut answers, keeping this question in mind can help thread a way through the dense foliage of political rhetoric.

The current Cuban version of democratic media technology development and usage echoes earlier dissident methods of organizing—for instance, when media played a key role in political resistance against the corrupt and punitive Fulgencio Batista regime. Arriving in power after a military coup in 1954, Batista's dictatorship was characterized by state violence and the repression of oppositional movements. During his tenure, "the CIA was a pervasive presence, . . . developing 'assets' and 'liaisons' throughout the political, social, coercive, and administrative fabric . . . and its state structure."[30] The establishment of Radio Rebelde, a clandestine radio station in the eastern mountains founded by Che Guevara, allowed the leadership of the 26 of July Movement (the guerrilla group headed by Fidel Castro) to update the people of Cuba about the resistance movement. By the time Batista left power at the end of 1958, ending the guerrilla war, thirty-two such provincial radio stations had been created and, with Radio Rebelde, formed the so-called Liberty Network.[31]

Radio thus played a key role in political organizing against Batista. Just as Howard Dean's 2004 presidential nomination campaign initiated "netroots" groups through the Internet—a strategy later intensified by the Barack Obama 2008 presidential campaign—so the rebels of the 26 of July Movement informed rural communities and organized support through broadcasts of Radio Rebelde from the Escambray Mountains. Political resistance became political power for the former Cuban dissidents who used not only radio but film, television, and the printed press to consolidate postrevolutionary society. Audiovisual media were oriented socially, to reflect national concerns and to continue the revolutionaries' commitment to a new Cuban nationalism and against imperialist capitalism.

Military victory was followed by the struggle against destructive foreign cultural values. Concomitant with the presentation of socialist ideals of volunteerism and responsibility, media content included materials guided by conservative political views. Rock and roll music, including the Beatles, and books by Cuban author Severo Sarduy and the Peruvian Mario Vargas Llosa were banned; *telenovelas* found new themes not representing bourgeois capitalist ideology. Such acts of censorship as defensive media strategy, intensifying from the late 1960s until the late 1970s, were characterized by the Communist Party as "resisting the penetration of the enemy."[32] Paternalistic, repressive attempts by the state to control mass media met their match in the Cuban people who listened to, or read in secret, all the smuggled portable media they could obtain. Even students returning from the USSR managed to bring in illicit paperbacks and vinyl records. Since then, the Cuban state has come to relax its stance and embrace reforms, excoriating its own past behavior. *Telenovelas* shape cultural debate, reaching levels of prerevolution popularity; rock and roll music, though sometimes still a source of repression, is a staple of Cuban radio (and of Radio Martí); Cuban state officials even attended the unveiling of a statue of John Lennon in a residential park in Havana in December 2000. As always, heavy-handed control of media by Party ideologues to limit official discourse to sanctioned democratic ideals produced popular resistance that in both content and practice expressed alternative concepts of democracy.

The novelty of television in the 1950s coincided with the energy of a victorious revolution. This opportune juncture particularly defined the medium as a powerful social and political tool. Fidel Castro appeared so frequently (and spoke for so long) that Cuban author Ambrosio Fornet came to reflect that as a "young man . . . [I] learned to be a Marxist through television."[33] A major part of the explanation for the character of state media, in fact, lies not only in the instrumental role it serves for the Communist Party, but also in its particular use by Cuba's "Maximum Leader." Through television, Fidel Castro forged a strong association between himself the party ideology. Through lengthy televised speeches, he became a constant presence in Cuban homes, instructing viewers on important matters of policy, ideology, and goals. In "*Fidel, el oficio de la palabra*," Gabriel García Márquez writes about this leader's oratory capacity. One week into the revolution, Fidel appeared on national television and spoke for seven hours. Cuban political life had acquired a new rhythm: "In the first few hours, the people of Havana, not yet accustomed to the hypnotic power of his voice, sat to watch the speech in the traditional way," García Márquez notes, but, after a while, they began to return to their daily routine, dividing their attention between their chores and watching the program.[34] Fidel's oratory power brought him into people's lives, defining the cadence of daily routines with elements of his style: endless repetitions, surprising details, diversions, and the familiarity with which he addresses his audience. His four-decade leadership, presence on television, and voice invade the private sphere of the home, solidifying a paternalistic role that obscures the boundaries between government and individual. In Cuba, politics comes in, sits down, and stays, and Castro came to occupy individual, private realms. García Marquez wonders if Fidel's compulsion for conversation comes of a profound need to discover the truth "amidst the hallucinatory mirage of power."[35] Fidel was said to be at ease when he approached people on the street, who would meet him without hesitation, speak to him directly, argue, and contradict him, and to be enlivened by the frankness of their discussions. The bond sanctioned his paternal approach and fostered a tolerance of his pervasive media presence. The sincerity behind the egomania of the "caudillo," his genuine wish for the good of the people, and his presumption of closeness to them could not, however, lead to a passive acceptance of his media dominance.

Through centralization, the Cuban government has monopolized all Cuban media, except those today used by a growing underground network. No longer addressing people publicly, Castro's "voice" has now migrated to the Internet. In 2007, while recovering from the extended illness that forced him to relinquish power, he was markedly absent from screens and airwaves. Once again defying ominous rumors of his imminent death, Fidel has continued sending missives onto government Web sites, where, rather like a columnist, he covers global and national topics: from corn-to-ethanol research and world hunger to the George W. Bush presidency and genocide. The Web page *Reflexiones de Fidel*, linked with the Web site of the official state newspaper and other official Cuban Web pages, is a new virtual place from which Fidel can steer political discourse.[36] Even if only representing him as spectral presence, *Reflexiones* supports Fidel's desire to communicate.

The difficult living conditions of the Special Period strained the loyalty of the people, yet Castro commands respect and attention around his declared causes even from those who raise their voices in disagreement. His 2007 commentary "Autocrítica de Cuba" (self-criticism from Cuba), which also reflects on Cuba's "energy revolution," excoriates those with access to foreign remittances who fail to conserve fuel. Typically unafraid to acknowledge the difficulties of life in Cuba, Fidel chides those consumers whom he views as profligate: "Real and visible inequality and scarcity of pertinent information facilitates critical opinions, especially from the sectors in greatest need."[37] Holding onto his immense political capital, the Cuban leader, through this editorial column, maintains his public presence and simultaneously reinforces the legend of his moral integrity as ideologist. Fidel's authority brought together multitudes, as vividly illustrated in the mass demonstrations opposing the Elián Gonzalez kidnapping by the boy's Miami relatives in 2000, an opposition brilliantly orchestrated as a television event to vindicate Castro and Cuba. Even absent, Fidel remains a singular presence in Cuban media; even its limited bandwidth manages to transmit his extra-large power. As a Cuban scholar quipped, in response to the title of one of my essays, "Will the Internet Spoil Fidel Castro's Cuba?" But Cuba does not belong to Fidel; Fidel belongs to Cuba.[38] The same is ultimately true of Cuban media.

The public response to such politicized use of media typically has power to produce political change. This was seen in January 2007, when memories of strict Communist Party politics were awakened in response to the apparent redemption on Cuban television of three high-ranking functionaries of the National Council of Culture (today, the Ministry of Culture) during the infamous "Gray Years," 1971 to 1976. Luis Pavón Tamayo, who had been "retired" in 1979 for abuses of power, reappeared unexpectedly, on January 5, 2007, on the national show *Impronta,* a program that pays homage to people in the arts, sciences, and other aspects of culture.[39] Armando Quesada of the Instituto Cubano de Radiodifusión (ICRT) and Jorge Serguera of the Dirección de Teatro del Consejo Nacional de Cultura, both leaders of these institutions during the same years, had appeared, weeks before, on national television shows as participants in discussions of Cuban culture. Their tenure in government had produced social exclusion through their extreme ideological policies and censorship resulting in homophobic attitudes and repression, their exceedingly narrow view of culture producing censorship and repression in the arts.

Assuming that the televised appearances vindicated the nefarious policies imposed by Pavón, Serguera, and Quesada during their tenure, the intergenerational intellectual community unleashed an overwhelming outcry on and off the island, an outcry that became an "e-mail war."[40] A single email sent to a broad mailing list by one outraged Cuban writer was followed by more e-mails, blog entries, forums, and e-journals among Cuban intellectuals representing greater Cuba. Desiderio Navarro, in a follow-up email, harshly questioned the legacy of the three early functionaries' policies and the reason for their televised resurgence. Is the men's legacy not one that "irreversibly damaged the lives of great and not so great Cuban creators [ostracized] in one form or another?" Did their censorship not "inundate us with the worst of contemporary culture from Eastern Europe?" Is Cuba a country "of such short memory that we no longer remember the woeful conditions that our cultural institutions were reduced to by the National Council of Culture?" A scriptwriter and essayist, Arturo Arango, in another email acknowledged the emerging texture of political culture: "We live in an intense and difficult moment, and I am convinced that the path that our country takes in a more or less immediate future is the responsibility of all of us." Cuban intellectual culture, he maintained, "has become more complex in recent years, and next to the existence of an obvious right-wing thought, inside and outside Cuba, there is a self-satisfied position . . . mixing market opportunism with the official preference for silence and obedience." The heated online controversy over the televised appearances eventually brought the online contributors on the island into a face-to-face debate that both lowered the political temperature and explored the legacy of censorship in the production of cultural memory. The official Communist Party response by Minister of Culture Abel Prieto sought to distance twenty-first-century Cuban socialism from errors of its authoritarian past: "Today the leadership of the country is very critical of that period of our history."[41] The powerful critical response by authors and artists brought to the surface the way the state constructed its political memory to give the impression of flexibility and change. Prieto acknowledged that a present and future Cuba must hold to the original intention of a broad cultural policy representing diverse positions that demanded real political engagement.

Like the Alarcón–student exchange, the online discussion of traumatic events in Cuban intellectual history heightened the level of online interaction, rapidly manifesting a willing, participatory, and vocal community as a newfound coalition of protest, facilitated but not created by the Internet. The continuous social tension generated by fluctuating levels of government transparency, by remembering and by forgetting, produced an atmosphere that vibrated in place, as citizens kept on edge insisted on rectification and openness as a part of healthy social exchange. The state insisted, and insists,

that this must entail a danger to society and therefore potentially dangerous for its citizens. The sequence of events that led a televisual "error" to
generate a broader digital debate ended in a closed-door symposium among
members of the intellectual community.[42] A difficult path to expand the
public space of discussions was seen in the absence, in electronic or print
media, of the January 2007 debates. These would finally be addressed on
Open Dialogue, another national television show, ten months later in November 2007.[43] The spirited and indignant online debate did receive an official
response from the Party, but also, by venting public political pressure,
worked to calm the situation. As a conduit for negotiation as well as information, digital media mediates the flow of political ideas between people
and the hierarchies of power, beyond political structures as well as within
them. Media continue to lend power to disagreement and opposition, but
also, in their present high-speed forms, can prompt communication that
closes gaps and hastens resolution.

Coming generations of Cubans may bring new kinds of political pressure from a wider base than would the intellectual community alone. The
political framing of Cuba's media within a national orientation and a social
function, whether to educate the people or to represent the nation before the
world, defines media practices with their emphasis on the collective.

Socialist Cuba is betting on its youth, aiming for high technological
literacy by prioritizing computer use in schools, structuring its computer
clubs in the form of neighborhood media centers, and sponsoring institutes
of advanced information studies. This is in line with Cuba's construction of
its economy, on a basis of education and technology, for performance in a
globalized system.

As the old guard draws to an end, the presumption exists that Cuba's
democratic ideals will naturally pass from the present generation in power
to the next. Media will obviously play a major role in the necessary transition, but, given the upcoming generation's exposure to new ideas and media
practices, there is strong desire for popular culture and its products. Young
Cubans naturally show interest in lifestyle choices potentially in conflict
with Cuban national identity, choices that are nevertheless often constrained
by discomfort with the material excesses of the West. Cuban youth identify
across the gamut of popular culture possibilities, from Hollywood and sports
celebrity culture to cultures of resistance and success expressed in hip hop
music and the world of rappers. Although Cuban socialism has been declared

eternal in the Cuban constitution, "It may all just be," as one frustrated Cuban remarked almost in resignation one day, "about personal satisfaction."

Elections, Representation, and Media

In the absence of acceptance of democratic principles (as defined by Held), the first democratic malfunction appears when presidential elections are either not held or not held regularly. From the perspective offered by Ruechmeyer et al., the institution of the electoral process provides the first measure of the existence of democracy. Yet, historically, elections, even with the requirement of universal suffrage fulfilled, guarantee neither Held's "collective decision-making about public matters" nor personal wellbeing. As the experience of contested elections shows—for instance, in the United States in 2000—the electoral process does not even ensure implementation of the will of the people.[44] (Interestingly, digital technology played an important role in the malfunction of the computerized U.S. voting system.) Regular elections and a representative electoral process more likely guarantee a safe economic environment for investors than provide safeguards for the economic crises regularly experienced by marginalized populations.

In the last two decades of the twentieth century, some observers argue, Latin America experienced a "third wave" of democratic consolidation, regional integration, and socialist renewal. This assessment follows the institutional reading of democracy in emphasizing the electoral process. Recognizing the blatant inadequacies of any economic systems in meeting people's basic needs, popular social movements have emerged to construct an open public space to lobby for fundamental changes, to what political scientist Leonardo Avritzer calls "democratic elitism."[45] Media have proven fundamental in presenting a new public face, as social movements carve out ways to confront the status quo, often using the Internet as a means of empowerment. In Mexico, for example, an online response has figured strongly against the claims of the two main conservative parties, the PRI and the PAN, as well as of the leftist PRD, to represent more than a privileged class.[46] Since 1994, the Internet has been key to the Ejercito Zapatista de Liberación Nacional (EZLN), popularly known as the Zapatistas, and since 2006 to the teachers' protest movement in Oaxaca, Mexico, transforming these struggles from local to global. Both groups have depended on digital media for social organizing, community radio, and distribution of documentaries and other evidence, supplied by the indigenous peoples, of mistreatment and abuse.

Even though the Zapatistas oppose the version of globalization championed within NAFTA, they use digital technologies to create a support base that is a model of global democracy in its provision of collective decision making.[47] Using digital and analogue media technologies available to 1950s Cuban revolutionaries, the Zapatistas have also proved again that connectivity for the community can be effective in bypassing the commercial and private model of media.

According to Avritzer, exposing the undemocratic nature of elitist power works to create fundamental changes in leadership and civil society, increasing participation of ordinary citizens in the affairs of political life. Although elections are the main measure of legitimate democracy as defined by and within nation states, grassroots organizing efforts, no matter how sophisticated, cannot achieve any form of officially recognized democracy, but instead seek change of the underlying system. The fight for civic rights as the third dimension of statist democracy needs to underpin the principles of global democracy, in place of a continual political drive recycling, and assessed by, elitist forms of power.

Assessed on the metric of elections, Cuba (along with other countries) usually finds itself in the minus column. However, since the beginning of the Special Period, Cuban electoral reforms have indicated a changed role for parliament, emphasizing improved accountability to constituents. E-government initiatives introduced in 2003 and 2005 stated: "Internet forum will debate democracy and elections in Cuba." A parliamentary representative responded to Internet user queries about elections. Candidates for office have always been allocated equal media exposure and resources, but political proselytizing in campaigns is forbidden by law. There are merits to this restriction, especially in contrast to the nefarious results from campaign funding that blankets media networks in the United States; however, one of the students in the Alarcón debate complained of the limited information and knowledge about the candidates for National Assembly elections. Electoral reforms, it should be noted, cover the election of representatives to the Asambleas del Poder Popular, which together make up the National Assembly of Popular Power, which in turn elects the Council of State and the highest government office of president.[48]

Historically, the Castro regime has responded to criticism about the lack of plurality in its electoral process by emphasizing that Cuba's democratic ideals "do not reside in the ballot box." Instead, in the transformed social and political landscape after the revolution, democracy became synonymous with social provision for the people. In 1971, when asked by a journalist in Ecuador why there were no elections in Cuba, Fidel Castro explained that Cuba was developing a different kind of democracy that was "much more direct . . . involving the debate of fundamental laws by all the people and all labor sectors."[49] However, beyond the significant achievements of health care, education, and scientific and technological development, social provision thus far has proven sorely lacking. Has the state therefore failed in terms of democracy as measured on its own terms? Castro claims not, given the strictures of the U.S. embargo. Judged by Daniel Cohen's measure of three levers, Cuba succeeds in creating the potential for a democratic model of government. Assessed on Held's principles, however, the state may come up short; although its complex, extensive, and inclusive system for selecting parliamentary representatives gestures toward collective decision making, it does not suffice. Cuba's recent use of the Internet in displaying the details of the electoral selection process cannot be viewed as increasing domestic transparency; however, it does demonstrate that the intrinsic levels of transparency and accountability of the system are high. Voluntary participation in the selection process is reported regularly to hit 90 percent, although political observers question the validity of these numbers. Given the many obstacles to Internet access for most Cubans, the main target audience for the government's display of its political process may be international. Cuba needs a global platform to validate its democratic credentials, and is well aware of the value of media technologies to help it gain such a position. Besides using the Internet as showcase and tool of conventional democratic practices, the state has begun to improve its international projection of Cuba's nontraditional democratic discourse. In communicating the crucial significance it attaches to the Internet and related technology, and to Cuba's leadership in the open-source software movement, Cuba is deepening and expanding its network of partners in practices of democracy based on improving human well-being.

"Cuban Democracy"

Cuba's path was rooted in distrust bred by the incoherencies and corruption of the Batista-era institutions and international capitalism. A rejection of past government practices and standard market economics has underpinned the nature of democracy in Cuba in the postrevolutionary period.

The erosion of legitimate state institutions prior to the revolution was, according to historian Carolee Bengelsdorf, key in the swift victory of the rebels over the Batista regime, and also contributed to the nature and scope of the institutional framework to follow.[50] As the first cultural institutions of the new state, ICAIC, UNEAC (Unión de Escritores y Artistas Cubanos), and Casa de las Américas signaled the importance of culture and media in the new society. ICAIC's emphasis and character as an artist-run organization showed the manner in which the new government would throw off the old baggage of Cuba as a capitalist, dependent nation. Newsreel footage of the era shows Cubans taking sledgehammers to the rooftop signs of Twentieth Century–Fox and other U.S. media headquarters. Political economist Joel Edelstein concluded in 1995 that a history of dependency factored significantly in the turn toward socialism.[51] Private enterprise, including Goar Mestre's broadcasting empire (discussed in chapter 1), thrived in prerevolutionary Cuba, and the economic engagement of private companies fostered reliance on external financing and partnerships, along with foreign technological innovation, but failed to build strong, inclusive, responsive national institutions. In Cuba's unfettered but exploitative economic environment, media corporations prospered. The revolutionaries thus inherited a strong media infrastructure, and they demonstrated a keen awareness of the utility of media in their quick redirection of the transmission capacity toward the public interest. Newsreels, for example, became exhortations to raise rural literacy levels or to help improve housing. Documentaries took up inherent conflicts and internal frictions that the social campaigns encountered. Reorientation of media also took subtler forms—for example, introspective cinema produced by ICAIC that served as mediation over issues concerning the nation. Films such as *Memorias del subdesarrollo* (Memories of Underdevelopment, Tomás G. Alea, 1968) aired the anxieties of a declining bourgeois class, while productions like *Suite Habana* (Fernando Pérez, 2000) came to celebrate the sturdiness of citizens during the trials and tribulations of the Special Period.

Castro's instinctive recognition of the need to nourish fresh political currents out of the revolution's cultural effervescence finds theoretical resonance in Jesús Martín-Barbero's 1993 book *Communication, Culture, and Hegemony*. A Spanish communication scholar working in Latin America, Martín-Barbero analyzes the importance of viewing the popular class, not as a separate political category disconnected from culture and ideology, but as a source from which culture and politics emerge.[52] Postrevolutionary, analogue Cuba established a democratic tenor utilizing signals quite distinct from those of a U.S.-dominated era and pointing to transnational circulation.

However, from the beginning, the stresses of the U.S. embargo and hostility were used to justify censorship and demagoguery. For instance, while championing democracy in its organizational structure as well as its output, ICAIC early on blocked distribution of material as apparently innocuous to today's audience as the 1960 Cuban film *P.M.* (Sabá Cabrera Infante), which documented the seedy nightlife of a Havana bar and was therefore considered potentially to expose Cuba to criticism at a politically sensitive time. In a sign of a renewed critical spirit, *P.M.* was screened in 1994, after having been censored for thirty-three years, during the annual Festival Internacional del Nuevo Cine Latinoamericano in Havana.[53]

Meanwhile, censorship for journalists became even more severe during the first half of the Special Period. Material deprivation had triggered the permitted exodus of disaffected citizens that became known as the *balsero* (rafter) crisis, and state institutions moved to contain public criticism. Homero Campa and Orlando Pérez reported that, in 1993, censorship was justified by Julio Garcia Luis, president of the Cuban Union of Journalists (UPEC), in a heated closed-door debate with Armando Rollemberg, president of the International Union of Journalists (IUJ). The controversial issue was the expulsion of Cuban journalists from UPEC because they had endorsed a political manifesto, which Garcia Luis saw as a violation of journalistic ethics.[54] Garcia Luis acknowledged related restrictions and censorship, but he argued that they were warranted in the face of horrendous CIA-financed attacks against the Cuban state. Giving a voice to disgruntled citizens would, he felt, be tantamount to giving ammunition to the enemy. This state view, as voiced by Garcia Luis, ensured that between 1989 and 1994 members of the Cuban public not only learned nothing of the debate about journalistic ethics, but also found out very little of the diversity of Cuban thought and the realities of hardships other than their own. In 1994, an editorial in *Juventud Rebelde* summed up the frustration at the disparity between reality and Cuban reporting: "At no other time has there been a greater need to know exactly what is happening. . . . We cannot conceive of the transformations and measures that are taking place if they are not accompanied systematically by information, an exhaustive explanation of causes, and clarity about what affects the life and destiny of citizens."[55]

The limited extractive wealth of the Cuban economy, and an agricultural economy that traditionally revolved around two products, tobacco and sugar, suddenly greatly devalued in international markets, meant that Cuba could not avoid economic catastrophe. The resultant internal pressures substantiated state suppression of media. Director of Ideology Carlos Aldana, the state official who publicly outlined media policy, was retired in 1993, a casualty of internal wrangling as the government strained to give an impression of managing the country's economic crisis. Forced to rebuff attack, especially during the Special Period, the Cuban state continued to be a force that maintained and defined a language of democracy. Not surprisingly, this meant that it sometimes contradicted its own values. In comparison with countries such as the United States, Cuba was, and is, more likely to be labeled undemocratic for its government's role in media interference; prohibitions on the media in the United States—the interdiction of publication of photographs of dead American soldiers returning from Iraq, the monitoring of the content of post-9/11 films—are seen as within the bounds of governmental responses during heightened moments of crisis. Cuba, whether overzealous in its protection of revolutionary values or, rather, opening up inherited structures in a reformative political drive and casting media in the service of society, is continually faulted for falling short of democratic standards; it is seldom given credit for being intent on achieving them.

As Edward Said noted in *Culture and Imperialism,* "the apparent challenge to American authority in the almost laughable case of post-Batista Cuba suggests that what was at stake was hardly security but rather a sense that within its self-defined domain (the hemisphere) the United States would not accept any infringements or sustained ideological challenges to what it considered 'freedom.'"[56] The ideology of democracy in Cuba is expressed in complex terms that bind the individual to a political identity, because Cuba's legitimacy is constantly challenged. It has thus relied on a notion of democracy defined by the state but upheld through a common project in collaboration with the people. Cuba declared itself socialist in 1961, embarking on an intellectual and political project that redefined Marxism away from Soviet Stalinism and established the social orientation of the revolutionary agenda as democratic. Democracy and socialism ended up at opposite ends of the political spectrum (a separation that Bengelsdorf attributes to the contradictions of the theoretical construct of Marxism itself).[57] The Cold War produced an anticommunism, equivalent in the United States to antisocialism, that associated the new Cuban regime with dogma, repression, and economic disaster. However, the end of the Cold War, new media technologies, and globalization are forcing a reconsideration of the terms democracy and socialism. Cuba now benefits from a resurgence of socialism in Latin America that relies on cooperation and integration in the region, where media technologies figure largely in international agreements. In forging new political and media connections, postdigital Cuba stands positioned to reframe the terms of democracy that are beginning to take hold internationally, if not globally.

The Politics of Access

In no way does access to the Internet equate with a potential for democracy. The determinist assumption behind such an equation assumes that access to more information and new tools to promote individual action leads to the creation of politicized communities able and willing to oppose hegemonic political and economic structures. Prescribing this logic for Cuba fails to consider inherent economic limitations (such as low wages and expensive hardware) that prevent the majority of the population from even owning a computer. It ignores obstacles created by limited information about technological developments. (Keeping up with advancements is difficult when information can only trickle in.) It does not take into account the economic divide between an embargoed nation and commercial service providers. (Cuban citizens accessing the Internet are presumed to be ready consumers and credit card holders.) Access to technology, then, though crucial for economic development, is not in and of itself a fundamental marker of democratic practices. Access provided with an orientation and intention toward social benefit would need to be present for deeper democratic practices to develop. Finally, Internet use is not free of control, as we have seen, in the wider global context where, so far, access to media technologies has depended on who and where the user is when attempting to communicate, view, search, log-in, sell, or buy Net equipment.

Outside Cuba, access to technology networks is typically privatized and designed by global media conglomerates that converge into the monopolies of a few global players. Media advocacy groups that thrive on decentralized networks and rely on savvy computer "hacktivists" resist the proprietary locks that protect much media content and technology, in defense of intellectual property rights driven by the profit motive. As they appropriate media technology to produce social awareness of monopolistic and authoritarian media practices, independent, Internet-based media collectives operate by targeting specific sites of political disturbance like the United States–Mexican border or the state of Oaxaca, Mexico. Although the economic divide is amplified globally by the relatively high cost of hardware, software, and connectivity, the open-source movement, along with electronic and community activism, establishes an alternative to the privatized realm of most Internet activity. Globally, democratic practices tend to develop out of combined approaches, vision, efforts, and technologies, as evidenced by the World People's blog (where human rights projects such as the Okinawa Women Act against Military Violence find a voice), Wikimedia, or digital art cooperatives in Cuba.

For Lage in Cuba, the fundamental advantage of the Internet lies in its role as a component of perceived global democracy, one that could allow the Cuban state to represent itself as part of a worldwide community of nations. When it uses the Internet to clarify and inform, the state seeks transparency of its political structure. Its single-party system, dedicated to noninstitutional democratic aims, is purported as adequate to achieve these aims, leading to the question of how the state can best represent the interests of individuals.

At present, the Cuban state uses national campaigns, policies, and the Internet to emphasize the extent and dimension of the U.S. embargo. The official Web site of the Cuban Republic reveals the central power of the Communist Party in Cuban politics, as well as the infrastructure of government, its branches, ministries, agencies, and political figures. Sites document ongoing campaigns in the Cuban courts against the U.S. embargo and terrorism.[58] Greater global visibility achieved through an online presence also has the effect of putting pressure on the government to extend its principles of democracy to full social equality, and possibly to allow multiple political parties. Cuban state caution about the implications of increased media access comes across as fairly reasonable, considering the historical leadership's own use of media to foment the 1959 revolution, and in light of the general conditions of poverty still pervasive in a country where social equity is allegedly a strong democratic value.

Increased access does not lie only in the realms of government control and personal funds. Access to the Internet is also limited when Cuban network security personnel block Web sites they consider dangerous, in response to U.S. aggression or when Microsoft blocks Cubans from using the instant messaging service from the island. However, this kind of "local" focus on how access is provided or denied by government or other source, as Chun puts it, "overlooks questions of infrastructure and connectivity" crucial for understanding how networks reveal their political character.[59] Cuban restrictions result in lower connection speed and scarce IP addresses, leading those excluded to create and use illegal channels of access. Examples abound of the power to be gained from illicit access to media technologies—again, as happened notably with the early Cuban revolutionaries' use of radio (and as seen during the NATO bombing of Kosovo in 1999 when Yugoslavian hackers were able to disrupt the flow of e-mail on the NATO Web site). Technology can in this way be used to circumvent official or well-established media, for Web sites and intrusive programs can provide and potentially disrupt, alter, and erase information. Satellite photographs of raids by government forces in Darfur can also be used to counter political maneuvering. Virtual sit-ins organized by political collectives such as the Electronic Disturbance Theater disrupt major Web sites to undermine political and economic power.

Even though legal or illegal access does not automatically herald a new culture of democracy, it leads to new activities by users that push against the established paradigms of power relations as information and information channels are directed to serve specific purposes. Cuba restricts access to prevent external subversion of its political aims; it also appears unwilling yet to trust its citizenry sufficiently to test whether they have adopted the goals of the state. Although students at UCI have been endowed with the government's trust, this trust has to be negotiated, as became evident during the Alarcón–student debate that circulated on YouTube. Disregarding the necessity of preexisting aims, reports by pragmatic consultants from large U.S. think tanks argue that the expansion of computer networks increases the prospects for democracy by providing outside information, and by allowing the sharing of ideas and coordination of activities. Kedzie claims that, even if regular elections do not occur, "Interconnectivity is a better predictor of democracy than schooling, GDP, life expectancy, ethnic homogeneity, or population, particularly in regions of newly emerging democracy."[60] Kedzie's view of connectivity is a familiar determinist perspective that sees technology itself as even more responsible for changes than is education. This view limits the role of culture and human principles in producing alternative models of democracy, such as those raised by Held, that might be considered irrational. To be a driver of processes of democracy in Cuba, connectivity needs to incorporate equal worth and dignity, agency, personal responsibility, consent, and so on.

In Cuba's predigital years, Carlos Aldana conveyed a resolute commitment to narrowing the political space for dissent. With the coming of the Internet, by March 1996, the space potentially to be controlled had grown much larger. State paranoia then had to extend to include the possibility of attack through virtual access to its territory (as occurred with AOL in 1996).[61] Tensions were heightened by a report from the Political Bureau, authored by Raúl Castro, that regarded research by the Party's own think tanks as a dangerous activity. The report suggested that academic studies in collaboration with foreign scholars could lead to ideological deviance, and mandated narrowing the scope of Cuban research scholars.[62] Earlier the same year, the leaders of Concilio Cubano, an umbrella organization for about 140 opposition groups, had met with repression and were denied permission to hold a public gathering in Havana to obtain certain rights in the political process.[63] The arrival of the Internet added more possible steps to the state's ongoing dance of opening and closing to control the spaces of communication.

As an event that combined personal, political, and religious dimensions, the visit of Pope John Paul II to Cuba in January 1998 was bound to push the limits of centralized media control. Appropriation of media technologies by user groups, including NGOs, is slowly pushing development of the Internet in all directions, whether state-sanctioned or in the interest of individuals. The meeting between the Pope and Fidel Castro, which Tad Szulc called "one of the most startling encounters in the modern history of religion and diplomacy,"[64] touched on many unresolved conflicts. The pontiff spoke out against the embargo, called for increased freedom of expression on the island, and requested clemency for a number of political prisoners. The papal visit brought journalists and visitors from all over the world to Havana and generated 1.5 million hits between January and February 1998 (more than ever before) on the Web site for *Granma International*. Cuban exiles, many of whom had not returned to Cuba for almost four decades, made an emotional pilgrimage to the island in the hope of witnessing the beginning of radical political change. Cubavision, the official television network, aired several regional masses during the Pope's stay, including one by a charismatic and powerful proponent of Catholic doctrine, Cardinal Jaime Ortega from Santiago province, an occasion also covered widely by the international press. Such wide television access for the Catholic Church has not been repeated since.

The Pope's visit was designed by the state as a mass media event occurring just two years after the country's connection to the Internet. The occasion functioned to some degree as a test of technical capacity, flexibility and security. Politically, Cuba was able to raise its international profile by showing increased tolerance and openness. The papal visit created a platform for Cuba to redefine terms of engagement while controlling and even experimenting with media technologies. The Internet was fully deployed as a means of communication and coordination in state and public service, and for the Catholic ministries.

In summary, Cuba's fin de siècle was heavily marked by two of the most transformative events of the twentieth century: the end of the Cold War and the emergence of an information society. According to Manuel Castells, social, cultural, and political changes have converged with a newly networked culture that, "is made up of many cultures, many values, many projects that cross through the minds and inform the strategies of the various participants in the networks, changing at the same pace as the network's members, and following the organizational and cultural transformation of the units of the network."[65] Castells's description assumes an open system and largely unrestrained individual participation, rather than the centralized and rigid control of access imposed in Cuba.

Vulnerability of an economic base inhibits flexibility. In the case of Cuba, social and political markers indicate willingness to restructure reality where the conception of a democratic world order defies the prioritization of personal access. Cuba chooses to organize its electronic space through networks ordered according to the dynamics of global democracy, and does so with characteristic resourcefulness and creativity.

3

TOURISM AND THE
SOCIAL RAMIFICATIONS OF
MEDIA TECHNOLOGIES

In 1995, the newly opened, Spanish-and-Cuban-financed Meliá-Cohiba Hotel in Havana placed a computer in the lobby. The screen featured a hypertext tour of the hotel's services and sophisticated accommodations, built solely for the visitor from abroad. In this monolithic ocean-front hotel, where an ice cream even then cost US$6 and a room upward of US$200, the computer provided a new interface between the physical and the virtual world, its foreign origin and funding and its segregated use and users unintentionally highlighting the political, ideological, economic, and social contradictions of Cuba's unique geopolitical space.

The Meliá-Cohiba hotel itself stood as a larger symbol representing the redirection of the Cuban economy in the 1990s that put capitalism in the service of socialism. The construction of this hotel complex, allegedly a copy of a Japanese counterpart, was to a large degree rationalized as a source of new revenue and jobs to help jumpstart the Cuban economy. At twenty-two golden stories of metal and glass, this first structure in the wave of post-Soviet investments generated controversy from the start (fig. 2).[1]

The scale of the hotel's postmodern architecture dwarfs its immediate neighbor, the 1950s American-style Hotel Habana Riviera. Although architectural contrast was not new to the Havana skyline—Cuban author Alejo Carpentier once described the city as having a "style without a style"—the Meliá-Cohiba towered over historic promenades and oceanfront walkways as a symbol of foreign capital. Its size and placement paid no regard to the vernacular or to the need for green and open spaces, advocating instead urban

———— 2. Hotel Meliá Cohiba, Havana, Cuba ————

development, with an eye to international capital. Consistent with the drive behind media technologies, from satellites to cell phones, the hotel loomed above and apart from the spaces these media were helping to shrink across the globe. An ostentatious product of foreign investment, the Meliá-Cohiba linked Cuba to emerging international trends.

Since connection to the Internet was still in the future for Cuba, the computer in the lobby only anticipated the new interface between people and global computer networks, creating the illusion of connection to the world of up-to-the-minute information and entertainment, for tourists and residents alike. The lack of international press on the hotel newsstand served, in contrast, to remind tourists of the ongoing U.S. embargo. The computer, a proudly showcased artifact in a sea of gleaning marble and lush tropical plants, would two years later be relegated to the business center (fig. 3). Here, as part of a local computer network used for hotel administration and guest

3. Lobby, Hotel Meliá Cohiba, Havana, Cuba

services, it provided an island of Internet access, offsetting the meager offerings at the newsstand.

The original virtual tour on the computer nevertheless was more than a sign of postmodernity in a new tourist space. The postmodern glow of the hotel could be experienced not only by looking at its shiny, reflective exterior, but also by traversing its digital interior via the computer screen. The use of hypertext turned the luxury space into code, through a graphic interface that exemplified the types of multimedia applications that served as "training wheels," in the early 1990s, for the World Wide Web. This software taught users to understand virtual space and information by clicking on-screen buttons.

Today, transformed from novel display to regular function in spaces of administration and personal computing, computers and their uses in Cuba challenge allegations of technological backwardness. Even under dire economic constraints, the country has consistently demonstrated the will to invest in modern technological projects, but citizen access to these services, particularly to the Internet, is dispensed by the state through carefully sanctioned spaces, which include the hotels along the Havana seafront.

The original hypertext tour in the hotel lobby was a symbol of the Sol Meliá Hotel Group's new push into telecommunications. As one of the ten largest international hotel chains in the world, the Spanish-owned Sol Meliá sought to differentiate its services in the competitive field of tourism by visibly featuring technology. More than a decade after the Meliá-Cohiba was built, virtual tours of most of its luxury hotels in Cuba are still featured on its corporate Web site. In addition, promotional videos providing 180-degree views of interiors and exteriors—advertising an image of excellence and elegance, fantasy and nostalgia—have been uploaded to YouTube.

The expansion in the 1990s of Sol Meliá to Cuba and Latin America intersected with Cuba's developments to expand its tourist economy. State and corporation both invested heavily in telecommunications to access the new potential of this expansion.[2] As Cuban professor of informatics Lázaro J. Blanco Encinosa has noted, the growth of tourism would not have been possible without an informatics or communications base.[3] Typically, hotels have had local computer networks, but, from 1995 on, they have been wired from inception to facilitate a multiplicity of services for foreign consumers (clients), making the social contradictions from the use of new media forms more evident. To enable this computerization, hotel corporations would import their hardware to Cuba; Cuba would provide the workforce and manage the online reservation system through Cuban tour operator HABAGUANEX. Amid the economic deprivation of the Special Period, luxury hotels became islands of opportunity and social dilemmas. As media spaces, they began to push both private and civic self-definitions toward expanded boundaries.

In this chapter, I explore the social ramifications of media technologies used not only to facilitate international tourism as an economic lifeline, but also purportedly to strengthen Cuba's socialist orientation. The media geography created by hotels' associated investment in new technology encompasses new social interactions and media practices, and the social patterns that emerge hold significant parallels to earlier eras of technological development. With defiant insistence on its independence, Cuba has redefined its place in a global era, while its people, too, increasingly appropriate the new technologies as a means of survival.

Cuban Tourism Then and Now

Cuba's late-twentieth-century venture into tourism constituted a new state project, an economic salvage operation that ironically capitalized on global tourists hungry for "one last look before it all changed." The new hotels, investments for mixed foreign and national capital and part of Cuba's new tourism-based economic directive, coincided with the island's incipient connection to the Internet. The modern, international, and only recently desegregated space of the Meliá-Cohiba reflects the restrictive way that the Cuban state has adopted digital technologies, just as the hotel's golden exterior reflects the state's decision to mine its complicated heritage for cash in an evolving but strangely consistent political present.

Tourism everywhere has always pointed to social contradictions while serving the economic needs of governments and elite entrepreneurs, continuing to expose neocolonial strands in the exploitation of capital and labor. The tourism industry established in Cuba beginning in 1910 created an "island paradise" for foreign visitors, functioning as an important economic and cultural sector that was off limits to the majority of the country's socially and racially stratified population. Cuban historian Luis A. Pérez Jr. contends, "Nowhere did North American demands reconfigure Cuban life as dramatically as through tourism."[4] Inside and outside Cuba, the radio, film, and print media promoted the image of tropical splendor to potential consumers, attracting hundreds of thousands of visitors from across the United States who took advantage of the island's close proximity. Repeated contact reinforced the development of an industry that catered to the tastes and preferences of North Americans, resulting in a tourist infrastructure with U.S. characteristics.[5] American films such as *Week-End in Havana* (Walter Lang, 1941), with top stars of the era like Carmen Miranda and Cesar Romero, projected fantasies of sexual abandon and "good neighborliness" onto the image of the island and its people, but also simultaneously displayed for movie audiences the lavishly modern spaces of newly constructed hotels. In these films, as in actuality, hotels separated tourists from locals, customers from workers. The reality of the uneasy class and race relations that resulted from tourism and American capital in 1950s Cuba are featured in two now-classic feature films: the Cuban-Soviet coproduction *I Am Cuba* (Mikhail Kalatozov, 1964) and Francis Ford Coppola's *The Godfather II* (1974).

American investment interests and design made possible the first era of Cuban tourism, creating hotels such as the imposing Hotel Nacional (1930), for half a century "the insignia hotel of Havana."[6] To accommodate more visitors and thus higher profits for a growing, and soon Mafia-supported, industry, the 1950s saw the construction of the Habana Riviera, Habana Biltmore, and Habana Hilton (later renamed the Habana Libre), among others.[7] The next wave of hotel construction would be deferred for four decades.[8]

The economic pressures arising on the island from the end of Cold War alliances in 1991 forced the Cuban state into inconvenient compromises, inviting capitalism back, but under socialist terms. The memory of hotels as sites of corruption during the 1950s had to be accommodated into a new social consciousness in which they functioned as socially inclusive spaces in a restratified socialist society. Restrictions on Cubans entering hotels, however, were in place by the 1980s. Symbols of a global tourist economy, hotels by the 1990s created particular kinds of impermanent social experiences to offer designed exotic pleasures and privileges to visitors and Cuban residents alike. American visitors dining with Cuban friends at hotel cafeterias would sense the pervasive feeling that Cubans were trespassers—even internationally renowned Cuban film directors. Restrictions against Cuban consumers inside hotels created socially awkward spaces where the foreign visitor had a clear advantage. As the sites of permitted circulation of capital, hotels embraced new strategies of service and entertainment, but only with great difficulty. In the new tourist service economy of Cuba, the needs of foreign clients became priorities, producing an uneasy accommodation for the often highly educated Cubans employed at bare survival wages to meet these needs. (Talk to a cab driver in Cuba, and you may learn that he was previously employed as a MIG fighter pilot.) An established filmmaker in the 1990s earned $300 Cuban (pesos) per month, the top salary. The actual legal prohibition of Cubans staying in hotels, along with the country's historic demands for equality, made restrictions to hotel use highly questionable.

The resulting social anxiety produced ample criticism from Cubans, especially those of the exile community. The starkly anti-Cuban film *Azúcar amarga* (Bitter Sugar, 1996), by Cuban American León Ichaso, explores the resentment of workers made redundant by the financially strapped state. Cuban filmmaker Daniel Díaz Torres preferred humor to show residents of Havana creatively surviving a situation in which the basic needs of citizens were subordinated to visitors' requirements, in comedies such as *Hacerce el sueco* (Playing the Swede, 2001). Anathema to a socialist project relying on ideals of social equity, the hierarchy of values and practices of the service industries heightened powerful social and political contradictions. As an industry that stood as symbol of global economic exchanges, tourism shielded the Cuban government from its direct role in reinstating economic discrimination against its citizens. Cuba continued to train doctors, high-tech engineers, agronomists, economists, biologists, and teachers, but from 1995, impelled by economic necessity, it found itself also investing in massive training for a service foundation for its new tourist sector.

Cultural Interactions and the New Economy

Service economy training exemplifies the way government priorities reflect an increase in the value of tourism for the Cuban nation. Tourism and for-eign investment have become dual engines driving the new Cuban economy, in the midst of the still extant U.S. embargo. The strategy has apparently been effective, given the depths of the crisis and Cuba's relative growth.

The nature of the economic changes in Cuba since the end of the former Soviet Union has transformed the way the Cuban state directs itself with regard to foreign businesses. The Cuban government responded to the emer-gence of the Internet by partnering with foreign investors—from locations such as Canada, Europe, Asia, and Latin America—in new modes of cultural interaction. This response heralded a shift in cultural exchanges in regard not only to personal interactions but also to media practices; for example, banking services were automated, gradually, during the 1990s. Reinventing the economy was a principal goal for the state, but it acted with a commit-ment to control and define the terms of technological appropriation. By rejecting the neoliberal economic model then prominent in Latin America and the Caribbean, it also further validated its critique of that model's emphasis on privatization.

The state also read the potential of global computer networks in the 1990s as a new opportunity to make the Cuban nation visible within the ongo-ing reconfiguration of world power, no longer prey to the backroom deals between the superpowers of yesteryear. Visibility became a political issue for Cuba—to help build a tourist industry consistent with its own priorities, to increase the nation's presence in global media, and to polish its international image even while buttressing its economy. To paraphrase Cuban filmmaker and theorist Julio García Espinosa, a nation that does not produce its own image simply does not exist.

The original computer in the Meliá-Cohiba Hotel has faded into the technological past, while the Cuban hotel-building program of the Sol Meliá Group, Club Med, and other European hotel chains proceeded apace.

———————— 4. Hotel Meliá Habana, Havana, Cuba ————————

Today, hotels like the Meliá-Habana (1999), a sprawling beachfront complex competing with the Meliá-Cohiba, set the new standard by providing guests with e-mail and other telecommunications and satellite television services (fig. 4).

Modern media technologies complement international hotel chains in ways that the Cuban state turns to economic advantage. The construction company that builds the new Cuban hotels is Cuban owned, as is the entity that designs and implements the telecommunications infrastructure, creating employment opportunities and providing new levels of expertise for Cuban telecommunication workers. The design of telecommunication systems is directly guided by the state. The goals are to transform the culture of limited information among Cuban citizens and to expand the ways in which the state does business and protects its political goals. All this represents a tremendous investment in creating a strong knowledge base and training among the citizenry; empowered citizens, it is felt, will want to reap the economic and personal benefits of technological advances along with the state that insists on directing the deployment of these new gains, and they will want to define openness for themselves as subjects of a networked society.

Public and Private Media Spaces

Experiences of media and technology vary according to social, regulatory, and political conditions determining function and value. Under the media restrictions of the Special Period (many of which continue), media reception for Cuban nationals has differed from that of foreign visitors and workers. The social environment of hotels in particular provides a meeting point of media technologies and their incoming signals even while the average Cuban home is only beginning to open up to multiple media channels or networks.[9] The typical home exists as a zone of control and sometimes of technological blackout. Cuban territory is an amalgam of gateways that allow prioritized residential customers to receive a television satellite signal or gain Internet access. The planned expansion of fiber-optic networks is too costly for the Cuban government, forcing it to delay use of its existing infrastructure. Critically, control of access is also influenced by embargo politics as the U.S. government restricts Cuban Internet connection to the private fiber-optic network running close to the island. According to Ramiro Valdés Menéndez, Cuban minister of informatics and communication, the U.S. policy has forced Cuba "to use a satellite channel with a mere 65 Mbps broadband for output and 124 Mbps for input," making the service anything but fast and capacious.[10]

As the result of both political and economic restrictions, the Cuban home is the intended purview only of state media (radio and television) and of video and DVD recorders, while the hotel spaces carry private, state, national, and international media, literally opening them to global currents. Contracts with European partners facilitate purchase of the prepackaged bundle of Sky Television programming on offer inside hotels. Cuba's participation (as one of five member nations) in the free pan-Latin Telesur satellite network, broadcast from Venezuela, means that this signal is both included in hotel packages and carried into homes. Meanwhile, the polyrhythmic flows of global television—MTV, Spanish TVE, Brazil's Globo, Italy's RIE, ESPN, and most typically CNN—spill over from lobby bars to find their way unofficially into homes, because limits on home access to satellite television are often bypassed by inventive viewers eager to expand their entertainment choices.

The practices, that is, of official media distribution in Cuba—streaming fast into the hotel, trickling into the home—are determined by the logic of complicated international political and corporate alliances.

Telephone service follows similarly, and needs to be considered against local experiences and the larger framework of global communication services. Throughout the world, telecommunication services are now considered "essential luxuries," and customers often pay high premiums for access. Increased numbers of foreign visitors to Cuba means increased need for telephone lines and mobile communication services. However, the AT&T-owned underwater cable that delivers international telephone services to the island has been inactive since the 1960s, when the United States seized funds designated for payments due the U.S.-owned Cuban Telephone Company, which had been nationalized by the Castro government. Hence, even while domestic telephone landlines primarily supply direct national access, hotels provide an internationalized if costly service that reveals the high premiums associated with Cuba's participation in the digital revolution. The long-distance call—crucial for keeping so many scattered family members in touch—is a luxury for the ordinary Cuban. To offset the scarcity of international telephone lines available and the increased domestic need to connect internationally, the Cuban telephone company, Empresa de Telecomunicaciones de Cuba, S.A. (ETECSA), facilitates overseas communication through prepaid telephone cards usable from public telephone kiosks. By 2007, ETECSA could point to success in reaching the planned goal of 4.5 public telephones per thousand people. This goal was driven by the conviction that nationwide expansion of telecommunications services was necessary to improve the economic growth of the country.[11] But economic necessity has largely confined the explosion of media channels (satellite, wireless, fiber optic), of systems of communication (Internet, local area networks, etc.), and of digital equipment (computers, cameras, mobile phones, fax machines, and televisions) to the new hotels and workplaces, establishing but also limiting Cuba's configuration within the coordinates of new flows of exchange and information. Viewing the hotels as an integral but intricate part of the island's media geography reveals how media networks, convergences, and locations differentiate the uses of social environments. A vacationing tourist can pay to send an e-mail from the luxury of the Meliá-Cohiba, but the hotel bartender must pay to use a public Internet kiosk. Both use the same media map, but differentiated political mandates force participants to take different and unequal routes.

For Cuban citizens and visitors alike, hotels became invested with complicated meanings in the context of a socialism reinvented with capitalist partnerships. Because hotel services excluded locals while meeting the demands of visitors, the hotels became the locus of awkward emotional experiences. But locals were not unilaterally excluded; some found their way into expensive hotel shops, restaurants, and bars. Today, as then, high prices reinforce a sense of exclusion in one's own culture; encounters with family members visiting from abroad are marked by both the joy and the painful passions of political disagreement. Disproportionate attention from security guards creates pervasive tension. And embarrassment and anger stir in response to not-so-secret signals that allow Cuban sex workers to enter bars and restaurants even when Cubans in general are prohibited entry. The role of tourism and telecommunications has appeared key in the transition to global economic bonds, and their growth necessary for developing and sustaining productive national forces. In twenty-first-century Cuba, the new tourist culture has come to feel less artificial and forced, but today a Cuban citizen visiting a guest at the Meliá-Cohiba still faces complex emotions.

Cuba may be more visible, thanks to digital technologies, but tourists still ask locals to retell history, to recommend the best place to buy cigars, and to answer the million-dollar question—what will happen in a post-Castro Cuba? Further, state-imposed economic constraints mean business transactions with foreign visitors are as likely to be illegal as legal.

Cuban filmmaker Ana Rodríguez captured the strangeness of Havana hotels in *Laura*, one of five shorts that make up the feature film *Mujer transparente* (Transparent Woman, 1991), by depicting her eponymous heroine waiting uncomfortably in a luxurious hotel lobby to be reunited with her long-exiled childhood girlfriend.[12] Privilege produces an unsavory taste in a socialist project that proposed to eradicate social advantage. The belated re-embrace of tourism has ushered in an unpredictable new reality, a reality with an unpleasant edge, to social interactions.

Digital Consumption of Cuba

Media have been highly important in encouraging a growing number of affluent, digitally savvy travelers to visit the island. Cuba as a tourist's fantasy entices through Internet images of a Caribbean paradise—images carefully crafted by tour operators, hotel chains, and travel agencies.[13] Professional and amateur photographs of smiling Cubans, crumbling or picturesque houses, lush tobacco fields, and perfect beaches appear in coffeetable books, calendars, travel guides, Web sites, and personal blogs. Cuba scholar Ana Maria Dopico points out that Special Period Havana in particular appears "as a synecdoche for Cuba," because the city has become "synonymous with the photograph [of Cuba]."[14] Dopico claims that the photographic image triumphed in exporting Cuba during the Special Period, when the meaning of the nation was up for grabs. Photogenic Cuba promised "clarity, transparency, and visibility at a moment of obscurity."[15] The Cuban image projected during the 1990s cultivated curiosity. New video production companies sprang up to fill demands for promotional ads to greet tourists in airports and hotels. Before Web sites became commonplace, paper publications such as the *Cubanacan Beach Magazine* offered tourists their choice of activities from ecotourism to fashion shows. Films from within and outside Cuba, whether professional or amateur, explored history and music culture, as well as controversies and lost homelands. Wim Wenders's *Buena Vista Social Club* (1999) tapped into the popularity of world music, and not only relaunched the careers of old Cuban *son* musicians but also supported the commercial success of a series of music CDs under the Buena Vista Social Club name. Through images and music, the West rediscovered Cuba as the last bastion of communism in the Western hemisphere and as a forbidden paradise for American tourists.

Facilitated by visual culture in general and the Internet in particular, Cuba became visibly consumable. Still, the U.S. embargo managed to direct the Western viewer and traveler's orientation in Cuba. Even today, cultural objects still function, behind the showcase façade, as Cold War remnants emanating traces of ideological conflicts. For the outsider, the incongruent fascination of 1950s American-made automobiles in the streets of Havana is not solely a temporal dislocation. The automobiles, along with cultural referents like the Tropicana nightclub, cigar rollers, and the former Bacardi Rum building in Old Havana, form part of the island's pre-Castro legacy. Meanwhile, the period cars are economic engines of another sort for their owners, who rent them out for weddings or taxi service. They symbolize older visions of progress condensed into the mobility of American car culture. Lovingly conserved, 1950s American cars simultaneously display Cuban ingenuity, the island's culture of survival, faded American privilege, and admiration of American style and wealth. Chevrolets and Fords (but never the Russian-made Lada) are held up as examples of excellent engineering and design, a measure of the longstanding cultural affinity between the United States and Cuba that persists even after, and in some ways because of, decades of embargo. Despite the fact that new Asian, French, and German automobiles are numerous on city streets, it is the vintage American cars that inspire tourist photos and YouTube videos accommodating a nostalgic view of the island.

Old Havana, with its 242 city blocks and four thousand buildings (of which nine hundred have "heritage value"), was already the island's major attraction prior to the 1990s tourist boom.[16] The historic center of the city, founded in 1519, was declared a UNESCO World Heritage Site in 1982. To expand capacity and refurbish the decaying, often crumbling structures, the Office of the City Historian (La Oficina del Historiador de la Habana Vieja) was, through Law 143 (1995), granted political status within the Executive Committee of the Council of Ministers. Along with tourism, architectural restoration projects operate with power and autonomy, directing the necessary financing to Old Havana projects and creating sufficient commercial enterprises to generate *divisas* (hard currency).

The restoration project is embedded within the Cuban informatics project, making it prominent on the Cuban digital media landscape. According to Eusebio Leal, director of the Office of the City Historian, Cuban city planners are designing sustainable spaces for residents and tourists alike. This goal is underscored by an ideological project to develop socially conscious tourism. In 1999, at the end of its first five years, the restoration project had generated seventy million dollars and completed work on 95 sites, with a remaining 58 in progress. Another 79 sites began restoration the following year.[17] This multifaceted endeavor relies on the latest data-processing technology and design and modeling software. It also includes technology in public spaces, in the form of information centers with Internet access. CENIAI, the central government entity providing connectivity, is located in Old Havana's historic capitol building. Metaphorically, reconstruction for residential and tourism purposes mediates the temporalities of the spaces involved, transforming colonial survival into a postmodern space of global capital.

As a medium characterized by decentralized networks, and consequently by broader public discourse, the Internet reflects the unstable, dynamic form of emerging technocultural relationships. In the mix of political and social flows generated so easily about Cuba, the Internet becomes both object and subject. Noted intellectual figures inside and outside Cuba use online journals like *Cuba Encuentro* to debate contemporary topics of relevance to Cubans everywhere.[18] Organizations like Reporters without Borders purport to have the Internet under surveillance to uncover violations of press freedoms, such as those published in an October 2006 report denouncing Cuba's access policies.[19]

But perhaps no other Internet phenomenon exemplifies the extent of debate so much as does the war of words over the definition of Cuba on Wikipedia, the free online encyclopedia created, edited, and administered by volunteers that "attempts to summarize all human knowledge."[20] As the controversy over words such as *democracy* in the Cuba entry heated up, the discussion was picked up by the Miami Herald.com Web site, which reported that the battle of edits of the Cuba entry (it received thirty edits, for example, on April 27, 2006) caused the article to be placed off-limits to first-time or unregistered users of the site and potentially subject to mediated discussion.[21]

However, ideas of Cuba do not spin solely in heated online interactivity. The expansive Internet space also features singular, one-way output in pre-web mode. Wi-Fi TV, an Internet television company that streams television and radio broadcasts from five hundred stations including Cuba's Cubavisión (which airs lengthy speeches by Fidel Castro),[22] affirms that the live news feed (too slow for easy extended watching), is often picked up by viewers and Internet users in the Miami area seeking breaking news from Cuba.[23]

Forms of Internet coverage draw on established media conventions and practices that range from reporting based on humanitarian principles and discovery of truth to the production and packaging of entertainment. The space of the Internet affords conventional use and traditional practice while also allowing their reinvention, subversion, and avoidance under the direction of advocates, activists, and citizens molding a terrain of public discussion. In the still-firm grip of socialist ideology, Cuba offers lively Internet territory to those celebrating or competing over it and over the country's future.

Diplomacy and Technology

Cuban history shows that the island is no exception to the rule that changes in communications technology generally follow economic development, each reinforcing the other. The significance of sugar in Cuba's development grew with the early emergence in 1838 of the railroad, key to the timely transportation of vast loads of sugar for export.[24] The expansion of undersea cables for communication in the nineteenth century followed the interest of imperial economies in expanding their markets, consumers, and political influence. In 1867, Cuba became part of an international cable network that included

England, France, India, and China, and reached the African continent in the late 1880s and early 1890s. As Armand Mattelart argues, pursuing the relationship between capital and technology in *Networking the World, 1794–2000*, the tightly entwined logic of trade and diplomacy meant that private enterprises could thrive despite ideological differences between governments: "The fact that the British undersea cable depended on private companies—unlike France, where it was placed under state control—changed nothing from a geostrategic point of view."[25] By 1902, the British cable network covered two-thirds of the world's nations and was supported by a cabling fleet ten times larger than that of the French. In expanding their reach across the colonial regimes of capital, private companies depended not only on economic power and access to natural resources but also on mastery of cable technology.

Historically, the relationship between private enterprise and diplomatic interests has relied on the design and control of technologies and communication systems that could facilitate trade expansion; for instance, nationalism, in the form of rallying popular participation for Herculean production efforts, helped Cuba control technological appropriation in the context of opposition by the dominant United States, especially (but not exclusively) after 1959. Issues concerning control of technology do not arise merely from competing ideologies, such as from Marxism or socialism confronting "savage capitalism." Rather, they stem from the way nations of whatever political types confront their place in the global economic order. For smaller nations, decisions about economic development and technology are frequently made with a view toward creating an enduring national economy without exploitative imported models.

How sugar proved a major engine and conduit for technological advances in Cuba has been examined extensively by scholars, who have produced both traditional histories and historiographies uncovering the cultural meaning of sugar in the creation of networks of trade and exploitation. In *The Sugarmill*, a classic work of historiography, Cuban historian Manuel R. Moreno Fraginals supports the view that sugar, as an important global commodity, was a decisive factor in the development of the transatlantic submarine telegraphic cable network.[26] As a major world producer of sugar, Cuba benefited from such early transoceanic communications, which united it primarily with Spanish and U.S. interests. The sugar industrialists, tenacious in their pursuit of profit, made Cuba a major sugar exporter.[27] Owners embraced advances in technology in nineteenth- and early-twentieth-century sugar mills even as it brought them to confront the issue of abolition of slavery. Technological advancements may have been tied to trade in Cuba, but they would come to serve a very different political and economic system from that of their origin.[28]

From 1959 until 2002, the production of sugar drove the Cuban socialist economy, rhetorically and culturally invested with a utopian vision of social justice. Slogans projected an inexorable and indefatigable independence, characteristic of the nation as symbolized by its sugar production. Cuban writer Antonio Benítez-Rojo contends in *The Repeating Island* that sugar represents the deepest "ideological presence" running through the history of Cuba, irrespective of the ideology of those in power.

> Its propaganda apparatus has elaborated, through time, such slogans as "without slaves there is no sugar," and "without sugar there is no country," and "the Cubans' word: ten million tons are coming!" Thus sugar is the same as fatherland, and to produce sugar is to be Cuban. Years ago, when someone sought to change the sugar world's status quo he was identified as an enemy and called a "revolutionary"; now he's called a "counterrevolutionary," although he is the same individual. The extremes bend to form a circle and they don't mean anything.[29]

According to economists Jorge F. Pérez-Lopez and José Alvarez, "so intimate was the relation between sugar and Cuba [that] it was hardly possible to talk about one without referencing the other."[30] When the colonial–mercantile plantation economy gave way to the socialist project, sugar acquired a new iconic and political value, expressed through citizen volunteer work in the sugar fields. For three decades, sugar remained the basis of Cuba's USSR-subsidized economic system—a system symbolized in the titanic and ultimately unrealizable undertaking of the 1970 campaign to harvest a record-breaking ten million tons of sugar. As world sugar prices fell to record lows in the 1990s and the former Soviet Union stopped paying preferential prices, however, tourism, mining, and biotechnology displaced sugar from its central role in the economy. Technological innovation and planning focused on tourism and its information relays as the new motors of the Cuban economy.

Oceans of Cable

Data pipelines were facilitated in the mid-nineteenth century by transoceanic cabling routes that made possible telegraphic transmission, and then, in the early twentieth century, by telephonic networks and, beginning in 1988, by digital communication networks. Cable technology connected Cuba not only to Europe and the United States, but, more crucially, to the logic of the communications system. Standards for measures and protocols for operability were required no matter what political system was in place. Until the revolution, Cuba met the standard practices facilitating the politics of communication, practices that in part defined its relationship with its trading partners as they simultaneously facilitated commercial transactions and transfer of profits. The established practices were undermined when, in 1959, private companies (IT&T and many others) found their holdings and profits nationalized by the new revolutionary government. Before the revolution, cable technology had fast become a domestic fact of life, with the modernization of the telephone system. This is evident from the 1958 Havana telephone book: the cover artwork celebrates modernization, with a background of new high-rise apartment buildings in front of which four muscular workmen guide the placement of an underground telephone cable from a giant spool sporting a large red sign, "More telephones for more people." Disappearing underground through a manhole, the cable promised not only to connect thousands of additional customers of the Cuban Telephone Company (a subsidiary of IT&T) but also to connect international business interests through the undersea routes (fig. 5). Revealing an emphasis on trade with the United States, Cuba has never had an underwater cable link with South America; finally, in the early twenty-first century, as a result of new agreements between Cuba and Venezuela and increasing attention in the Southern Hemisphere to regional integration (orchestrated through ALBA), a fiber-optic cable between Cuba and Venezuela is being laid and is projected for completion by 2010. In contrast with the physical and political constrictions of Cuba's present digital system, the considerable increase expected in bandwidth reflects the continued willingness of the state for engagement with Latin America.[31]

In the 1970s, as a result of early insertion into the cabling architecture of new communications technology, and as a consequence of sugar's importance to the national interest, socialist Cuba pushed for the creation of a data transmission network. To support the goal of the ten-million-ton sugar harvest project, scientists developed data networks and incipient uses of computers to collect information. In a 1983 study, published during a period of strong anti-imperialist ideology revived by authoritarian dictatorships in

———— 5. Cover of Cuban 1958 telephone directory ————

Chile, Argentina, Brazil, and Central America, Mattelart and Hector Schmucler examined the defining role and potential of information technologies
in the region. Their study analyzed the interconnected logic followed by
communication technologies in Latin America. Written in the shadow of
the murderously authoritarian, procapitalist regimes mentioned, the analysis is influenced not only by a Marxist reading of culture industries, but by
the repressive conditions that gave notions of democracy and freedom a
critical immediacy.

Seen in the study's lens, revolutionary Cuba represents an interesting
example of defiance and invention, given the state's decision to create an
autonomous computer industry as Cuba simultaneously embarked on its
most orthodox pro-Soviet policies. Mattelart and Schmucler note that Brazil
and Cuba made the greatest effort in Latin America to establish a policy
that would spur a national computer industry. Early in 1970, "a group of

researchers at the University of Havana proposed the construction of a digital computer to resolve the problems of rail transport of sugar cane."[32] As noted by Pedro Urra González, director of *InfoMed*, Cuba's medical computer network, the computer scheme was no mere assembly project.[33] The Cubans perfected the prototype of a native minicomputer, and moved on to specialize in computer production for particular requirements. Mattelart and Schmucler also found significant that the Cuban "data transmission network [was] made possible through Cuba's national technology."[34] Computers thus became intertwined with the state's subsequent project to position Cuba at the forefront of scientific and technological innovation.

As I discussed in chapter 1, as long as Cuba had an economic partnership with the former Soviet Union, its economy followed the centralized pattern of state command economies. While still fundamentally centralized, Cuba's economy soon took on a new structure, charted by the reforms of 1993, gradually making the state, in the words of economists, more "agile and efficient." All administrative functions were transferred to individual companies, which were given autonomy to move into foreign markets, handle their own finances, and control their own resources.[35] The arrangement set up a paradoxical relationship between centralization and decentralization, one that is, according to Cuban economist Silvia Domenech, the essence of the nation's economic reality.[36] She finds that decentralizing the enterprise sector could make centralized economic planning effective, and this radical change has indeed been responsible for the growth, though modest, of Cuba's economy.

One instance of decentralized entrepreneurship has produced an interesting conjunction of Cuban tourism, retail, and technology enterprises with its military. The armed forces now operate hotel chains (Gaviota), a national airline, and even stores (TRD, or Tiendas de recaudación de divisas). In August 2006, under the interim leadership of Raúl Castro, Revolutionary Commander Ramiro Valdés Menéndez took over as minister of informatics and communications, after heading a technology enterprise. This was the younger Castro's first ministerial appointment after taking control, at his brother's behest, on July 31, 2006. The ministry is responsible for policy, design, and implementation of information and communication technologies, and serves as an example of what non-Cubans criticize as growing militarization. Given the strength of military culture in Cuba, it should come as no surprise that the armed forces play a vital role in managing aspects of the nation's economy. As the origin of the Internet in the U.S. defense-funded

ARPANET shows, military interests are tied to information technologies throughout the world.

As set forth by the Cuban Communist Party, Cuba's post-1993 economic system is a practical response to the problems that plagued centralized command economies under the former Soviet Union model. In the old structure, centralized decision making contributed to short-term problem solving yet it also created overblown bureaucracies, over-regulation of economic activities, and absolutist decision making. The process of decentralizing the business sector creates autonomous structures where managers are able to set salaries, create goals, invest, and manage their own costs. The Communist Party remains the central authority for guiding the development of businesses, setting policies, and rejecting neoliberal models that would allow markets to establish economic value. Essentially, the state continues to be the guardian of Cuba's future, responding to social issues by providing the social services that have been the fountainhead of national development during the socialist era. Even as education, medical facilities, and medicine were stretched thin during the Special Period, the government (and, in many instances, foreign aid) focused on maintaining the state's role in social services.

Cuba's ownership of the fixed-line and wireless telephone companies, ETECSA and CUBACEL, prevents regional price gouging in telecommunications services and creates a "social" model of telecom services for the population. As a state priority, the telegeography of this model spans the national territory even when ownership is structured as a joint venture with foreign investors. In the midst of global deregulation and restructuring of telephone companies throughout the 1990s, and with the emergence of mobile telephony as a new economic force in the following decade, Cuba's continued ownership of its national telephone service has presented a different information paradigm, with the state well aware of its lucrative potential.[37] Cuba's nationalized telecommunications infrastructure supports Mattelart and Schmucler's claim that control of information is based on national specificities (such as Cuba's centralized media ownership) and on the "multidimensional character of information as raw material," as information contributes to a reformulation of the "planetary order."[38]

In 1994, Mexico's Grupo Domos and the Telecom Italia/Stet formed a joint partnership with the Cuban state to control 49 percent of ETECSA. Pressured to withdraw by the United States, and unable to raise the needed capital for the venture, Grupo Domos sold its share of the partnership in 1996, leaving

Telecom Italia/Stet with a 27 percent interest. ETECSA then merged its two cellular phone providers, CUBACEL and C-COM, and by 2004 controlled 100 percent of mobile telephone services and 73 percent of fixed-line service.[39] Rather than follow the pattern of privatization of telecommunications, in short, Cuba chooses to control them and, thereby, their key role in the economy.

In 2003, the executive committee of the Council of Ministers issued Decree 275, which extended until 2019 the concession to ETECSA for the operation of fixed telephony, cellular mobile, and Internet access, among many other services. Cuba was not in the sprouting fiber-optic and telecom network brought about through the North American Free Trade Agreement (NAFTA) pact among the United States, Mexico, and Canada; instead, benefits of cooperation among telecommunication enterprises have, for Cuba, been directed toward South America, with new economic and political pacts with Venezuela expanding the realm of possibilities for twenty-first-century socialist partnerships.[40]

International cooperation has brought liberalization of trade barriers to create more competition within each nation's territories, which ironically has not lowered prices. Telephone companies in Mexico promoted computer use in the early years of the privatization of the Internet (mid-1990s), since these companies stood to gain more customers, higher revenues, and larger territories. Teléfonos de Mexico (Telmex), for example, increased the number of computer users by offering free computers to customers who signed up for Internet access, thereby helping to build international trade, foreign investment, e-commerce, and e-government. Phone companies, following a European model, also shared revenues with Internet service providers to provide a free Internet service as part of a telephone and data package. Under this structure, privately owned telephone companies in Mexico, though competing with AT&T and other international carriers, dominated the national market, making telephone service rates in México one of the highest in the hemisphere.

Old Yet New Technologies

Economies based on inequities of exchange and resource control produce hybrid cultures, where "new" and "old" technologies coexist. The term *hybrid* defines more than a material reality; it defines approaches to being in the world. Employees of global industry can work in telecommunications factories yet have insufficient means of access to the products they make. This holds true in developing countries, including those previously colonized, where different sectors modernize at different rates, often as a result of residual neocolonial industrialization patterns. The overlapping existence of multiple forms of modernity, and the visible incorporation of a variety of cultural practices into mostly urban landscapes, generate an interface between material conditions (such as utilities and their regulation) and technology linked to political and humanitarian goals (such as social media). Thus, although agricultural processes in Cuba had long been mechanized as part of the push to create a modern socialist nation, the country continued to depend economically on the former Soviet Union and preferential prices. Modernization entailed all sorts of survival strategies relying on both old and new machines, and on incorporating impoverished or antiquated circumstances of the present into the utopian goals of state planners. In the mid-1990s, even while technological advances connected Cuba to information networks (albeit initially through a slow satellite link), withdrawal of former Soviet subsidies and the ensuing economic catastrophe in Cuba drove other technology backwards. If the Meliá-Cohiba Hotel had offered a virtual tour of the Cuban countryside in the mid-1990s, it might have taken a visitor on a drive, for instance, to the orange groves on the grounds of the international film school in remote San Antonio de los Baños, west of Havana. There, the visitor would have encountered the "idyll" of a peasant and his oxen, in postmodern counterpoint to a tractor nearby, its rusting gas tank utterly empty. Another perspective, inspired by eco-activism, would construe this contrast between farming methods as a dialogue between sustainable and mechanized processes.[41] The early phase of the economic crisis indeed sent farmers back to plowing their fields with oxen, a reminder of the vulnerabilities of technology and its requirement of political stability. The crisis anticipated a phenomenon of scarcity now becoming worldwide, the result of global economic and political conflicts. In Cuba, the crisis produced what appeared a temporal dislocation, exposing relations among political interests. Understanding relations between old and new technologies and rural and urban needs was revealed as essential to determining their function and value to society.

Ideological Forces

New opportunities and interactions become evident from the introduction of varied economic exchanges, as they were accompanied by technological interventions and advances. Although economic factors set the parameters of material infrastructure and potential (for example, limiting the expansion of fiber optics throughout the island), ideological currents and their concrete results shaped cultural interactions (as when the U.S. embargo made it impossible for Cuba to link to existing fiber-optic networks). The geopolitical and ideological framework that defined Cuba's economic opening in the 1990s required the reinvention of social and political concepts. In the context of tourism, notions of *foreign* and *national*, always significant in the historical process of Cuban society, were redeployed against the backdrop of forty years of revolutionary thinking and the material constraints of a heightened crisis. The space of Cuba's luxury hotels has been imbued with discomfort because it underscores the differing political and social status of *extranjeros* and nationals. Internet use was characterized by the same uneasy ambivalence; utopian visions of a disembodied cyberspace might provide an antidote to this duality, but state-imposed restrictions reinforced prevailing inequalities. Foreigners (and their hard currency) have been welcomed as guests and potential investors, with Cuban residents enlisted as workers in a subordinate, circumscribed capacity. Legal regulations barring broad Internet use, as well as adopted social behaviors, have defined related socioeconomic interactions, themselves linked to Cuba's complex history of neocolonial and capitalist interactions.

To justify its investment in a tourism-based economy, the state has had to demonstrate how its new economic model would serve the continuation of the established moral order of its socialist society. Created throughout four decades of revolutionary ideology, this social construction avows an investment in ideas of universal justice, independence, and equality. Depending on *the people* to build the model society, the state has repeatedly mandated sacrifice, discipline, and solidarity, with the meaning of these values also responding to the particular historical moment. The early sacrifices of the 1960s, for example, were experienced with euphoria as worthwhile, tangible examples of social progress. Reordering the society and abolishing social hierarchies set new priorities, aiming to bring those most disaffected, disadvantaged, and discriminated into parity by affording equal opportunities. Universal literacy is the most widely recognized Cuban accomplishment of this period. Such social projects gave citizens a concrete stake in the redefined nation, although younger generations subsequently may have felt restrained by them.

Later, during the Special Period, the notion of sacrifice varied, reflecting different levels of scarcity and the changes brought about both by reforms in general and tourism in particular. Videos on YouTube show images of solidarity in 1989, as the winds of political and economic change began to blow: a poor, middle-aged woman declares passionately, "Even if I had to live on one potato, I would support Fidel until the end of my days."[42] By this time, a shift in commitment from "building socialism" to "saving socialism" had begun to emerge. The revolution's powerful narrative of struggle and triumph met a sharp challenge during the 1990s. Ideas of community, solidarity, and shared goals were rearticulated through a focus on the social benefits of the Internet, orienting Cuba's embrace of advanced information technologies and tourism with conscious understanding of their divisive potential.

At stake since the Special Period has been the sense of legitimacy for the Cuban people, a legitimacy hard won through ongoing sacrifices and through belief in, and commitment to, a shared project. The social inequalities (in terms of access to dollars, the Internet, and satellite television, for examples) that arose during the Special Period exposed the frailty of the revolutionary project and its inability to sustain a pure socialist moral order without economic subsidy. Foreigners and nationals experienced the new sacrifices differently, however. Social stratification was touted not as a shift in the moral understanding of society but as an economic strategy, a *mal necesario* (necessary evil). Rationalization by the official press of the negative situation cast citizens as obligated to continue a social contract—a contract formalized by the state in the 2002 constitutional amendment establishing socialism as irreversible course.

Even as it addressed and, to some degree, resolved severe problems, the new economic direction produced social unease not only through the enduring of material hardships, but also through the actual experience of disparity. Inequality increased with the new economic measures, such as the granting of forms of nonsocialist property that allowed for the creation of economic joint ventures and corporations, like Comercio Interior Mercado Exterior (CIMEX), that have, however, brought investment and diversified the range of economic activities on the island. CIMEX has become a huge corporation, with eighty subsidiaries across the country in economic sectors from import/export, free trade zones, and tourism to transportation, digital communications equipment, car rentals, and audiovisual production. Entities like CIMEX facilitated the construction of Meliá-Cohiba and other tourist hotels throughout Cuba. Yet luxury vacation resorts in Varadero Beach and other provincial sites offer tourism products and help insert Cuba into the competitive, global flows of ecological, medical, and cultural tourism. Even the very idea of a socialist island has been packaged as an attractive commodity for tourists.

The state instituted the legal boundaries prohibiting Cubans from accessing the new spaces of luxury (the hotels) as guests, a measure taken from wariness of contact with the bourgeoning numbers of foreigners, as well as in an effort to fend off prostitution and corruption. Ironically, exiled Cubans returning to the island enjoyed open access to hotels, while family members who had not chosen to abandon the country were excluded. This humiliating contradiction was a springboard for the circulation of countless blunt jokes. Riffing on Cuban poet Nicolás Guillén's poem "Ahora sí," which celebrated open access to Varadero beaches for everyone alike after the Castro government came to power, "Así, sí" delivers a harsh and literal condemnation of the new measures. A Cuban tries to enter a hotel in Varadero Beach when he is stopped at the entrance.

Oye, compañero, no puedes entrar.
Mire, yo peleé en la Sierra.
No me importa compañero, esto es para turistas.
Oiga, que yo peleé en Girón.
No compañero, te he dicho que no puedes entrar. Esto es por
    dólares.
Mira chico, no me has entendido, yo fui casquito y peleé en la
    Sierra contra Fidel, despues vine en la invasion de Girón y me
    cambiaron por compota, y ahora estoy aqui por la comunidad.
Ah, perdone Señor, pase, pase.[43]

Listen, comrade, you can't go in.
Look, I fought in the Sierra.
I don't care; this is for tourists.
Look, I fought in Girón.
No, comrade, I've told you that you can't go in. It's in dollars.

Look, man, I don't think you understand me. I fought in the Sierra against Fidel and later I was part of the Bay of Pigs Invasion and they traded me for baby food, and now I'm here as part of *la comunidad* (exile community).
Oh, forgive me, Sir. Please come in!

Cubans can vacation on the state's payroll one week a year in Cuban-owned, non-luxury hotels as part of a reward system. The unsavory regulations, which echoed prerevolutionary race and class exclusions, when beaches, clubs, and hotels were off limits to working class and Black Cubans, were finally lifted in March 2008. Originally, universal access had only come in 1959, when the revolution opened the beaches and made hotels affordable. That the subsequent 1990s restrictions were so unpopular also attests to the level of social inclusion that had been gained after the revolution.

Negotiating the social tensions generated by exclusion of Cuban nationals shapes the way individuals (foreigners and residents) established relationships in public and private spaces, hotels or homes. The regulations have found their match in the ingenuity of Cubans and foreigners alike; for example, foreigners can check into a Sol Meliá Hotel in Varadero, the beach mecca of Cuba, with fortunate Cuban friends by pretending marital relationships. Other tricks are also used consistently to circumvent restrictions to Internet access. Just as political systems accommodate practical trading and communication necessities, individuals act on their personal transactional and communication needs under any governing ideology; the scope of digital technology has increased and diversified the ways in which both forms of adaptation occur in Cuba.

The development of the telegraph and the computer both reveal social investment—the first in association with modern capitalism, the second in conjunction, in Cuba, with consolidation of a socialist regime. Cuba's drive to be a world power in medicine, biotechnology, engineering, and education represents another important component of the state's ideology: a strong and persistent nationalism. In Cuba, national identity and socialism are key ideological and rhetorical factors driving the acquisition and deployment of technology, as well as access to it. Even as the world is defined increasingly in postnational terms, Cuba's desperate outreach to Venezuela and Bolivia for economic and ideological support reveals the importance of formulating nationalism within broader geopolitical interests: regional and transnational integration becomes vital for the survival of the "national."

Needs and Uses of Technology

Technological development in the Special Period followed Cuban needs and interests as well as those of new investors, encompassing, for instance, the modernization of information facilities for the medical sector and the updating of the telephone infrastructure. As Raymond Williams has argued, the causes and effects of technology, whether foreseen or not, make understandable the social needs behind them and the degree to which these needs are met.[44] The Cuban state not only proclaimed public ownership of new information networks for science, information, and communication; it also created the Ministry of Informatics to implement regulations to direct development and access. In Cuba, the government has constantly weighed its claim to run an open society against the perceived risks of openness. No stranger to popular analyses of the Internet, the Cuban regime forecast a windfall of benefits around the acquisition of information, geared to undermine the all-encompassing obstacles created by decades of embargo policies. It was not, and is not, helpful to view technology in Cuba as a panacea for poverty and underdevelopment; the state has not promoted technology in this way, nor has it directly recognized the negative ramifications of its policies. Instead, it has pursued links to the creation of a sustainable economy and network of trade to carry Cuba into the post–Fidel Castro era.

The convergence of the digital revolution with the remaking of political paradigms, and the uncertain future of post-Castro Cuba, feed incongruous and conflictive social relations. Benítez-Rojo writes about the history of the Caribbean as a series of repeating historical traces, referring to unforeseen relations among Cuban phenomena as "a dance movement and the baroque spiral of a colonial railing."[45] The dance metaphor takes in the highs and lows of the spiral, down to the ubiquitous sight of foreign men and women who come to Cuba's hotels for business or pleasure and partake in the burgeoning prostitution trade. This uncomfortable reminder of colonial era racial and sexual relations exemplifies the problems faced by an open socialist state. The acceptance by the Cuban government of the investment brought by the foreigners brings its own reminder and irony; as wryly noted by cultural and political observers throughout Latin America, the return of Spanish investment to the entire region in the 1990s felt like a second conquest.[46]

Wendy Chun contends that "global networks are always experienced locally"[47] as the local populations respond to the technical conditions of each network. At the level of architecture to meet local demand, restrictions, and uses, the network is also political. In Cuba, where the "network of networks" arrived during an epochal shift alongside social, economic, and cultural forces, the Internet was presented to the public as fascinating and even mysterious. Popularly, its inner workings were little understood and were shrouded in the taboo of state control; it generated tremendous discussion about old and new topics, for example, opportunities for circumventing economic sanctions, the dangers of on-line pornography, and the possibilities of new kinds of interactions between human beings and technology. Social factors in Cuba and innovation in information technologies influenced the orientation of policies and their implementation, through the state's definition of, and prescribed uses of, the Internet.

Like countless other nations, although for different reasons, Cuba vested political and economic importance in the Internet's future. For the Cuban government, the prospect of the Internet resuscitated dreams that a viable socialist (rather than neoliberal) economic model might still be possible. For a society already heavily invested in the promotion of scientific knowledge, the Internet offered ways to generate financial return from its science-related endeavors. Amid general consideration (in the international press, specialized literature, and interest groups) of the empowering potential of the Internet for people and governments, Cuba took hopeful but cautious steps to open to the perennially double-edged sword of information. The nationalistic fear of being left behind helped motivate development and hopes of potential benefits. Security software, firewalls, and political controls, it was felt, would help navigate the dangers.

The Internet was introduced and integrated within existing political, scientific, and administrative governmental structures, with access restricted to specific control points. Its development was prioritized as essential for economic growth, scientific discovery, and culture. As Cuba launched its "social" approach to the Internet, international reaction termed the restrictions to private access yet another sign of Cuba's authoritarian dictatorship. Internally, Cuban computer scientists, medical experts, information specialists, and artists officially embraced their privilege, conferred in times of economic hardship, while unofficial criticism predictably decried the restrictions, which increased as the new technology led to unprecedented conflicts such as the proliferation of unauthorized copying.

Limits and constraints aside, it needs to be acknowledged that the "social" orientation of the Internet in Cuba, which flies in the face of its largely privatized development elsewhere, has produced tangible social benefits, most notably in the form of *InfoMed*. Politics, cost, and data volume concerns set technical limitations on the growth and size of networks. Today, prioritization of "social" rather than private application persists, and institutional development of the Internet continues to feature restrictions, for as long as the state fears that dissenting individuals within or enemies without may attack Cuba's networks.

The Cuban state uses the Internet to capitalize on its economic and educational potential and on the newfound, postmodern romance of foreigners with the island. Emphasizing education means financing hardware and infrastructure upgrades, revamping the existing computer sciences curriculum to include new developments in Internet protocol (IP) technology, building new facilities, and training the specialists needed to transform the structure of technology on the island. The resulting expert labor force in software development and network design has created a national resource of engineers, programmers, and hardware specialists. Existing institutions such as the ISPAJAE and the Youth Computing Clubs provide practical computer training within communities throughout the country. As in other parts of the world, computer science and training have supplanted other subjects in the curriculum, and the importance of computer-related studies in the national economy has increased.

The control of uses of the Internet serves many interests for the state besides privileging social applications over private communication and entertainment. Through centralized control, the government hopes to prevent the emergence of large local multimedia groups. As Mattelart and Schmucler point out, "the process of concentration of the cultural industries . . . shows the extent to which the new technologies are becoming increasingly an instrument for the concentration of economic power."[48]

Cuba's interest, beginning in the 1970s, in the potential of information technologies to generate social and economic gains facilitated the swift deployment of digital technology away from private usage. The high cost of peripherals created a user profile requiring higher levels of income and good foreign connections. The same was true for most of Latin America (if not most parts of the world), where the majority of Internet users reported salaries upward of US$50,000 a year, extremely high salaries for the nations involved.[49] The dire economic conditions of the Special Period in Cuba further inhibited the development of private uses because the dwindling salaries of even the highest-level professionals made computer purchase prohibitive. Hardware is still typically acquired through donations or gifts from friends. Among the digital technology specialists in Cuba designated by state planners as the principal Internet users are those who experienced the publishing crisis of 1992 due to the scarcity of paper and reduced access to other information channels. Resuscitating the publishing industry today forms part of the goal, strongly held by many Cubans as well as by the state, to create an image of Cuba capable of altering the influential perspective imposed during the Cold War. In this way, investment in media technologies continues to reflect an ideology of progress, even as it ironically also continues to limit the sources, and therefore the range, of available information and opinion.

Yet the Cuban government recognizes that, regardless of the complex web of institutions and bureaucracy erected around Internet access, the restrictions on personal expression (to what extent people express their opinions in a government-monitored public sphere), and the legacy of a compromised press (all media owned by the government), the Internet will become an unstoppable force as Cuba enters further into the global economy. Gonzalez-Manet shares this opinion, observing that the history of technological development and use in Cuba is deeply rooted in relationships of past dependency (on the USA and then on the USSR), with resultant unequal levels of economic exchange. Further, he warns, views of the Internet as a great equalizer overlook its power to marginalize, given that three-quarters of the so-called third world population "barely has access to 10% of communications media, 5% of the computers, and 2% of the satellites."[50] From this point of view, a government responsible for directing social responses to technological change becomes the only force against a savage marketplace where coherent policies are lacking. The need for such direction, however, can only be met through more centralized control of information flows and connections, precisely the most contested aspect of the development of Internet infrastructure both within Cuba and worldwide.

Although Manet's position is shared by other cultural critics who focus on the downside of the globalization of media, the position requires a

Marxist perspective that divides culture between the economic superstructure and the base: in other words, the understanding of technology as an ideological function of either the state or of the economy. From this point of view, the ability of technology to generate culture beyond these realms is invisible. Manet's focus on dependency theory with its long understood limitations precludes his examination of broader implications and unpredictable aspects of culture, appropriations of the Internet in Cuba, and national contradictions.

The unequal relationship between North and South, with its long and troubled history, certainly influences technology policies in Cuba. However, the picture is incomplete without a look at the unofficial responses to policies and governments and the disruptive potential of "Caribbean rhythms."[51] Cuba's crisis in the 1990s led to a search for ways to generate income in order to lessen Cubans' dependency on state support.[52] The same search applied to the Internet. Some Cubans have created illegal IP personal networks that have allowed them to pirate or informally rent limited access codes and share e-mail accounts. The Internet in Cuba operates in overlapping spheres of legal and illegal activity, respectively serving predominantly social and primarily individual needs. Those who now share e-mail accounts may once have shared use of the telephone, when telephone connections were not always reliable or available in the island.

The antecedents of a technology, how and why it comes to exist, must be examined in the context of historical, social, and political forces to avoid restricting its meaning to recent social causes and effects. For Latin America, and for Cuba in particular, such a study means examining historical relations with Spain and the Iberian Peninsula, with North America, and especially with the former Soviet Union, and then locating the social forces affecting technological development in a domestic context. For Cuba, it is necessary also to consider the political and social burden of the revolutionary nationalist agenda and its need to "supervise" development through state control, as well as the nation's infrastructural limitations, its crisis of the 1990s, and the degree of recuperation achieved during the first decade of the twenty-first century. Further revealing interconnection is the correspondence of technology with those who envision its evolution, access, and uses, along with the socioeconomic conditions.

Cuban tourist hotels as international media hubs demonstrate the principal types of exchange brought about by converging media technologies and an international tourist culture; however, media interactions extend to the home and to more customized appropriations. When legally sanctioned to receive non-state media, homes demonstrate a complex range of media practices. Home access to satellite television can only be granted by special dispensation from a government agency; the subscriber pays the fee in hard currency, a sign that this activity is a privilege in the socialist system, intended to reward merit. The private home and the TV room become the locus of particular kinds of foreign media experience that cultivate a comparative, outside-in view of domestic programming, provoking complaints about poor local television, complaints voiced as if from the "virtual elsewhere" presented in foreign programs. For other Cubans, homemade satellite dishes, special boxes rigged next to the television set, and other forms of signal modulation provide unique television viewing situations where residents can watch local and satellite channels simultaneously.

The political and personal significance of reception and signal appropriation becomes most apparent when they overlap. For the 1996 Atlanta Summer Olympics, the Cuban local network ran a tape-delayed version of the opening day ceremony, editing out a performance by exiled Cuban singer Gloria Estefan. This version of the event could be watched (by those with the special boxes) alongside NBC's live coverage of the opening ceremonies, in which Gloria, Tito Puente, and Sheila E. performed for two billion viewers. The rich layering of the experience exposed the constructed nature of any message, the political importance of media, and the personal significance of participation in a world event, dimensions that collapsed at that moment into one. Media appropriations, official and unofficial, are key in monitoring the adaptations seen in social relations, as individuals and self-organized groups of people across the globe engage one another within and outside of official networks.

The increasing engagement of Cubans and the state with media technology in the face of scarce resources leads to appropriation with a view to individual and political advantage. To avoid the political and financial constraints on individual access, homes become innovative, sometimes unauthorized zones of cross-cultural appropriation that take Cubans outside their country, stimulating a counter-discourse rooted not only in personal lack and frustration but also in community. Tourist hotels again bring the world to the island, acting as places of strained cultural interaction—vital to the economy of Cuba, yet contrary to its politics and expressed social goals. Simultaneously interface and firewall, the hotels provide productive ideological and individual collisions but have yet to yield equitable and just environments.

4

FILM CULTURE IN THE DIGITAL MILLENNIUM

Working in his bedroom at his parents' Havana home in 1996, Miguel Coyula, then eighteen years old, began crafting special effects for his personally created films on a 486 personal computer. The computer processor was eight times slower than the machines he would use twelve years later to render the effects for *Memories of Development* (2010), a sequel to the 1968 masterwork by Tomás G. Alea, *Memories of Underdevelopment*. In the time it then took to render a single, simple effect, today he can make complex and beautiful composite images. In Cuba in the 1990s, blackouts lasting up to eight hours made the completion of projects a heroic endeavor. Coyula made his first two shorts, *Pirámide* (1996) and *Válvula de luz* (Light Valve, 1997), in the bleak conditions of the Special Period and prior to his attendance at film school in Cuba. *Válvula* was shot sequentially on a VHS camcorder "edited in the camera" and on a 3/4-inch U-matic videotape system without direct sound recording.

In his experimentation with reality, narration, and form, and in his expanded range of expression and themes, Coyula characterizes the international generation of media producers who have integrated digital technology and the Internet into their mode of filmmaking. As a Cuban filmmaker, he embodies through his work a transition into the digital era that understands individual practice, productivity, and expression that are complicated by institutional involvement. Although Coyula's emergence has become celebrated in Cuba (if not always in film school), he now lives and works in New York. He demonstrates typical Cuban inventiveness under constraints that have become part of his style. His is a brand of creativity begun in spite of, and informed by, difficult conditions. Cuba, with its insistence on social purpose, has not seduced him with its long record of filmmaking support and its involvement in content, production, and distribution. In fact, Coyula spills out of the history of Cuban filmmaking with an individual, lucid approach that challenges the central position of the state. He represents a democratization of filmmaking that is molded by digital innovataion and new creative interactions among political, cultural, and social factors.

Coyula is not alone. As I show in this chapter, the political and social culture of Cuba offers a dynamic view of factors interacting in the digital, global era and yields insights into popular and political responses in filmmaking as well as their adaptations in terms of content, production, and distribution. By reviewing the utopian views of filmmakers, as expressed in manifestos such as "For an Imperfect Cinema" (Julio García Espinosa, 1969) and "Manifesto of Poor Cinema" (Humberto Solás, 2003), along with the work of new filmmakers, I reveal the adaptation of Cuba's media discourse to the digital age. Applied to the Internet, these filmmakers' theories provide fresh emphasis, and question the orientation of media in general. In forecasting the empowerment of audiences and users to do away with elitist artistic production and distribution, García Espinosa and Solás embrace the potential of digital media to strengthen local expression in the face of dangerously homogenizing corporate globalization.

In this chapter, I also examine the cinema of the Special Period in the context of what anthropologist Arjun Appadurai calls a mediascape, which reveals media as one of several cultural flows overlapping in global dimensions. Media extend beyond national dimensions of culture onto multinational capital, technology, diasporic communities, and ideological groupings.[1] The cinema links and embodies these overlapping aspects of global culture. Since the 1990s, Cuban state film production has survived in various ways: expanding partnerships with international networks for coproduction; encouraging independent producers, internal and external to Cuba, who increasingly move between market and noncommercial interests; and building the infrastructure of computer networks (described here in chapter 1) that have increased the global presence of Cuba through improved circulation of information and images.

Backstory of an Industry

After the revolution (especially in the period 1959–1979), cinema was used to encourage cultural survival and social change and to aid new governance systems. As a cultural and political project, Cuban cinema served to integrate the vernacular into national culture to reinforce cultural memory. Ideas of cultural survival find new currency in light of the greater cultural exchange made possible by greater numbers of visitors to Cuba in the 1990s, the evolving infrastructure of transnational productions (coproductions), and heightened economic restrictions concurrent with greater circulation of culture, all providing new understanding into cultural production as the terrain of both the state and the individual. Encountering the contingencies of Cuba in the Special Period, as well as the emergence of new media tools, these ideas find fresh expression through digital media and the discourse that gives such media cultural meaning.

Until the late 1980s, state support, combined with the commercial and critical achievements of Cuban film, insulated Cuban filmmakers from the onslaught of market-driven industrial concerns, at least at the level of production and local distribution. In an interview, Cuban filmmaker Gerardo Chijona wryly described his position prior to the 1990s as one of "the spoiled children of Latin American cinema."[2] Indeed, other filmmakers have described the 1980s as a "fat and democratic" era in filmmaking, a time of assured financing for film projects. State support of film thus produced democracy, seen as the provision of resources for, and the protection and nurturing of, creative production. This view of democracy could prevail against the form envisioned in the free market: filmmaking unprivileged by the state, with film practitioners, although formally unrestricted, forced to pander to market forces in order to survive. The arrival of digital technology in the Special Period saw its quiet adoption by veteran and younger Cuban filmmakers steeped in the experience of scarcity and constraint; it thus brought a third perspective of democracy: democracy predicated on artistic freedom and freedom to exhibit, and facilitated by the technology itself. The development of filmmaking in Cuba thus demonstrates the intertwining of political, social, and personal factors with technology to a point where digital tools give the individual the edge and defy any state prescriptions for democracy.

Unlike their predecessors, Cuban filmmakers starting out in the 1990s trained at the Instituto Superior de Arte (ISA) and the Escuela Internacional de Cine y Televisión (EICTV), overseen by the Foundation for New Latin American Cinema, established in 1985. The new filmmakers may also practice and learn to make films with amateur groups, or by working in the nascent commercial media sector. Such a digital ICAIC presented a greater dilemma than did InfoMed and general educational computing in terms of potential to foster the means of dissent or of a potential departure from the long established role of Cuban filmmaking as a social and cultural project.

The Cuban revolution had guaranteed financial backing for its cinema through strong support for ICAIC (1959) and the appointment of filmmakers, rather than bureaucrats, to high-ranking ICAIC positions. Able to define the terms of its autonomy, ICAIC produced, distributed, and exhibited national and Latin American films, negotiating strict protectionist deals with international distributors. As part of its original cultural mandate, ICAIC broadened the perspective of Cuban audiences by introducing them to world cinema through international programs, amateur film clubs, and festivals.

By the 1980s, the general social climate and the structure of apprenticeship in ICAIC fostered creative renewal through an intimate artistic culture, mentorships, and professional partnerships, many of which endure to this day. Filmmakers became socialized both through practice and through the institution of ICAIC, benefiting from its productive environment and its professionalization. In general, the 1980s promoted aesthetic diversity while adhering to revolutionary values. The then-extant institutional culture facilitated creative risk-taking by filmmakers, simply by obviating the strict exigencies of financial procurement for their projects. Thus, until the Special Period, ICAIC ensured the completion, distribution, and exhibition of approved film projects.

The important safety net for Cuban cinema also allowed it to support the development of Latin American cinema, often assisting (publicly or indirectly) in the completion of films made in other countries. This situation did not last beyond 1989; the major economic restructuring weakened the state's ability to maintain its cultural institutions. The film industry had not only to endure the resulting scarcity of resources and disruptions to production, but was also forced to become much more politically sensitive. The new vulnerability of Cuba proved again that there were limits to state tolerance of criticism from within. This was demonstrated spectacularly, at the moment of entering the newly named Special Period, with the scandal over the fully Cuban-financed film *Alicia en el pueblo de Maravillas* (Alice in the Town of Wonderland) of Daniel Diaz Torres (1991). In hindsight, *Alicia* seems more forgiving than films made later in the decade. Written in the late 1980s, the film reflects the institutional and thematic concerns of the time: anxiety about a withering socialist domain, about an ideological vacuum, about the seeming endlessness of sacrifices. The film unleashed a wave of negative reaction from conservative political leaders and the state-controlled national press, which attacked the film, hurling insults and labeling it inopportune and harmful to Cuban culture. Its filmmakers were seen as traitors and opportunists trying to gain favor outside Cuba.[3]

Only astute political maneuvering by Alfredo Guevara as ICAIC's returning director ended a government attempt to dissolve ICAIC by merging it with the more conservative Instituto Cubano de Radio y Television (ICRT). Extinction avoided, drastic changes followed, under the direction of non-filmmakers. Despite the strength of talented filmmakers who fought to preserve a climate of tolerance, openness, and plurality at ICAIC, by the late 1990s the leadership of Alfredo Guevara, which had helped to build a climate of experimentation and international cooperation and renown, had reached a limit; ICAIC dissolved the three working groups (led by Tomás Gutierrez Alea, Humberto Solás, and Fernando Pérez) established by former director Julio García Espinosa in the 1980s. With this stroke, the Cuban film industry lost the largely democratic creative infrastructure that had fostered open artistic dialogue.[4] By 1996, with the death of premiere director Tomás Gutierrez Alea, an era of creative flexibility and broad vision had come to an end. Different values and practices, adjusted to hard commercial realities, colored administrative decisions at EICTV, changing the nature of international support to the student body. Nevertheless, although the harshest period of stagnation in production would abate by 2006, the economic viability of the institute continued to be undermined by reduced state subsidies and bureaucratic centralization.

The bankruptcy of the Cuban socialist state and the resultant financial crisis for ICAIC directly affected Cuban film producers, removing their central support. ICAIC retained control and provided some buffers, but the problems that concerned Cuban citizens on a personal level in the 1990s—food shortages, transportation delays, housing problems—along with the surrounding dilemmas and contradictions, hit filmmaking in many ways. Extreme shortages of materials, from gasoline and electricity to food and film stock, led to the production of fewer films and documentaries.[5] Equipment failure increased, while repairs became impossible. Film processing labs and exhibition venues closed. The national theatrical circuit suffered, and international film purchases fell (fig. 6). Film completion dates became a mirage.

6. Acapulco theater in Havana, Cuba, which played some foreign films: *Die Hard 2*

Trained film personnel (art directors, actors, writers) endured long periods of unemployment, and many left the country, leaving behind skyrocketing costs, in which fuel and meals, typically below-the-line expenditures, made up the greatest portion of budgets.

The crisis affected all levels of the industrial infrastructure of filmmaking. Between 1991 and 2001, approximately thirty-one features were produced, at an average of three per year (with none in 1996). In the same decade, approximately thirty-eight shorts, mostly documentary, were produced through ICAIC and many more through EICTV. The time when ICAIC produced ten features and fifty documentaries per year seemed a distant memory. The production of newsreels, which had been handled through ICAIC and had long documented the history of revolutionary Cuba, simply ceased. The Cineteca Nacional, part of ICAIC, saw its operating budget reduced, and became secondary to the central operation of ICAIC. The reorganization truncated the development of the Cineteca's valuable cultural, educational, and promotional resource, one ripe for utilizing digital tools for improving archival projects, had investment been available. An internal institutional battle also ensued for the right to commercialize archival materials, which would generate hard currency for the Institute, and to control video concessions of ICAIC productions.

From 1991, cinema produced through ICAIC ventured into the international coproduction sector to secure its survival.[6] The increase of such films (mostly through partnering with Spain) was accompanied by an increase in production of both documentary and fiction films *about* Cuban culture from a vantage outside Cuba, as well as by the emergence of an independent cinema reliant on digital technology. The resulting films and the conditions that surrounded their production show how the emotional geography of Cuba was moving beyond social revolution, beyond the island, and toward the self.

Economic disruption increased the need for the state to promote a renewed political vision. Cuban films, however, began to reflect the emptiness of this vision in the face of hardship and continuing demand for sacrifice. Filmmakers, like everyone else who had to deal with the pressures, adapted their methods to survive. The Cuban state's long-established revolutionary values, and its democratic–paternalistic tradition of public debate and of investment in individual talent in prioritized fields insured the film industry against a crackdown that would reduce it to a mere instrument of propaganda. Given the increasing potential of film to foment dissent, however, the state would not risk technological investment at the level seen in the fields of medicine and education. Instead, it permitted—and tapped—its adaptation to the economy.

The digital age arrived at ICAIC during the second phase of the forty-year tenure of Alfredo Guevara. While ICAIC was mired in internal political squabbles, confronting economic devastation and a changing media paradigm, information about new digital media was slow to arrive and almost nonexistent. It would not be until 1998, two years after Cuba had officially connected to the Internet, that ICAIC would establish a Web site. Yet, while appearing reluctant to embrace the Internet, ICAIC leadership encouraged and participated in broader cultural debates about media globalization. Through seminars, and on the pages of the *Cine Cubano* journal, analysis of the changes in mass media became the starting point for any investigation of cultural and historical change.[7] The debates often focused on the negative aspects of globalization, views that coincided with the official party stance toward globalization and the Internet. Institutional vulnerability postponed a significant discussion about the practical benefits of the Internet or about the philosophical changes facing artistic communities, in favor of salvage efforts and future prospects. The difficulty of acquiring a new technology, given the paucity of information about innovation, and given the prohibitive costs of funding projects, reinforced the direction of investment according to central planning. The limitations of a small industry and market, and of that industry's limited distribution possibilities, also contributed to the expansion of noncentral practices, including coproduction.

The profound crisis of the Special Period transformed the nature of Cuban filmmaking. Cuban cinema could no longer be contained within the boundaries of the island nation or sustained by the industrial model established in 1959. The 1990s saw the state's claim fail over an industry it had helped to create, an industry that was escaping both the grip and the comforting embrace of the state and venturing into a wider filmmaking world that offered new and different supports, opportunities, and conditions. Cinema made with and without foreigners, and with or without the participation of film, of digital, video, and editing tools, and of the Internet, embraced new genres and displayed an emerging sense of self at odds with the state's version of reality.

Adaptation to digital technology and its network connectivity demands political and economic adaptation; in Cuba's case, there has been a contrast in approaches between the slow, patchy adaptation to the digital environment that connectivity has permitted for the Cuban film industry, and Cuba's overall deployment of computer training, medical and education networks, and tourism (fig. 7). Modern filmmaking tools make it harder for the state to use film to serve only the socialist project. Digital technology and filmmaking interact in the realm of personal creativity, which is less easily harnessed than are knowledge and infrastructure. Digital filmmaking tools facilitate greater levels of expressive opportunities for either trained filmmakers or amateurs than could 35 mm film or analogue video technology. Low-cost digital equipment easily integrates with computers, audio composing and recording, special effects generation, and automatic uploading to the Internet for distribution. The automatic nature of synchronized sound and image manipulation, without the need for film laboratory processing, means that individuals can produce films, videos, or blogs with little or no institutional collaboration. Digital filmmakers like Coyula represent both continuity and dissonance with Cuban filmmaking as established in the 1960s, which was immersed in discourses of Cuban national identity. Coyula's individuality, creativity, and rejection of corporate machinery ironically align with a

7. Avid workshop for ICAIC editors, led by visiting filmmaker
Roger S. Christiansen, Havana, Cuba, 1995

state that regards itself, rather than private enterprise, as the prime agent of industry.

Seeking Imperfection

As much as Miguel Coyula looks back with wry disappointment in *Memories of Development,* his point of view and digital method in some respects represent both continuity and dissonance with the earlier 1960s generation so often focused on the complexities of national identity. The emerging work of his own generation, who are using today's multiplicity of avenues for expression, shows there is also the possibility to decentralize analytical focus. The work makes it possible to look at personal and institutional expressive cultures, at where they overlap and influence each other. Even while a strand of discourse adheres to a national–social perspective, another strand decidedly slides past a national focus to tie into a personal one.

In 1969, Cuban filmmaker and theorist Julio García Espinosa (second director of the ICAIC) wondered whether the technological conditions for spectators to become active viewers were beginning to exist. In his most well-known manifesto of the era, "For an Imperfect Cinema," he wrote:

In the realm of artistic life, there are more spectators now than at any other moment in history. This is the first stage in the abolition of "elites." The task currently at hand is to find out if the conditions, which will enable spectators to transform themselves into agents—not merely more active spectators, but genuine co-authors—are beginning to exist. The task at hand is to ask ourselves whether art is really an activity restricted to specialists, by extra-human design the option of a chosen few, or a possibility for everyone.[8]

García Espinosa anticipated by more than thirty years the debates about media and democracy re-enlivened by the emergence of low-cost digital cameras, editing systems, portable computers, and social media networks. His critique, with its postcolonial perspective, was rooted in the belief that film, as a mass medium, has the potential to engage and transform its audience through the confrontation between old and new artistic languages. In the 1990s, political, academic, and popular considerations about digital media in a global era generally echoed García Espinosa's earlier concern over the possibility of producing art that did not respond to dominant models. Recent debates about the impact of globalization on cultural production have expressed fears that culture was becoming increasingly homogenous at the hands of corporate media conglomerates economically capable of eclipsing richly layered local expression. The Special Period saw a renewal of the impetus of the manifesto, an impetus rejecting the idea that films could not be made unless one had access to advanced technology. "If these were available, they were welcome. But it was not a question of waiting to have them in order to express our anxieties."[9] The search for a space of artistic practice independent of the "perfect," mass-produced products of mainstream media was re-enlivened by the creative explosion facilitated by digital media tools.

Inspired by the potential of the revolution to effect significant transformation at the level of artistic culture, García Espinosa called for a cinema that would be "imperfect." The use of this adjective has often been misinterpreted as a call to make cinema of poor quality. García Espinosa acknowledged the misreading and clarified the usage in a follow-up essay, fifteen years after the original call. Imperfect Cinema was a provocation, asking artists to consider their role in artistic practice as either reinforcing elitist modes of creation and spectatorship or creating a space of "interested" and committed art. Artistic practice could formulate new expressive forms and meaning from a new engagement, thereby renewing not only the arts but society at large; art would no longer be produced by a minority of elites, but by everyone. In 1969, when written, in the historical context of fast-developing space technologies (satellites, lunar probes, space photography), the first landing by humans on the moon, and the resounding international successes of Cuban cinema, the 1969 version of the essay "Imperfect Cinema" forcefully intervened in an ideology of progress—the ideology of a progress identified by standards of quality set by interests—whether scientific, political, or artistic—that formed elite hierarchies. By doing away with hierarchies of production, and by challenging the standards of quality set by self-interested corporations, the production of "imperfect" art created expressive communities that cultivated process instead of producing forms marketed to mass "common-denominator" markets.

Coyula, a personal filmmaker formed in the Special Period and producing in globalized times, has no interest in filmmaking defined by "national" preoccupations. He does, however, hold an aversion to reproducing the seamless continuity of space, time, and movement typical of realist cinema. He and his colleagues in the present generation of Cuban filmmakers—armed with their bought, borrowed, or rented digital cameras—work independently with computerized editing systems. They may train on commercials, create animation, design Web sites and graphic art, build installations, and record experimental video. Some of their work is featured in the Annual Muestra de Jóvenes Realizadores, an international event in Cuba showcasing works in digital and analogue formats produced through independent production companies and *Televisión Serrana* (Community Television in the Mountains). Digital tools make it easier for Cuba's twenty-first-century filmmakers to enact cinematic "imperfection," as espoused by García Espinosa, as they expand cinematic language beyond established conventions, thus helping to create new relations between films and spectators. They go beyond habitual codes of meaning, and they challenge production strategies and industry standards to probe representation, hierarchies of knowledge, and rules of engagement.

In advocating decentralized production and access to digital tools as a means of liberating users from the tedium of consumerism, García Espinosa posits Internet technology as potentially freeing individuals from constraints.[10] His early film *The Adventures of Juan Quin Quin* (1967) shows just such evasion of convention, and represents the most promiscuous example of Imperfect Cinema. Among other techniques, it uses direct address, jump cuts, shifting acting styles, and juxtapositions of narrative forms. Implicit in this artistic strategy is the challenge to established codes of meaning, the filmmaker constantly rewriting their potential signification.

Digital technology greatly facilitates the same sort of alteration of metaphor, meaning, and experience, and today assists Coyula's imperfect vision of wildly stylized and constructed worlds as it contrasts drastically with the neorealism that inspired his predecessors in the 1960s. He is not interested in realism or in recreating verisimilitude. Elements of the natural world, such as falling snow, can become a fragment of the real to be repurposed within the context of a new image. The real is broken down into usable digitized assets as raw material that precludes the use of CGI software to create an "organic non-reality."[11] The no-budget reality of independent filmmaking influences, and is influenced by, Coyula's solo style as he produces, directs, edits, writes, shoots, and composes his films' music and sound effects. In a completely individual process that itself informs the product, he edits as he shoots, using computer software to produce atmosphere, weather conditions, backgrounds, graphics, and so on. The attraction to the dynamic creative potential of digital technologies provides the possibility of "creating worlds from scratch [fig. 8]."[12] In Coyula's cinema of graphic layers, cutouts, collage, and animation, the "real" enters as counterpoint and backdrop. "You can play with all these elements," he says, "music, theater, photography, . . . controlling every single aspect" to create a desired atmosphere.[13] He is reminiscent of a self-conscious Tomás G. Alea in *Memories of Underdevelopment*, when the filmmaker, playing himself, explains, of the form of film he is making, "I'm experimenting with the idea of collage, putting different things together, we'll see how it turns out." Typical of Coyula's films, *Válvula de luz* has a style that contrasts with the realism of the work of indirect mentors such as Alea, bearing an indelible visual imprint of Japanese anime (a childhood fascination), accompanied by an elliptical narrative. Literature and the comic book form have inspired Coyula to seek the diversity and imperfection of composition that becomes evident in the shift of style from, for example, sentence to sentence or frame to frame.

The Internet assists filmmakers as they live up to the spirit of García Espinosa's call for diversity and adaptability of resources, for example, by facilitating creative collaboration, making possible the sharing of software, aiding problem solving, and providing access to organizations like Creative Commons (CC) with its CC-licensed sound and image content libraries.

———— 8. "Eres intenso," animation still from *Memorias del Desarrollo* ————
(Miguel Coyula, 2010)

Characteristic optimism about the potential of the Internet to subvert the
entrenched power of the market as regulator of taste relies on a philosophical connection to the foundational spirit of the sixties; the question of access
to the Internet, however, particularly for filmmakers still in Cuba, raises the
shadow of the tough controls that have long limited Cubans' Internet usage
and regulated discourses perceived as counter to the state's.

Finding Individuality

Social renewal, formal experimentation, and proto-utopian expectations
were at the center of revolutionary culture in the Cuba of the 1960s. Radio,
television, and film acted as catalyzing social agents expressing and recording the transformation begun with the Cuban revolution. The project of
building a new culture drew on collective dreams and the continual desire
to connect national ideas with the larger vision of a better world. This project evolved through a thirty-year long independence struggle against Spain
(1868–1898) and later the U.S. economic embargo, and a passionate desire to
build autochthonous identities.[14] Film of the 1960s entailed a Cuban national
aesthetic, an aesthetic made up of diverse styles and influenced by international currents—neorealism, modernism, and formalism—but blended
with a nationalist orientation. Cuban filmmakers expanded the efforts of

international film pioneers from the 1920s and the 1930s who had called for the social orientation of documentary and fiction film.[15]

The touted promise of digital and mobile media technologies for democracy lay in decentered, social, and plural uses. García Espinosa sought a new relationship between film and spectator by expanding cinematic language beyond established conventions and reinforcing the production of meaning that was rooted in national and local identity. He and late Cuban filmmaker Humberto Solás (*Lucía, Cecilia*) embraced the potential of digital media to strengthen national and local expression in the face of corporate globalization.[16] Reinforcing a plurality of popular expression would produce a national identity out of local culture, one that did not reside in a singular national culture. The arrival of digital technology, however, coincided with the faltering of the guiding ideological, social, and political structures (*patria, socialismo, pueblo,* and *partido*) in the stressful decade of the Special Period. Individuals, including filmmakers, had to contend with the increasing complexity of a society losing its fundamental meanings or, at the very least, in which meanings had to be reconstructed. Many, like filmmaker Juan Carlos Cremata, renewed meaning by incorporating a philosophy of local and national identities that would appeal outside Cuba. Without a personal history of revolutionary experience to inspire social ideals or the goal of Imperfect Cinema, and confronted only with hardships, many young filmmakers have preferred to concentrate on the individual freedom of artistic practice offered by digital tools (see *Frutas en el café,* 2005, and *De generación,* 2007). Today, young Cuban filmmakers echo their predecessors' discontent with commercial homogenization and domination, but their quiet concentration on personal digital production is, until now, its own counter-discourse to notions of film contributing to any larger identity or expression.

The rejection of standardizing corporate film industry frameworks is a mark of continuity with earlier intellectual thought. It is joined by the impulse to create a new vocabulary with images. In 1948, French film theorist Alexander Astruc's notion of *caméra stylo* (camera as a pen), as described in "The Birth of a New Avant-Garde," foresaw that film language would be steered by the film author's ability to "write" with the camera. The writing instrument, today, is a cell phone or computer program. Cuban filmmakers like García Espinosa (and Brazilian Glauber Rocha, Argentines Fernando Birri and Fernando Solanas) used the camera in the 1960s and 1970s to foster aesthetic, intellectual, and political questioning, negating the tendency of artistic celebrity to define the quality of a work of art. Today, the proliferation of visual languages that has developed out of digital methods in Cuba and elsewhere gives partial credence to the predictions of 1960s manifestos. The celebration by Cuba and U.S. critics of filmmakers like Vivian Lesnik Weisman (*Man of Two Havanas*, 2007) and Coyula, however, as it invites filmmakers to visit to receive honors at events in Cuba, indicates how digital technology remains as neutral as any writing tool. It fails to further the "imperfect" dream of evaluating art without reliance on establishment standards and sanction.

Rejecting Poverty

The driving spirit behind Espinosa's manifesto was to destabilize dominant centers of media production, a potential that, thirty years on, he conceded was lost as "the market grew more powerful, imposing force over reason."[17] In a 1999 manifesto, "Cibernautas de todos los países periféricos, uníos!" ("Cybernauts of Peripheral Countries, Unite!"), he responds to vanishing ideals, finding in the Internet a new weapon (fig. 9). Humberto Solás added to the theme of Imperfect Cinema in his twenty-first-century digital manifesto,

9. Julio García Espinosa at his home in Havana, Cuba, 2006

"Manifiesto de cine pobre" ("Poor Cinema Manifesto"). Like García Espinosa's earlier proposition, Solas's makes clear at the outset that "poor cinema doesn't imply a cinema lacking ideas or artistic quality." Rather, "it refers to the cinema of restricted economies being made not only in less developed or peripheral countries, but also in the heart of economically stable societies through official, independent, or alternative production programs."[18] Such cinema acknowledges the decentralizing potential of low-cost digital tools to prevent what Solas calls, in the manifesto, "global vandalism," through the promotion of new social groups as producers and distributors. The focus on multiple sources and sites of production recalls Solás's contemporaries' earlier manifestos, such as "Third Cinema" (Fernando E. Solanas and Octovio Getino, 1969) and "Aesthetic of Hunger" (Glauber Rocha, 1965), as along with "Imperfect Cinema" and other manifestoes that helped to define the New Latin American Cinema Movement in the 1960s and 1970s; all were influential in postcolonial discourses about culture and cinema from 1965 on.[19] Not only did these works continue to expand the idea of cinema as a political act, a tool for liberation, along with a radical aesthetics, but the manifestos were produced from reflections on the practical work of the filmmaker. Revealing the influence of the Special Period, the historical moment that produced *cine pobre*, Solas's manifesto focuses on economic themes at the heart of much cultural production in the 1990s.[20]

Cine pobre led to the exhibition of low-budget international cinema through an annual Cine Pobre Film Festival, supported in part by ICAIC. The obstacles that inspired Imperfect Cinema still endure, and aesthetic and economic domination by Hollywood and global entertainment conglomerates have even accentuated, with lack of access to distribution channels, limited financing, and the repercussions of the end of the Latin American Cinema movement (in the 1980s). Cine pobre rearticulates the strategy of Imperfect Cinema that focused on processes of creation, generating broader distribution of alternative media practices through digital networks. (Private ownership, in the earlier concept of Imperfect Cinema, produces a supposed perfection that confines innovation to repetition of standards serving the interests and profits of culture-producing corporations.) Increasing personal use and appropriation of digital media, along with the resulting production, distribution, and copying (authorized or not), may increase the freedom of artists to create, but it also renews concerns over corporate ownership and control of information and copyright of works of popular culture.

An irony exists in the impatience of filmmakers with Cuba's intellectual debate. Continuing poor conditions made filmmakers' practice of cine pobre an obvious, necessary choice rather than an intellectual or political one. And emerging Cuban filmmakers are finding success disproportionate to their numbers in competition with filmmakers from backgrounds of high availability of tools and training, notably where careers are largely geared to corporate production. This comparative success of "poorer" filmmakers may well stem not from deprivation itself, but from the advantages proposed by cine pobre— primarily access derived from digital tools, state support, and decentralization of production. As in other fields, such as athletics, however, this phenomenon suggests value also in the intensity of focus, careful usage, mentorship, and historic example incidental to poor conditions, along with perhaps a stronger cultural current shaping filmmaking in Cuba than is consciously recognized.

Cuban Digital Cinema

The long history of acknowledgment in Cuba of the power of film as a cultural product has continued into the twenty-first century, even as the state still grapples with the issues aggravated or raised by digital access. In the mid-1990s, with the introduction of the Internet in Cuba, and in an approach typical of Cuban concepts of democratic practice, ICAIC organized official debate on the topic of digital media. Under the extreme economic circumstances of the 1990s, digital technology promised low-cost access to production equipment, greatly desired to help ensure the survival of the institute, which was not prioritized for investment. The Havana International Film Festivals of 1997 and 1998 explored this potential through special seminars that examined digital media ramifications, costs, and viability. The seminars expressed caution about the deep reach of media globalization, raising fears about economic impact, threats to cultural heritage, and concerns about the widening economic gap between North and South. These early conversations attested, at the very least, to intellectual reflections about change and new directions, and how the leadership of ICAIC orchestrated a strategy commensurate with previous goals. And, in spite of the concerns discussed, video technology—both digital and analog—did indeed provide access for many Cuban filmmakers, and facilitated the forging of new visual perspectives outside the province of ICAIC.[21]

The Annual Muestra de Jóvenes Realizadores (Havana New Directors Film Festival), established through ICAIC in 2001, provides a platform for emerging talent.[22] Initially, noted film critic Juan Antonio García Borrero presided, and acted on his long-held concern with decentralizing film culture in Cuba by setting up a Semana de Crítica Cinematográfica (Film Critics Week) in Camaguey province. Today, both the Muestra de Cine and the Semana de Crítica represent attempts by filmmakers and critics to renew the discourse of cinema in Cuba, improve support for Cuban filmmakers, and foster digital production for individual intentions. Each year, aspiring filmmakers screen their shorts, documentary and fiction, as well as experimental and video art to a jury of critics, filmmakers, and artists. Working independently, and using any means possible, but principally employing digital technologies, filmmakers who came of age during the 1980s and 1990s are reshaping the parameters of industrial cinema in Cuba. They are a diverse mix of practitioners, engaged or not in larger intellectual considerations of the role of Cuban cinema and globalized media. The embrace of digital production is key for this group, but its members are also savvy about the economics of the industry, and aware of marketing and of the international market. Filmmakers like Juan Carlos Cremata, Humberto Padrón, Miguel Coyula, and Pavel Giroud (*Edad de la peseta*, 2006, and *Omerta*, 2008) who were first recognized through the annual Muestra have gone on to make independent coproduced features. Exhibition and material support by ICAIC for independent productions represents official sanction by the state of cultural renewal and expansion in the face of tough economic realities, if not encouragement of personal careers and advancement. Success, subsequent to the Muestra, came for Cremata's first two features, *Nada* (2001), which garnered awards and critical praise, and *Viva Cuba* (2005), a family-oriented story that drew large Havana audiences during the summer of 2005. *Viva* went on to win a series of awards, and was sold to international markets at various film festivals, making Cremata one of the most successful of the new generation of directors. With renowned actor Jorge Perugorría as producer, Humberto Padrón directed *Frutas en el café* (Fruits in the Coffee, 2005), with a commercially oriented storyline that relies on some of the habitual characters of the economy of the Special Period: foreigners, *jineteras* (sex workers), black market thieves, criminals, and the good cop (played by Perugorria himself). The film is Padrón's second digital project. His previous film, *Video de familia* (2001), structured as a video letter, also displays a keen interest in provocative topics. In *Frutas en el café*, a young Cuban man who emigrates to Miami informs his family in Havana (through a video) that he is gay. The father's angry response reveals his intransigence and intolerance—particularly given his membership in the

Party—as the "old" set of values; predictable melodrama then ensues over the clash of generations strained by the emerging openness of gay sexuality. Meanwhile, cheaper digital production has facilitated projects that explore content still controversial in Cuba (*El hombre y el bosque*, 2008) but less risky and potentially viable internationally.

The seeds of Cuban digital production were sown by the nongovernmental group Movimiento Nacional de Video de Cuba (National Video Movement of Cuba), founded in 1989. The group provided training, seminars, and information to videomakers throughout the nation. During the Special Period, when already shaky conditions became extreme, the group attracted amateurs seemingly unfazed by difficulties; underwater videographers could be seen carrying their cameras on bicycles, building special waterproof housings for their equipment, and producing videos at any cost. The National Video Movement developed into an important venue for amateur directors, artists, and writers, especially those outside the center of production in Havana. Gloria Rolando, known in the United States for her work on the African diaspora, was able to create Imagenes del Caribe (Images of the Caribbean), a production group under the auspices of the National Video Movement. Many of its members also worked in television and publicity, either for the tourism sector or for organizations like ICAIC and other entities producing commercials, music videos, graphic art, and animation.

The new independent generation is not the only one moving to digital production. Humberto Solás went for a decade without making a film, returning to the screen with *Miel para Oshún* (Honey for Oshun, 2001), shot in digital video to international acclaim. His second digital film, *Barrio Cuba* (2005), a Spanish coproduction and part of the cine pobre aesthetic movement, was supported through ICAIC, but also moved away from the established industrial model. Solás emphasized the digital medium to encourage films that departed from what he called the elitist model of cinema.

Mata, que Dios perdona (Kill, God Forgives, 2005) was the debut feature of Ismael Perdomo, a filmmaker who worked as assistant director with celebrated documentarian Santiago Alvarez between 1996 and 1998. Perdomo has also made music videos and collaborated with international production companies. The more experimental narrative structure of *Mata* creates a view of the past that eschews the familiar articulation rooted in a realist perspective. His personal vision also expresses an unusual perspective on Cuba and national cinema. At the screening of his feature in the Third

Festival Internacional de Cine Pobre (International Festival of Poor Cinema) he stated, "Here, we no longer have transcendent dreams, but rather the harsh certainty of a transient presence . . . [my] intellectual references, 'spiritual teachers,' professional formation, [are] more due to a VHS player or television where I've seen millions of images a day, than to a Bergman or Rossellini film seen in a theater."[23] Negation of neorealism and modernism, two aesthetic tendencies of the New Latin American Cinema Movement, may well characterize the newer generations of filmmakers. Perdomo from the new generation, Solás from an older one, both relying on independent modes of production, strive for recognition as part of a broader audiovisual field.

The different digital production groups are in no way mutually exclusive. Both point to a maturing film industry. In Cuba, survival in the industry depends on coproduction and the independence and irreverence of a generation educated within the social context of the Special Period. Digital filmmaking in Cuba means navigating state restrictions, economic and material scarcity, and the obstacles and opportunities that come from film as a cultural preoccupation. To view a Cuban digital film is to see the surface as many layers, piled thick in the form of responses to regulations, questions, and difficulties, particularly valuable to compare with the merged layers of composite corporate experiences.

Digital Content and Discontent

At its core, Coluya's *Válvula* explores the increasing failure of human communication and the rise in alienation as video games and Internet chatting attempt to simulate emotional responses and warm human contact. In resourceful style, the filmmaker cast high school friends as the youth of the film's stark, modern society. Special Period Havana lends itself as an ideal post-apocalyptic set for a film that is part science-fiction, part surreal dreamscape. A staccato, dissonant soundtrack saturates the images with uneasiness. *Válvula* serves as a sumptuous advertisement for the power of computer tools, in the hands of a talented user, to overcome resource constraints. In terms of response to the conditions in which it was made, the film features a nuclear explosion as metaphor for the critical energy coinciding with a time when the established symbols of power had shifted and revolutionary culture appeared distinctly "old." Admiring the anarchist drive of Coyula's films, Cuban film critic Dean Luis Reyes writes that "facing the possible craving in demand for altruistic conclusions, or a positive stand, Coyula chooses annihilation."[24]

Controversial content and difficult subject matter typify the films of the generation that grew up in the 1980s and 1990s, amid worldwide disenchantment with the socialist project.[25] Crisis and discontent have generally been conducive to artistic inspiration. Searching for new forms of meaning, individuals in Cuba reconsider everyday life in terms of the mobile and virtual world around them, as well as in terms of the identities inherited from the revolutionary project. In Carlos Díaz Lechuga's and Claudia Calviño's short, *Cuca y el pollo* (Cuca and the Chicken, 2005), silent cinema language, black-and-white photography, and digital special effects are combined in a hilarious look at food shortages and a waning socialist solidarity in the face of hunger. Special digital effects give the film the old look of a scratchy and dirty film print. Obviously inspired by the comedic cinema of Charlie Chaplin in *The Gold Rush* (1925) and the ideas of the "Imperfect Cinema" manifesto (1969), these young, modern, no-budget filmmakers comment on their low-budget era with sophistication and wit. Set in the midst of the harshness of the Special Period, the short follows several people in a Cuban neighborhood as a chicken is offered as reward to the winner of a bicycle race. The disappointments begin when the prize turns out to only be half a chicken, and the solidarity of neighbors gives way to the search for personal advantage. As in other Cuban films of the 1990s and 2000–2009, black humor successfully turns a digital focus on the madness and discontent of the times.

The new generation of filmmakers does not work only in Cuba. Working both in and outside his home country, Coyula essentially launched his career in the "micro cinema" movement in the United States. Richly textured, his first feature, *Red Cockroaches* (2003), has the feel of a low-budget *Blade Runner* (Ridley Scott, 1982), the classic postmodernist, science fiction film. The signature incest plot in *Cockroaches* is a throwback to Cuban *radionovelas* (radio soap operas) of the 1950s. But its narrative texture, borrowing from the steamy and baroque science fiction artistic design of the 1980s, illustrates a depleted environment where acid rain falls on New York City, a viral epidemic encroaches, and red cockroaches represent nothing unusual to beleaguered citizens. The exaggerated colors of *Cockroaches* are the antithesis of the stark black-and-white achieved with *Válvula*, which accentuates the desolation of characters that "chat balanced on the edge of evanescence."[26] In *Cockroaches*, Coyula mixes animation and digital images "scattered like graphic footprints"[27] amid live-action melodrama to compose a foreboding yet playful style forming a familiar yet strange reality. Coyula represents how the digital-era filmmaker in Cuba is coming to terms with the role of artistic practice at a critical moment of renewal and critique.

Drawing to the end of the first decade of the twenty-first century, the horizon for cultural production for filmmakers in Cuba's restrictive environment is energized in good part by the easier access that comes with digital tools. Such access may not produce outright dissent but it does facilitate complaints creatively conveyed in digital films. Cuba's digital dilemma gains a nuanced dimension when Cuban films signify both creative success and social failure.

From "Barbaric" to Civilized Cinema: Decentralized Digital Media

The Festival Internacional de Cine Pobre enjoys the support of ICAIC and a host of international nongovernmental sponsoring agencies. Held annually in Gibara in the province of Holguin in the eastern part of the island (where Columbus first disembarked in Cuba), it attracts an international cast of participants interested in working with digital tools and lining up with the cine pobre manifesto's advocacy of digital technology to promote democratic alternative media practices.

Significantly, the regional location of the festival challenges the centralized location of cinema culture, if not specifically its funding infrastructure. In addition, the regional focus attempts to create an alternative space for audiovisual practices to help, in the words of Solás's manifesto, "bring down the wall controlling film distribution by a major or transnational group, which alienates audiences when they do not have access to the work of national authors."[28] Solás indicates his strategy can be fruitful only when "governments take legal action to support the production and distribution of their autochthonous film industries."[29] Then, and only then, "will the cinema have moved on from the age of barbarism."

Cuban digital media help, as the country emerges from the Special Period, to trace the new relations of production locally and internationally. Such relations are tied to tensions and fears that generate new meanings to be found in the filmic texts produced in and outside the island. What Appadurai calls a "landscape of images" reveals media as forming several cultural flows and a complex pattern of territories of digital production. Established filmmakers, film schools, commercial productions, regional tele-centers, independent cultural institutions, film festivals, and formal government institutions increasingly channel their work through international and national networks.

Solás established his worldwide reputation with elegant, expensive historical dramas, but digital technology provided him and an impoverished film industry the opportunity to reimagine the parameters of filmmaking. The cine pobre festival supported a new attitude toward media productions inspired by conditions of the Special Period. Its thematic nod to the past incorporates the present to foster a critical and creative engagement with the new conditions of globalization. Development of a new perspective can also be seen in ICAIC and its difficult exchanges with the Cuban government as a result of political attacks and brushes with globalization. Centralized planning has played a role, too, by expanding ICAIC's approach to international coproduction, but lacks economic investment in film industry infrastructure and training. All such factors relate to a broader media sphere.

All Cuban media continue to be in the hands of the state. Through the ample use of Web sites, radio, television shows, the press, billboards, and the like, the state has continued to deploy ubiquitous political messages and thus the perception of unified discourse. Although signs of change have begun to appear under Raul Castro, the continued controls on citizens' access to media technology and television programming that many perceive and categorize as dogmatic, along with increased sloganeering and a decrease in leisure activities, contribute to the present complexity of life in Cuba. This paradox is an important indicator of why Cuban audiences continue to embrace film: despite decreased output and worsening conditions of exhibition, Cuban cinema still provides a space where people may recognize themselves. Digital tools may be available to most Cubans only through educational venues, but once available they allow unprecedented capacity for expression. Use of digital tools in filmmaking and other media production is also helping to make such expression less "barbaric." With the introduction of the Internet in 1996, Cuban filmmakers and artists resuscitated dreams from earlier decades for the cultural expansion of their work.

The number of national television channels in the late 1990s grew to four, to accommodate two new educational channels. The international arm of one of the national networks, Cubavision International, increased its audience as its satellite footprint expanded throughout the Atlantic region and to parts of Europe. A decade after the expansion, ICRT agreed to broadcast some previously censored Cuban films, though films from the Muestra still do not appear on television. *Strawberry and Chocolate* (Tomás G. Alea and Juan Carlos Tabío, 1993) was the first screened on national prime time—in the summer of 2007, thirteen years after its theatrical run.[30] Greater circulation of media has become possible as satellite television makes international programming—including the Central Chinese Television network—accessible, though mainly to select Cuban citizens, foreign business people, or travelers through the island's hotel sector. And newspapers and journals in danger of disappearing due to paper scarcity, have returned, in a limited way, with many migrating to desktop screens.[31] Radio had its brushes with commercialization, and a number of independent production outfits capitalized on cheaper audiovisual digital technology to produce commercials, as well as industrial and personal videos.[32]

As a final broad stroke on a very rough larger media map, a booming underground media market exists, supplying hardware, IP numbers, and film and music titles. Underground video clubs have blossomed and operate a neighborhood service, stocking international films, television programs, and some national titles. Video clubs filled the void left by neighborhood film clubs that closed as the new stock of films in theatrical release decreased from budgetary cutbacks and theaters closed from poor maintenance. As illegal businesses, the clubs had been under heavy attack by the police, but the world of media duplication is sophisticated and resourceful, creating strong, if not vast, demand, albeit illicit. Because cash remains short, pirated DVDs, VCDs, MP3s, and music CDs still abound. The Cuban mediascape is shifting, out of necessity, driven by a combination of entrepreneurship, politics, and digital technology to create the larger context in which Cuban cinema and its particular complexities must articulate post-Special-period survival in a globalized twenty-first century. It remains unclear whether this digital era will be more "civilized," but Cuba's filmmakers and their work provide clues and perhaps hope.

5

DIGITAL COMMUNITIES AND THE PLEASURES OF TECHNOLOGY

So much music coming through the vent—you think you're in some-one else's apartment. Body reawakens by sun, physical contact, stick on cowbell. Cigar smoke. Inside of conga drum as storage. Clocks don't work. Son. Cha cha cha. Bolero. Romántico. "Alitas de pollo" or "Fried chicken wings." You have to be there to turn off the water when the cistern fills. Un café claro. Air, clarity, distance rushes from the sea. Ay mamá.

—E-Poetry, Loss Pequeño Glazier, *Territorio Libre*

A home television satellite dish, mounted on a makeshift skateboard, sits on the terrace of a home in the Nuevo Vedado district of Havana, ready for quick removal from the sight of thieves. This is not an illegal satellite antenna, as are so many throughout the city's growing satellite television "market." This home is licensed to receive the costly service as a benefit of the inhabitants' work in the arts community. Not far from this location, however, a web of unruly cables links pirated satellite signals throughout the city, in an expanding private business that distributes satellite television into homes without the required permit. This type of circumvention of the Cuban government's prohibition of home satellite dishes makes for many interesting anecdotal anti-Cuba news stories, and illustrates certain challenges for law enforcement. In 2003, a Miami news story for the local Univision Spanish news broadcast on Channel 23 interviewed an anonymous satellite hacker in Havana who revealed the ingenious branching maneuver needed to create a satellite delivery system. The signal, stemming from a single source, branches out through cables, routers, etc. that do not allow control of channel selection or time of viewing. For the privilege of connection and watching someone else's viewing choice, he said, customers paid about ten dollars a month; in one instance, a single signal served fifty to sixty homes. These scattered satellite dishes are known colloquially as the "fourth network." Police raids against the illegal network can fine users up to one thousand dollars. The reporter plays up this angle; Cubans, she says, are so desperate to see anything other than the government's television network that they risk the steep fines to view television from Miami.

Minidramas of domestic action by underground satellite and Internet users against prohibitions have become a part of everyday life in Cuba, and occur in tandem with efforts by the government to circumvent the restrictions of the U.S. embargo. Restricted and centralized, media consumption in Cuba occurs not only legally but illegally. This makes it difficult to study the patterns of digital expression springing up within the malleable contours of such practices as the satellite television "network." Uneven, sometimes secret, often unpredictable viewing, surfing, blogging, and chatting provide at best a provisional snapshot of a larger social experience. My reading in this chapter of expressive space attempts to apprehend the myriad astonishing things that people do with digital media—and the ways that they do these. The electronically composed and published work by Buffalo, New York, poet and visual artist Loss Pequeño Glazier with which I have opened this chapter builds on the notion that "inscription is not simply about recording ideas but [is] about inscribing language in a specific medium."[1] Glazier sees meaning as partly determined by the material space in which that meaning is created. The result is that the "recorded text is not an ideal or definitive one but merely one articulation of many possible ones."[2] The Web-based electronic poem *Territorio Libre* alludes to a place, Cuba, through street sounds, images, and a Babylonian touch in its mixture of phrases in both Spanish and English. Multiple interpretations are possible, each based on the reader's understanding of either or both languages, responses to sound and rhythm, speed of reading, and how many times the text is modified while reading. Capturing the piece at any moment gives it one of many possible, chance states of permanence. Its meanings are also contingent on the social and historical context.

Greater, or even open, access to the Internet seems certain to occur in the next few years, despite Raul Castro's warning on July 26, 2008 (during the annual celebration of the 1953 attack on Moncada Barracks that commemorates the beginning of the Cuban Revolution), that hardships in the midst of global financial and food crises lay ahead. Dire predictions aside, a focus on individual experiences shows how Cubans are increasingly using digital technology to explore their own existence and its social and cultural context.

This chapter examines the use of electronic genres by Cubans, and provides a view of forms of mediation and social architecture. It allows the comparison of emerging practices and niche identities and their impact on the evolution of socialism and of personal freedom. Online chat and e-mail bypass and increase communication to, from, and on the island. They also extend emotional lifelines to friends and colleagues in exile, as occurred during the "e-mail war" in 2007. Blogging creates personal platforms and intellectual communities, and tests the boundaries of censorship and expression, as evidenced in the Cuban blog *Generación Y*. In my investigation in this chapter, I seek to provide a perspective on particular interactions, social uses, and private appropriations as they stand highlighted in Cuba's overlapping zones of digital expression and experience.

Cuban digital technology practices respond directly or indirectly to political geographies formed by the ongoing conflict with the United States, which continues to define present-day Cuba. The creation of home pages, blogs, personal spaces, and videos published online produces digital communities of complex personal, political, and psychological economies; anxieties, passions, and gatherings feature strongly; as spaces of representation, these online communities offer the possibility for the displaced to become both "discursively emplaced" and "virtually present."[3]

Exilio culture, formed by numerous topics of exile, migrates to the computer screen in the form of Web sites created by individuals, social and political action groups, businesses, and educational projects in those nations that exhibit nostalgia for Cuban regional cultures, quotidian objects, ephemera, and product brands. Paradoxically, the diversity involved in such online nationalism reveals the intricacy of the national identities that complicate and enliven the island's history. History is crucial for defining national struggle and sovereignty, and personal histories, told in photographs and other documents, provide evidence that can supplement, enrich, amplify, repair, undermine, or correct an official record—functions greatly facilitated by digital media. Many online spaces that focus on narratives of exile deliberately attempt to rewrite and discredit official Cuban discourse. Numerous Web sites encourage denunciation, activism, consumption, historical revision, and an opposing view in general of the Castro regimes. From the beginning, the Internet, as a virtual space of expression and a sphere for passionate politics, memory, and xenophobic and extremist discourse, has begged a reconsideration of the spatial logic of exile.

People use digital technology to experience the world in ways that extend or go beyond their everyday lives. This technology helps to build creative social experiences that reshape the contours of virtual and real life, and produce new personal and social infrastructures. Cuba's Internet access restrictions coincide with the evolution of forms of citizenship and democracy crafted out of digital expression. As in other parts of the world, bloggers, citizen journalists, and programmers navigate around internal firewalls, putting pressure on official channels and on the opposition by adding another layer of discourse as they link with global action groups. Information gathering becomes one more of the black-market practices that help everyday Cuban life function. Such practices are in no way homogenous or driven by identical interests. Like the complex sociality of hacker practices examined by anthropologists Gabriella Coleman and Alex Golub, blackmarket practices related to Internet access in Cuba respond to a democratic morality of openness as much as to solving everyday problems.[4] The mechanisms that define their existence can vary from instance to instance—where users live, where they work, and the like—and in the support required (access to international contacts, for example) to carry out intent. The scope of user interaction may be limited to an undefined community or it may be tied to a specific political aim and/or a formal organization. The range, existence, and frequent use of all these digital activities show, however, that they hold in common a confidence in the technology to be used to fulfill individual aims. Still, apart from counts of user numbers or Web site hits, objective evaluation of success or failure to achieve ends through digital means rarely features in digital exchanges; engagement in digital community itself seems to provide sufficient satisfaction.

In the mid-to-late 1990s, online activities joined fictional and nonfictional literature, theater, film, and visual arts as terrain for the contest of identity and history, as clearly seen regarding all things "Cuban." Nascent Web sites revealed a range of understanding about what a networked system of exchange could contribute to knowledge and culture. From progressive health information networks to entrenched xenophobic excesses and individual memories of another era, official and unofficial online communities tended to merge past and present in a collision of news with nostalgia, archives with personal journals, official accounts with intellectual analyses, and so on in an unmanaged mix of personal and public flourishing. Since Carlos Lage first welcomed the Internet for Cuba in 1996, the increase in the number of official Cuban Web sites has provided evidence that the government uses the Internet to position itself as a player in the worlds of capital and digital capitalism.[5] Scientific discourse also benefits, as does the economy, as the state rebuilds an entrepreneurial business culture, domestic and international communications, and a reform-seeking cultural sector. Cubans, however, unsatisfied with the approved Internet access plan, engage in a popular response that includes a search for ways to circumvent restricted streams of entertainment and information. The formation of community around real political exile and controls also sees emotions run high, mainly within informal parameters necessarily not contained within political structures. Indeed, Cuba shows how digital communication flows more turbulently in restricted waters.

The exchange described below between digital text and live event illustrates one way that digital technology can become humanized. It shows, too, how the zones of digital invention in Cuba represent the spirited culture of protest and détente between U.S. diplomatic representatives on the island and the Cuban government. In 2005, Cuban officials featured the downloaded, globally circulated images of Abu Ghraib torture, enlarged and displayed on billboards in front of the U.S. Interest Section building in Havana (location of the U.S. government diplomatic representation in Cuba, where there is no U.S. embassy or consulate since there is no formal diplomatic relationship between the two nations). The words *fascism* and *murderers* emblazoned the horrific imagery located along the seaside Malecón. The American diplomatic representatives responded by installing a digital billboard on the roof of the main building to provide "real" news in bold red text. The intention of both iconic attacks has several layers. The Cuban state denounces the hypocrisy of the U.S. regime, links its own protest against terrorism to global human rights protests, and uses the set of Abu Ghraib images as a transformative agent. By providing news from around the globe, the U.S. digital broadcast atop its building in turn reminds the Cuban people of limits on information and of plurality. The Cuban regime effectively blocked the rooftop broadcast by strategic placement of dozens of flagpoles of just the right height in front of the building.

Digital tools thus offer new ways to draw opposing geopolitical lines. However, the use of such tools alongside traditional syntax of national identity such as flags shows that the edge, in terms of communication and representation, stems from the cleverness of the tool's user rather than from the tool itself.

Governments create their own myths to develop social cohesion. During the Special Period, the perceived situation of individual Cubans grew progressively more at variance with the state-propagated myths of Cuban identity (fig. 10). Good medical care and high literacy rates and standards of education were simply not enough to dispel the hopelessness, frustration, disillusion, fear, and boredom stemming from economic hardship and unemployment. Today, officially unacknowledged symptoms of repressed affective domains, these emotional currents continue to erode the state's hold on society. This has led to new crises of self-identity and to mass migration—the *balsero* crisis—as the overarching vision of a socialist collective unravels. Nevertheless, even as the majority of Cubans remain dissatisfied on several basic and civic levels, they continue to prepare to carve out a life

10. "Victoria de las Ideas," banner in Havana, Cuba

adapted to officially constructed territories of consumption, creativity, and expression. How do they accomplish this in digital times, and how much of this readiness to adapt comes from the relief and diversion facilitated by digital technology?

Official Stories

The tale of Elián Gonzalez, the six-year-old Cuban boy found barely alive and alone, floating on an inner tube in the Florida Straits in November 1999, is of special importance. The media barrage set off by the news story exposed the dynamics between Cuba and its exile community to a worldwide audience, and over an extended time. The death of the boy's mother in the risky ocean crossing created a custody dispute between the boy's distant relatives in Miami and his father in Cuba. The Miami relatives argued, through U.S. Senate members, that in Cuba the child would return to live in an environment of Communist indoctrination that his deceased mother had wished him to escape. The father argued, supported by the Cuban leadership, for his right to custody. Round-the-clock media coverage, especially of the young boy's dramatic rescue from the Miami relatives by federal agents of the Border Patrol Special Unit, revealed the complex layers of U.S. immigration policy pertaining to Cuba. The unsuspecting child became a symbol of the struggle between two Cubas—the defiant island and the exile community based in Miami. The position of both sides soon appeared on Web sites that tracked the daily events of the drama. Sensing from the start a strong chance of victory, the Cuban government also implemented a strategy of comprehensive coverage. A general media campaign steered coverage toward national and international advantage, demonstrating an official confidence in, and sophisticated deployment of, digital technology.

The boy's name and photo appeared everywhere in Cuba. Cubaweb, an important official Web site at the time, linked to "Elián," the official Elián Web page with hundreds of documents, including speeches by Fidel Castro, video clips, cartoons, and news.[6] The official press covered daily developments and later presented them as an official chronology. *Granma* in particular denounced the position of Elián's Miami relatives and the exile community as immoral, labeling their lifestyle "deviant." The multilingual *Granma International* Web site also covered the event, using a banner image with the bold title "Kidnapping in Miami."[7] This site featured a photo gallery and a press archive, containing over two hundred different articles from *Granma* alone, spanning the six months of the conflict. Internationally known writers, including Nobel laureates and intellectuals from the Latin American Left, supported the return of the boy to his father in Cuba. All the principal Web sites in Cuba, including the Cuban Chamber of Commerce,[8] featured a link to the Elián site in a digital and virtual public show of Cuban solidarity. The Cuban government's orchestrated media campaign thus directed digital communication in combination with more traditional means, which included daily radio and television coverage about the controversy, as well as mass demonstrations.

The Miami-based exile community in turn generated politicized Web sites—like those of the Cuban government—filled with anti-Castro content and criticism of the American government for its "betrayal" of the Cuban exiles. The Liberty for Elian site (taken offline December 2003) established a "Help Elian" task force, raised funds for the fight's legal expenses, and posted extensive articles from the exile press as well as photos of the immigration raid that recovered the boy from his great-uncle's house in Little Havana.[9] Although addressing a wide audience, the scope of the site was decidedly regional. Using a simple collage style and symbolic iconography, Elián's appealing face was set in the foreground against images of a white dove, Fidel Castro, and the Statue of Liberty. Privately made, unofficial Web sites held up an emotional, quasi-ideological torch in this media parade, and battled with public, official messages coordinated and concentrated to maximize political gain from public sentiment.

Both English- and Spanish-language television networks in the United States treated the case as a media event. The press followed the escape from communist Cuba, the travails of the Miami relatives as they tried to keep the boy, and the contradictory impulses of U.S. policy toward the Cuban government. Presidential candidates weighed in on both sides of the issue, radio stations held discussions on the topic, and the rescue raid received 24-hour coverage. The absurdity of the situation came to the fore when Janet Reno, then the U.S. attorney general, suggested that the United States could not decide custody of a minor based on the political ideology of the parent. In its legal decision, the U.S. government uncharacteristically sided with the Cuban leadership, though many in the U.S. political arena disagreed with it.

The divisive issue simultaneously re-energized and damaged the public image of the exile community in South Florida. Although the community encompasses varying viewpoints, the most politically conservative anti-

Castro voices have consistently monopolized public opinion and political power since the 1960s. The Elián Gonzalez case revived anti-Castro discourse as no other issue had, and brought back the dogma of earlier decades. But, just as U.S. media outlets helped to bring national attention to the anti-Castro lobby, they also linked the Cuban exile community's acts, after the government raid, with images of rioting, violence, vandalism, and political extremism. Televised marches and demonstrations showed angry protesters hurling insults and threats at the opposing side; that is, the U.S. news media story featured damaging photographs of conflict, contrasted with stories of celebration in Cuba. The test remains for the Cuban regime: would it ever distribute analogous images of rioting Cuban residents? So far, given state control of media and state power to suppress as well as publicize any nationally significant issue, it seems unlikely that digital and general media treatments of nationally significant issues would be allowed parallel development.

Other political issues, such as the 1999 trial in Cuban courts against the United States, in which Cuba sued for reparations for damages from the 1961 Bay of Pigs invasion, shared space on Cuba's official Web site, with a nightly slot on the television schedule. Moreover, digital and analogue tools have been jointly employed around an ongoing campaign to free the "Cuban Five."

In June 2001, five Cuban nationals living in Miami were arrested by the U.S. government, charged with espionage, convicted, and given life sentences. Early on, official Web sites in Cuba denounced the arrests, challenging their legality and the veracity of the criminal charges. As the case gained attention, a San Francisco (CA)–based grassroots organization, the National Committee to Free the Cuban Five, expanded their initial efforts into an international human rights campaign calling for the men's release. This campaign relies on e-mail and Web networking as fundraising tools for support of the Cubans' legal defense and for media campaigns—including a large billboard in San Francisco (fig. 11). The organization's plans have included such international events as marches in Washington, DC and conferences in the United States, Mexico, Canada, and Brazil. The focus has been on contesting what the organization perceives as the U.S. government's duplicitous view of terrorism. The group orchestrates support for the prisoners through letter writing, lobbies for family visitation rights, lists a calendar of related protest activities, and provides an outlet for the prisoners' own political artwork and editorials. Although it functions independently of the Cuban government's ongoing campaign to free the five, the committee's Web site

11. Billboard, sponsored by FreeTheFive.org, in the Mission District in San Francisco, California, 2008

not only provides a space for sharing photos among the prisoner's families and supporters but disseminates relevant documents to support the campaign.[10] This is, in short, a well-orchestrated international media strategy, made effective through a network of support for human rights. Cuba's official coverage and use of political issues, from the Elián incident onward, presents an integrated digital and nondigital media paradigm by a government that is in controlled communication with its public and has learned the potential of digital social networking.

Personal Stories

The debate over representation of the island and its history plays out in the exile community as nostalgia for an era, a way of life, and a place, and as hatred for the Castro regime, as the NoCastro Web site shows.[11] Many anti-Castro positions have found open channels on YouTube, where the video of Fidel Castro falling after giving a speech has had almost a million views. Narratives about the past define much of what is said about Cuba, and emphasize the duality of lived experience, the difficulty of moving on. An exiled individual frequently endures a liminal state described eloquently by film and television scholar Hamid Naficy: "Incorporation or assimilation is neither total nor irreversible . . . for most, liminality is a continuous state, a 'slipzone' of denial, ambivalence, inbetweenness, doubling, splitting, fetishization, hybridization, and syncretism."[12] Any cultural space that "structurally encourages analysis and reconfiguration of deep values," Naficy argues, "is [also] capable of breeding radicalism, conservatism, or in general extremism of all kinds."[13] The space defined by exile is also contingent upon length of stay, cultural and historical signifiers, and, in the case of Cuba, geographical proximity and the similarity of the natural environments of the lost home and the present place (Cuba and Florida). For the Cuban exile in Miami, or for those in Cuba who share the emotions of exile through division of their families, Cuba lies almost within sight across the strait—as it does for Celia del Pino, a character in Cristina Garcia's novel *Dreaming in Cuban*: "Celia del Pino, equipped with binoculars and wearing her best housedress and drop pearl earrings, sits in her wicker swing guarding the north coast of Cuba . . . Celia cannot decide which is worse, separation or death. Separation is familiar, too familiar, but Celia is uncertain she can reconcile it with permanence."[14] Radical anti-Castro exiles, particularly in Florida, are immersed in an overwhelming nostalgia for prerevolutionary Cuba, believing that only those who fled "old" Cuba are the "real Cubans." According to a recalcitrant seventy-five-year-old expatriate in Miami, "The new generations have been tainted by a Stalinist upbringing. When we die, there will be no more real Cubans left."[15]

Increasingly, that view is being eclipsed by pro-dialogue forces in the exile community. More moderate observers realize, especially after the Elián standoff, that continuing divisions, rather than stimulate reform, contribute to distorted memories and an essentialized cultural identity. Max Lesnick, outspoken critic of the Castro government yet a proponent of easing tensions and encouraging closer relations, speculates on a different version of the future, where "Those who became exiles in the 1960s [himself included] are beyond the possibility of exercising political power in a future Cuba."[16]

In past decades, political debates among the exile community garnered attention through local radio, television shows, and newspapers. The Internet, through Facebook, Twitter, chat groups, blogs, and Web sites, expands the sphere of influence of these ongoing debates that represent Cuba through information from the exile community and from the island. Such online representation can change and expand the discourse, if not always its tenor.

As numerous personal stories show, the Internet potentially transforms the exiles' longing and intensifies their temporal and spatial dislocation. The way the Internet offers a capacity to explore and convey the unsettling memories felt by exiles is an example of how it helps to redefine the notion of community, realizing in its own transience and nonlocation a gathering space for feelings of suspense and separation.

A brief survey of forty years of exilic discourse brings characters and histories into relief. Miami has the largest Cuban population outside of the Cuban nation, with more than a million Cubans living in South Florida (where the exile community is legendary for its anti-Castro politics). Beyond Florida, the Cuban diaspora exists in New Jersey, New York, Spain, Mexico, Venezuela, and Canada, among other places. Without negating the influential nature of other host cultures or the constitutive power that such cultures bring to life in exile, a focus on the South Florida community is instructive. Groups like the Cuban-American National Foundation (CANF), Alpha 66, Brothers to the Rescue, and others have saturated the media with incendiary rhetoric and extreme political views; a particularly vociferous critic of the Cuban regime is Lincoln Díaz-Balart, a Florida representative in the U.S. House of Representatives (since 1986), and Castro's nephew (which makes clear how the U.S.–Cuba conflict breaches deep family ties).[17]

Cuban migration to the United States since the 1959 revolution has been characterized as a series of waves, each with new challenges for the Florida-based exiles, challenges that in turn redefine the community.[18] Those who left Cuba arrived in four distinct periods. During the first, from 1959 until 1962 or shortly thereafter, emigrants consisted primarily of the elite, whose economic interests were being overturned. The group included the 14,000 children of Operation Peter Pan (1960–1966), sent unaccompanied to the United States by their parents who feared for their safety and dreaded their communist indoctrination.[19] The second wave, from 1965 to 1974, consisted of the "freedom flights" that Pan American airlines provided daily and free of charge from Varadero to Miami, which eventually transported 260,000 people. The "Mariel boatlift" of 1980 brought an additional 125,000 Cubans to South Florida, many of whom were political prisoners and deemed "undesirable" by the Cuban government. The last significant exodus, the "balsero crisis" peaked in 1994 (though, as sociologist Silvia Pedraza has pointed out, balseros had undertaken the crossing since 1985);[20] upward of 33,000 Cubans left their country in makeshift rafts during this "crisis." Within each of these groups there were both those who rejected the Castro government and those who had at first been supporters, and in some cases even held government posts, but had become disillusioned.

Beginning in 1980, the mass migrations included people who had lived in revolutionary Cuba for twenty years or more, among them former political prisoners. Many Cubans already in exile treated the new arrivals, including those punished for their opposition to the Castro regime, with a mixture of hospitality and hostility. Early exiles often considered later ones to have been "poisoned" by communism or to belong to an inferior social class. The former imprisonment of some exiles by the Castro government led to some arrivals being labeled criminals by the original emigrants. The dominant interpretation, in any case, was that the successive mass emigrations were further evidence of the failure of Castro's government. In time, initial clashes abated, as refugees made their way into the economic and social fabric of their new communities. Those Cubans arriving in South Florida after 1980 generally found a warmer welcome than did the second and third waves; over the years, they have become part of an exile community closer in demographic terms to "old Cuba" itself. Indeed, the Cuban population in Miami today has become more layered racially and politically.

With the aim of building a counterrevolution, the conservative wing of the exile community has traditionally used every communications medium at its disposal, voicing its political views about the Castro government in strong emotional terms.[21] The changing nature of life in exile can be traced through newspapers, literature, theater, and community events—marked in the first generation by a hope for return, and in the second by partial resignation to continued stay. Significantly, the personal accounts of both generations show that the members defined themselves not as immigrants but as exiles residing in the United States temporarily until Castro could be overturned.[22]

While generations born in the United States have been largely assimilated into American culture, the island of Cuba continues to be a referent for the construction of their identity, in a community that never loses its *cubanness*.[23] Nevertheless, four decades of successive migrations have altered the political discourse, helping to shape a uniquely Cuban American identity and culture. Spanish-language radio and television programming reinforces the community's cultural compass by maintaining popular interest in the tense coexistence of its differing views, as well as in the future governance of, and relations with, Cuba. Digital media provide another point of contact and political mediation, facilitating communication and increasing scope and reach. New media channels resulting from digital technology provide a platform for even strong views on any issue, including powerful opposition (primarily by the Cuban-American Washington lobby) to ending the embargo. Those who object to a dialogue with Cuba vie online with those who do not, with much more personal style and engagement than is possible with traditional one-way media. The flows, peaks, and troughs of such communication project the effects of in-person exchange, binding, interrupting, and extending virtual communities—and therefore real ones.

Personal investment in early Web sites foregrounded the suspended experience of exile, calling, whether through individual exhortation or organized political action, for a shift on one side or the other of contested boundaries. From the start, online nostalgic remembrances of historical Cuba have mixed with political rhetoric, all aimed at the global Cuban diaspora. Today, online groups attempt to recreate family and to locate friends and neighbors. Some discredit the official news coming from the island. Sites like those of independent press services and human rights organizations present content with a political tenor obviously in contrast to that of official Cuban Web sites.[24] Independent Cuban journalists regularly report from the island; their coverage is posted on the Web site for U.S.-based CubaNet, a Spanish-language site hosting the Buró de Periodistas Independientes (Bureau of Independent Journalists)—whose ties have often been linked to funding from the U.S. government.[25] The political impact of CubaNet is more significant within the exile community than within Cuba, given the island's access restrictions.

Like Internet use in Cuba, exile Web sites have become a way to represent the nation and contest the island's historical record. Unlike those inside the country, exile Web sites create virtual impressions of individual separation and lost community that, through physical disconnection, now exist only like singular entities produced by memory and imagination. Digital preservation, intangible and impermanent, injects a powerful sense of community for those who practice it, and one that can accumulate deep meaning for persons estranged from their original environment.

Emotional Geographies

The past becomes fetishized in Web sites dedicated to Cuban cities and regions like Cárdenas, Cienfuegos, Camagüey, and Güines. City stories recall prerevolutionary culture and dispute the revolution's discourse from afar, tilting their own histories at the government's revolutionary nationalist narrative. Often replete with personal recollection, the sites commonly convey the generational character of their owners; their regional focuses display local forms of Cuban identity. Cosmopolitan Havana recedes, as regional centers much less exposed to modern international influence come into view. Paying homage to cities, the Web sites create memorials to the homeland and to an idealized lifestyle. They retain this function, while evolving stylistically and digitally, as successive generations of Cubans embrace technology and new cultural references, narrative styles, imagery, and politics.

The City of Cárdenas Web site has been online for more than a decade, updated continuously by its creator, Ernesto J. de la Fe, with videos and information.[26] Known as Banner City in Cuba, Cárdenas is located about two hundred kilometers east of Havana, and is the site where the first Cuban flag was raised, in honor of independence from colonial Spain. Because it is also home to Elián Gonzalez, the site's author weighs in on the debate about the Gonzalez case. De la Fe belongs to the "one-and-a-half" generation—born in Cuba but raised in the United States—and dedicates his site to his "parents, grandparents, and family, as to all 'Cárdenenses' and their ancestors who, over a period of 170 years, built a small village on Cárdenas Bay into a prosperous and progressive city."[27] His personal identification, he notes, is closely entwined with the ideal of independence symbolized by the city's development. The current physical decay of Cárdenas, in contrast with its portrayal in the Web site's many photographs and videos, pains De la Fe, and he admonishes the revolution for abandonment of the city. A *virtual* place of his childhood, compiled from the tales of two generations, replaces a real location of early life. De la Fe states that his return to Cuba awaits the country's "freedom." But his Web site exhibits the "real tug of home": a video of the author's road trip to Cárdenas in 2002 today welcomes visitors to the main page.

On this site, the city as hypertext document is made up of new and vintage photos: an array of segments of society, including hospitals, factories, and schools. The self-referential linking structure takes us through Cárdenas's private schools, constructing an historical record extending back to before the revolution and illustrated with a series of graduation photos beginning in the 1940s; the simple layout testifies that the Internet is available to minimally trained practitioners, and heralds its democratic potential. The Internet also channels private emotional geographies into public media space; Web authors like De la Fe highlight personal landmarks of life and mind—houses, streets, churches, official buildings, Cárdenas Bay. Captions provide viewpoints: "Looking southwest on Calle Real with the once proud 'La Dominica' Hotel on the street corner in the foreground. Carts, bikes and carriages are about all you see on the main street these days."[28] The desire to hold Cuba, to contain it, has passed down from the father, now deceased and memorialized on De la Fe's Web site, who inspires the author to virtual reconstruction.

This type of nostalgic refiguring, fueled by selective memories of the homeland, often comes, from the imagination of first-generation exiles, in nondigital form. A different Web site, Guije.com, features various cities, including Cárdenas.[29] Created in 2008, the site proposes to be a nonacademic cultural and historical study of Cuba; visually, it imagines Cuba through recent and old photographs, collectible postcards and posters, and many other traditional Cuban symbols. Acknowledging that Cubans live all over the globe, it uses a decidedly apolitical language; its view of Cuban culture however, is constructed by referencing colonial-style buildings and prerevolution statistics and cultural production. Online, the city fills an interstitial territory between the reality of personal and political restrictions and the realities of imagination and memory. Such an emotionally compelling Internet vision of Cuba relies on the existence, somewhere in time and space, of a complex, living original. Creation only of a surrogate generated according to personal requirements reflects perhaps a superficiality of digital media themselves, where active democratic usage links and extends over the surface of screens but simultaneously depends on a sophisticated, largely invisible infrastructure, an infrastructure of complicated social and political origin.

Personal history sometimes connects old and new media technologies, on Web sites like that of Beam Radio, for instance, where the owner of a successful radio communications firm and member of the former Bay of Pigs invasion force, Brigade 2506, reveals his connection to the history of Cuban broadcasting.[30] Pride in the media connection can also be found in the archives of oldradio.com, and in an online article by Manuel A. Alvarez about the history of Cuban radio, based on the personal and professional experiences of his father.[31] As an early radio pioneer, the senior Alvarez experimented with one of the first radio stations in Cuba, in the province of Caibarien, before the full launch of commercial radio.

Responding enthusiastically to my email request for more information, Alvarez provided a hard copy of a book he had authored about Cuban radio and his and his family's experiences. The ease of my discovery of, and connection with, Alvarez also shows how the Internet further develops the ways that radio used to connect the Cuban diaspora, for radio use was limited to one-way communication of information. Maintained and updated, Web sites exist as places of contact, transmitting memory to sustain place and person, a human function served by media throughout the course of history.

Communicating Passionate Politics

Cubans in exile have excelled in creating political organizations. On the Web site of the Cuban Information Archives, scores of Cuban organizations are listed—from the most prominent, the Cuban-American National Foundation, to less prominent ones such as Cuban Committee for Democracy, Brothers to the Rescue, and Coalition of Cuban American Women.[32] From as far back as the first group of Cuban émigrés, before the revolution, Cuban exiles have formed hundreds of political organizations, often competing ones. One, the powerful, outspoken, and virulent Cuban-American National Foundation (CANF) has often served as a barometer for the state of other organizations. Its tenor shifted in 1997, after the death of CANF founder Jorge Mas Canosa, to represent the perspective of a younger leadership as well as the changing political character of an aging exile community. CANF's Web site provides a dissident perspective helping to modernize and prolong the politics of CANF amid what the organization's critics have called a failed U.S. Cuba policy. In this sense, Web sites help to take politics beyond personality—and could contribute a more flexible space of ideas in the politics of Cuban exiles, as the increasing age of the most ardent anti-Castro exiles and of the Castro brothers begins to lessen their individual influence.[33]

The Cuba Free Press project hosts the Bureau of Independent Journalists, which, in spite of the uneven quality of reporting, still provides a view from inside Cuba.[34] Not necessarily trained as journalists, citizen observers who possess varying levels of analytical skill report on all aspects of Cuban life; reports cover a broad range of topics, including information about censorship, political prisoners, conditions on the island, events, reaction to television programs, and personal observation. A story in 1999 discussed the appeal of American sports, and based its premise on the fact that New York Yankee and Florida Marlin baseball caps were being worn in support of the Hernandez brothers who had defected to the United States. The reporter wondered why the new Cuban entrepreneurs, seeing the interest shown by young people in adorning themselves with the symbols of their heroes, didn't take the lead and sell baseball caps for Cuban teams to wear as both a sign of club loyalty and a silent protest by the wearer against the centralized state control over sport. Later, while in Havana's Chinatown, he noticed a young man wearing a baseball cap, not from Industriales or Santiago de Cuba (two teams in the amateur national playoffs), but instead supporting the Habana, one of the most popular Cuban baseball teams of the past. The reporter continued, "I tried to trade him a Yankee cap for the old Cuban one, but the young man warned me that I shouldn't waste my time considering such a foolish notion." He wondered "why a Cuban would prefer to wear a symbol from a bygone era, and why . . . manufacturers found more success from making vintage caps of professional rather than amateur teams." The intended audience for this kind of online post is not necessarily other Cubans residing on the island, who must, like the reporter, grapple with limited Internet access. The reporter is, however, writing about emerging entrepreneurial, taste, and consumer cultures. Small observations about a new fashion or about recurring graffiti on a wall, products available at farmers' markets, celebrations, and so on play an important role in "filling in the blanks" of mainstream national news. "Citizen journalist" reports seek truths or reflect on the occurrences of everyday life; digital technology provides an avenue for developing the skills involved—from observation, analysis, critique, and articulation to negotiating restricted electronic access.

DesdeCuba.com is an example of a portal for citizen journalists who are self-described "regular citizens," not trained journalists or political scientists, and are interested in sharing their views about everyday life. They operate outside the scope of official media and comment about ideas and policies covered in television, newspapers, and radio, changes occurring in Cuba, and international issues of relevance to Cuba and Cubans. Because such sites involve a multiplicity of views and tackle political questions, they represent another way that Cuban use of digital technology exemplifies democratic practice. Arrayed with personal, business, and official Cuban sites, they allow a survey of concepts of democracy in the quotidian as well as the overtly political.

Blogostroika

Despite the limits to Internet access, with their resulting social tensions, the current era in Cuba will be deeply affected by the professional, amateur, unpolished, biased, utilitarian, promotional, and oftentimes outrageous work that appears on blogs. Although it is difficult to determine the veracity of claims, the increasing volume and response to the postings forces serious consideration of the cultural legacy of this activity. The generations that have come of age since the late 1970s are attracted to and adept at using electronic media. The reports of these citizens seek international attention on global networks.[35]

Blogs exist as new spaces alongside those sanctioned by the Cuban state, facilitating the formation of territories of individual exchange within personal, commercial, artistic, recreational, political, and intellectual networks worldwide. No matter what controls exist, inside these areas of interaction individuals are preoccupied with mobility, identity, intimacy, and self-expression. The resulting exchanges respond to local and external desires that reveal the complexity of historical relations and boundaries. As postcolonial scholar Achille Mbembe remarks of the emergence of alternative regional networks creating integration "from below" in Africa, they are "not merely regional, for these interstate exchanges are connected with international markets and their dynamics."[36] Using digital tools to relay symbolic language and political metaphors, bloggers reach beyond Cuba and connect with groups worldwide, whose members define democratic practice in varied ways.

Based in Cuba, the *Generación Y* blog by Yoani Sanchez has been online since April 2007. For her candid and shrewd reporting, Sanchez received the 2008 Digital Journalism award from the Spanish organization Ortega y Gasset. The award positions Sanchez within the values established by international claims to justice. Online international media such as the BBC, *El País*, and the *New York Times* covered news of the award and of Sanchez's inability to attend the award ceremony in Spain, given government travel restrictions. *Time* magazine named her one of the hundred most influential people of 2008. Sanchez writes from her home in Central Havana, making several entries a month, or as often as she can negotiate the limited access conditions. Her blog and several others are hosted through the DesdeCuba.com portal. Sanchez is a self-described "thirty-something," university-educated Cuban who trained as a philologist but dreams of becoming a journalist. Her objective as a citizen journalist is to write from the personal about the political. Her entries focus on the obstacles of everyday life—inefficiencies, insufficiencies, infrastructure problems, impractical policies—as well as conversations with neighbors and fellow bus riders, capturing through their candid comments the ways that Cubans face difficulties. Her writing (in Spanish) avoids political rhetoric and reveals that she is not part of an inner intellectual circle but rather of an independent community of aficionados committed to expanding the content and participation of media in Cuba.

July 21, 2008. *Cyber Mutilated.*

Let's see if I can understand the twisted logic of our virtual space: a Cuban citizen cannot buy a domain name on a local server, but is accused when they manage to host a site in another country. Official bloggers reflect reality, but alternative bloggers are seen as puppets of a foreign power . . . In addition to being mutilated in our society, we have come to the Internet with several of its pieces missing.[37]

February 18, 2008. *Habeas Data.*

Behind us are the times when official newspapers, the national television network, or Cuban radio were the only source of information—or disinformation—that we had. Technology has come to our help. Now, despite all the limitations to access of the Internet, the news reaches us, we watch satellite television programs, and listen—without interference—to short wave radio.[38]

For Sanchez, in her *Habeas Data* entry, technology as salvation ironically echoes utopian claims by Enrique Gonzalez-Manet in 1969. Sanchez's perspective, however is not at all in line with that of Gonzalez-Manet. In the view of a twenty-first-century blogger, digital technology rescues individuals from the monolithic confines of a tyrannical state. In gaining international visibility—her blog is, as of this writing, translated into seventeen languages including English, French, German, Russian, and Chinese—Sanchez has also gained a broader following through social networks such as Twitter.

The unruly activity of bloggers and activists would not persist were it not driven by personal conviction and the need to be informed, express frustration, and call for sensible reforms that would give increasing power to the voices of individuals, voices not mediated by the state. As an alternative "island" in the state-patrolled sea of digital technology, the barely formed Cuban blogosphere, like the illegal DVD supplier who bicycles contraband merchandise, forms a tenacious zone of digital activity. Blogging in Cuba takes the personal further than can a Web site of recollection or protest because it often charts a course through immediate experience, imbuing the interface with illegality and the pleasures and danger of digital trespass.

Cubans are thus not as totally isolated as many journalistic accounts contend.[39] Online journals, such as *La isla en peso*, the literary gazette *Lengua suelta*, and telemedicine forums provide community spaces of work and intellectual exchange, as do the personal and entrepreneurial Web sites that list rental housing and Santería ceremonies on the island.[40] Incorporated into cultural traditions, digital formats offer different approaches for displays of the personal, provide entrepreneurial opportunities, and multiply underground activities. Consumers of digital tools reinvent themselves in social rituals. Independent filmmakers create with a digital arsenal. Video letters articulate a new type of intimacy. And underground DVD businesses serve growing numbers of entertainment customers. *Oppiano's Coctel*, an independent blog, of uncertain frequency, by Cuban writer and poet Victor Fowler, evokes the mad humanity and artistry behind the contraband process:

> May 24, 2008. *Variación Jaula, II.*
>
> They copy neurotically. Belong to some club, although not referred to as such, at least, not yet. They meet with certain regularity and exchange what each has been able to capture, pilfer. Paranoid, no meeting place is precise. Something without details, a space, with chairs, tables, the necessary elements. While exchanging news about the latest, they enjoy an isolated drink. They are sweepers of the web and of trusted collections, and when added up, they embody a huge market of which they are only the messengers, only the tip of the iceberg.[41]

It is impossible to perceive all the sublevels of culture occurring in the midst of the real or performed clamor for change, the official speeches, the utopian claims, and the tireless entrepreneurial efforts. Bloggers in Cuba convey the sense of participation in aspects of culture that evades official eyes and is missed by disinterested or exhausted others. Fowler attests to this in covering an event held at the Espacio Aglutinador, a private home cum art gallery that, since the censorship of artists in the 1980s, has hosted underground art events such as the "We are Porno. Sí!" Fowler, who was present, observed that not one of over one hundred attendees was part of Cuba's established intellectual community.[42]

Cubans are increasingly seeking ways to transform their lives; for example, a writer might supplement an insufficient income by engaging in a personal side business for profit, even if operating such a business is illegal and subject to steep fines. Digital technology enters into some choices; for instance, the same author might decide to use the small computer facility provided to members of the Cuban Writers and Artists Union (UNEAC) in order to advertise for a marriage partner online with the aim of marrying a foreigner and emigrating to Europe. Dissatisfaction is expressed through whatever means are available, making digital technology desirable not as a luxury but as a potential avenue for self-realization outside the parameters demarcated by state bureaucratic mechanisms.

Through its use in leisure activities, celebrations, private events, home, and work, digital technology is increasingly assimilated into daily life, allowing attainment of familiarity and skill that provides literacy with new media tools.

Beyond the media infrastructure that luxury hotels provide, digital technology and tourism combine in another way. For example, marriage has become part of the tourist economy. Large numbers of Spaniards, for instance, married Cubans in the 1990s, becoming involved in complex cross-cultural relationships like those portrayed in the cinema of both countries in films like *Cosas que dejé en la Habana* (Gutierrez Aragón, 1997).[43] A UK Web site, Cubanmarriage.co.uk, helps to make "marrying a Cuban national easier."[44] The traveler cum marriage partner originating from a place of privilege in global culture can choose to navigate Cuban bureaucracy for the benefit of love, passion, or obsession. Meeting presumed demand for marriage-as-travel-adventure, Cubans have embellished the wedding ceremony—and their income—aided by digital sites that offer lavish wedding cakes, parties, wedding videos, and photo albums. A tourist can just as easily plan a wedding at the Dupont House in Varadero Beach as set the ceremony in a castle in Italy. Cuba Wedding Planners offers a service through a legal Web site that facilitates the virtual planning of ceremonies, legalities, events, gifts, invitations, and photography.[45] Hotels, seeing all this as a lucrative aspect of Cuban tourism, offer special wedding packages. Havana offers couples the opportunity to set their nuptials amid colonial or modernist architecture, or they may select spectacular beach resorts. Memories are piled into photo albums beautifully reproduced with digital imagery for families in Cuba and elsewhere.

This luxury contrasts with the affordable marriage ceremony, a byproduct of socialism that made matrimony after the revolution possible for more than the elite.[46] Dresses could be rented from the state, fees were almost nonexistent, and the liberal divorce laws made (and still make) marriage highly repeatable. The absence of digital display from this domestic "poor cousin" wedding adds to the impression that technology today is aiding an online departure from the postrevolution weddings of predigital days.

Quinceañeras, the enduring female coming-of-age celebrations, also demand digital photography. Using graphic software to process and enhance images reveals a domestication of technology in private life and leisure.[47] Color balanced, elbows cropped, images are speedily reproduced and laser printed, or are burned to a disk and supplied with a cover like a popular DVD. Unlike the use of technology to blog or book from a business Web site, technology here enhances everyday life, though at a less politically colored level than prevalent in many uses.

With the globalization of markets, the appropriation of digital technology has spread swiftly, playing a role in ever more aspects of Cuban life. Its own mobility of function and application assists the movement of its users physically, socially, and psychologically, as seen in various trends. For example, the generation that grew up with the revolution sang the songs of idolized rock musicians, often improvising their own lyrics, while today's teenage rap fanatic downloads the lyrics from the Internet and repeats them word for word—understanding, say, Eminem's rhymes. Young Cubans fascinated by Black American culture who invest social value in both its language of resistance and its material culture and fresh hip-hop look can copy the style of rapper Tupac Shakur from a Web site. Wanting to emulate the flashy style of Black American basketball players, Cuban youth can select favorite tee-shirts and sneakers from the online NBA store, for purchase and delivery to the island, by visiting U.S. friends and relatives.

In idle conversation, young women express the frustration of many who grew up during the tourist boom of the Special Period, when the social sphere expanded through contact with a growing number of international visitors; like many of their contemporaries, the women wonder about leaving Cuba to find work and create new lives. The pseudo-diplomatic openness afforded Cuba by the Clinton administration, which all but disappeared during the harsher policies of the George W. Bush administration, allowed many to migrate in "orderly" fashion to the United States, Mexico, Europe, and elsewhere.

Digital technology today allows residents of Cuba both to assuage and to increase their frustration. State controls may limit the exposure of technologies of information, entertainment, and goods and services, but the communication facilitated through government approval ensures that constraints will be breached. As a result, Cuba becomes a distorted microcosm of digital technology use where the squeeze of official and external restrictions produces spikes of intensified activity in social, economic, and political realms. The counterpart patterns tend to run flatter in free market economies of greater personal mobility and freedoms. Cuba shows how digital technology can align to the pace of any user and to the needs and desires of all of them with its unprecedented capacity to supply and reflect the personal.

Videostroika

The YouTube videos of the Alarcón–student debate at UCI (discussed in chapter 2) epitomize video documentation and distribution on the Internet that has "real life" impact. Beyond covering events in Cuba, a variety of uploaded Cuban videos continue to make the country and its people more visible abroad. Although the conditions of production, the name of the host, or the profile of the author are not always explicit, the amateur video community found on the Web represents a broad sample of life in Cuba. Although, in general, music videos remain the largest category available on YouTube, scores of other videos represent real Cubans speaking about contemporary changes and hardship—and documenting neighborhoods and public and private moments, sometimes with stunning impact. News stories about Cuba also make their way onto Internet videos sites, where the intertextual nature of digital media is fully deployed. The UCI student story is one such example; another is "Cuba's Youth: Restless but not Often Political," which appeared on the *Christian Science Monitor* Web site, about the social critique of rapper Bian Rodríguez's lyrics.[48]

Web sites provide expressive potential for the exile community, but live videos capture the nostalgic, entrenched, obstinate, melancholic, and hopeful character of individual Cuban lives. Since the 1990s, a number of visitors to Cuba have filmed their trips and uploaded videos that reveal naïveté about the usually willing subjects they encountered and their surroundings. Cubans making return voyages tend to film crumbling architecture, road trips, walking tours of the old city and of UCI, and deplorable conditions, along with creative ingenuity, in the countryside. Uploaded feature films, shorts, animation, family videos, and ongoing video projects by filmmakers like Miguel Coyula add to a wide-ranging, if incomplete, Internet-accessible vision of Cuba that poses interesting dilemmas for the government's attempts to maintain control over online activity.

Although the broader impact of Cuban bloggers and media makers is still emerging, their online contribution can be likened to the quantitative internationalization of artists from all over the world. The comparison illustrates the complexities that lie ahead in assessing new contours and languages of expression as journalists, amateur filmmakers, and citizens become more embedded into global networks. Reflecting on the effects of globalization on artistic practice, Cuban art historian and critic Gerardo Mosquera wonders if Cuban artists are "contributing or not to the transformation of a hegemonic and restrictive situation into active plurality, instead of being digested by that situation."[49] Digested or not, digital media tools provide Cuban artists new narrative activities and ways of working, either alone or communally, that also demand critical engagement with the new forms and their infrastructures.

Cuba's reticence to embrace personal digital telecommunications could have long-term influence on the creation of plural social identities and on their production of digital content. The postponement of a privatized network structure might suggest alternative architectures and uses from those of the consumerist model dominant in the capitalist world. Such alternative models would likely involve a continuation in some form of restrictive government mechanisms that use tools that easily erase, duplicate, upload, and download all sorts of potentially problematic messages. System openness in Cuba would remain contingent on the acquisition and implementation of the kind of improved national security controls now prevalent in most countries.

Despite overwhelming economic odds, digital media tools and venues have dispersed in Cuba through people's lives, work, and user communities. Artists working with traditional tools like paintbrush and canvas incorporate digital photography and sound design to create multimedia installation spaces. Electronic media expands the exposure of the locally situated art gallery.

The independent Havana-based art gallery Espacio Aglutinador, founded by artists Ezequiel Suárez and Sandra Ceballos in 1994, became a "zone of tolerance" when an exhibition of Suárez's provocative paintings at an official gallery was cancelled by officials prior to the opening. The artists' home and painting studio became the new gallery space that could exhibit "an incoherent, hybrid, undefined, chaotic, almost casual work of art [because it] might

be the only adequate reaction to the state of a world with similar characteristics and the best way to represent it."[50] Aglutinador as virtual space is
embedded in New York–based interdisciplinary artist Coco Fusco's Web site
supporting the independent status of Aglutinador's curators and expanding
their presence in international artist networks.[51]

Contributing to discussions about the use of new technologies and the
promotion of artistic and cultural values, the Centro Cultural Pablo de la
Torriente Brau, under the auspices of the Oficina del Historiador de la Ciudad
de La Habana, with support from the Dutch International Humanist Institute
for Cooperation with Developing Countires (HIVOS), the Empresa Telefónica
de Cuba (ETECSA)'s Cubasí Portal, and the collaboration of ICAIC, UNEAC,
and the Museo Nacional de Bellas Artes, organized Cuba Digital Art: The
Exhibit 2006. Exploring the relations between art and life, works examined
an impressive range of themes, including emerging spiritual geographies,
everyday life and its contradictions, and the language of music videos and of
advertising. According to Cuban cultural promoter and critic Victor Casaus,
"the significant number of Cuban electronic media entries for the event was
proof of growing domestic interest despite the limits of infrastructure."[52]
Despite state restrictions to Internet access, state arts institutions have been
effective in garnering strong international financial support for events such
as Cuba Digital Art.

The multiyear international collaborative project Sharing Dreams: Cuba
and the U.S. Cross the Digital Divide brought together digital artists from
both nations, who used visual design, spoken word, and digital technology
to create work in pairs that spoke to each other's realities. For the project's
2006 theme, Love Conquers All, concern infuses Pedro Juan Abreu's graphic
art as he observes that, in daily life,

> electronic messages replace more and more personal exchanges and
> face-to-face communication. Conversations, smells, sounds and kisses
> become synthesized icons in the e-mail software and chat halls. Vir-
> tual contact is replacing simple conversation and meetings of people,
> making us feel next to each other. We believe we know each other very
> well and we are very near each other when we spend long hours sitting
> before the display reading between lines and light dots.[53]

Cuban curator Luisa Marisy notes, of Fast-Forward, the video art installations held in 2006 at the Centro Cultural Pablo de la Torriente Brau,

"Fast-Forward accurately describes what is happening in the context of Cuban fine arts with the use of video and digital technologies."[54] Established to preview work in progress, forums such as *Fast-Forward I* and *Fast-Forward II* reveal that new digital tools have found their way into the creative processes of artists, leading them to pose new personal and aesthetic questions. Marisy points out that the forums comprise "a group of renowned artists, with indisputable talent . . . that places them in the national and international art scene . . . using video and digital technology to make very diverse works—video-installations, video-performances, animation and experimental films—always maintaining the consistency of the formal and conceptual discourse they have been developing for some time."[55]

It may be difficult to make sense of such complex experiences without falling into the familiar trap of lamenting what alternative networks are not. *Fast-Forward* seems to avoid the "chaotic movements and atomized practices" that, as Fowler says, "only reach unity in the barely measurable horizon of private consumption."[56] Cuban artists, writers, filmmakers, politicians, and citizens have not yet become the type of wireless "smart mobs" envisioned by Howard Rheingold, author of *Virtual Worlds*, however. Rheingold suggests that instant access and the evolution of wireless technologies is transforming cultures and communities by revolutionizing the sensorial and temporal relationship of an individual to place and space. "[M]ore important than the evolution of color and video screens in telephone displays," he contends, "is the presence of 'location awareness' in mobile phones . . . [where], increasingly, handheld devices can detect, within a few yards, where they are located on a continent, within a neighborhood, or inside a room."[57]

This rendering of information and commodity pleasures does not represent the situation of the millions of users and consumers of technology whose consumption is structured, and therefore limited, by the economies of less affluent societies and the failed policies of governments, policies in desperate need of reform. These realities notwithstanding, Cubans are acutely aware of their location within the "old" geopolitics of the Cold War and the personalized politics of the twentieth century. New social interactions are emerging from the ever-turbulent crossing of currents between capitalist politics and alternative political imaginings of a more socially equitable and responsive world. The Cuban government's resistance to investing in neoliberal capitalist models that have proven detrimental in other parts of the world appears to coincide tactically with the current realignment of models of regional cooperation around a new socialist, Southern Hemisphere vision. As the regional realignment continues, Cubans will continue, whatever bureaucratic or technical barrier confronts them, to find their way onto global networks, using every avenue of digital expression and digital tool so far invented. Single and merging streams of Cuban social, political, and artistic tenacity flow into global cultural currents, becoming part of an unmanaged, democratic digital remix. Cuba demonstrates how political proscription and restriction fails to contribute to the health of that mix. Not only does a vigorous, socially constructive digital future need the kind of active plurality proposed by Mosquera, it may depend on it.

CONCLUSION

In July 2007, Fidel Castro's forty-eight-year presidency gave way to a "new" political administration—his brother Raul's. Fidel's public presence thereafter has become virtual, a pivotal juncture substantiated by his regular Web site postings, "Reflectiones," televised images, or printed opinion pieces. That his presence still looms large in the consciousness of citizens was evident at Raúl Castro's second 26th of July address to the Cuban people, gathered to commemorate the fifty-fifth anniversary of the attack on Moncada barracks, the event that launched the revolution. Standing before a huge and colorful image of Fidel, Raúl began by referencing one of Fidel's speeches from 1973 and affirming the validity of its vision.[1] The younger brother repeated the assertion he had made when he took over as president in February 2008, "The conviction of the Revolution will continue to follow Fidel's correct analysis." He continued: "Fidel is Fidel, and we all know this. Fidel cannot be substituted, and the people will continue his work long after he is no longer physically present. His ideas have made possible the dignity and justice that our country represents."[2]

Fidel Castro embodies the symbolic weight of the revolution, which, as the driving force of the nation, has had a tremendous impact on the culture and people of Cuba. A generational change of leadership will follow the Castros, and, with this shift, fresh interpretations of, and different solutions to, internal and external problems will follow.

For the incipient post-Castro society to confront models of globalization will require a clear understanding of how life is lived, survival negotiated, and official norms challenged in twenty-first-century Cuba. Cuban revolutionary imagination has encompassed the evolution of a socialist ideology since 1961, developing and upholding the current forms of power. Official Web sites make use of symbolic and exemplary individuals, slogans, and images that synthesize the essential struggle of a small nation under constant threat from a powerful nearby enemy. The resolve of the political leadership's revolutionary project has been the mainstay in the fight to exert a sovereign identity and place in the global economy. Over the half-century since it began, the struggle over legitimacy has existed by rallying the spirit of individuals alongside the larger cause of nation building. Established institutions of the revolution have become the representatives, indeed the presumed conduits, for individual needs and desires; at least, this is what Cuban leaders sought to address through a centralized structure of power. Unofficial blogs and Web sites make apparent that twenty-first-century Cubans are concerned about economic survival and alternative social identities, and not necessarily concerned with revolutionary reality. To address emergent forms of cultural and social organization and greater democratic participation, the Cuban government seeks to resolve the disparity between revolutionary ideals and current conditions in symbolic ways that sustain its culture and its people.

Separate from the overarching officially generated metanarrative of revolution, knowledge and ideas are as important as material resources to Cuba's course of development. Digital media seeps into the everyday life of Cubans just as currents of political transition breathe greater dimension to individual expression and visions for the future. The generation of Cubans joining the digital era are grandchildren of the revolution, without firsthand memories of its victories and accomplishments. Their lot has been defined by the hardship of extreme times. This generation and its aspirations, complaints, and desires is changing and intensifying the nature of opposition to the government through fresh forms of expression. The call for new approaches to reform, expressed by citizens and the Cuban-based opposition, is informed by different roots of discontent than those underlying the demands of hardline exiles. The clamor from inside Cuba is infused with rebellious racial politics, plainly evident in Cuban popular culture, in response to an immediate sense of exclusion. New avatars of citizens appear on new media channels, relating personal stories and experiences through blogs, electronic discussions, journals, artworks, and local community organizations. A new social imagination has begun to shape the future of Cuba, taking it beyond earlier rhetoric even where that rhetoric is digitized.

The European Union lifted all sanctions against Cuba in June 2007—an act of major historic importance that met with the usual U.S. response that such actions are "insufficient" and only help the Cuban government. The changes implemented early on by Raúl Castro's administration stirred expectations of imminent political openness, expectations that have begun a transformation of the existing social fabric. As of 2009, Cubans are participating in traditionally monitored official debate and animated direct exchanges, but they are now also talking and "talking back" online, amplifying the conversation and taking it outside Cuba through the electronic constellation documented and analyzed in this book.

The expansion, consolidation, and even imposition of "democracy" have become foreign policy tools for the United States, which defines democracy on its own terms. But for Cuba, democracy and democratic institutions have a complex historical legacy that must be the starting point for any analysis of how to improve a democratic system. The deployment of the Internet through official institutions is defined as a way to help build a civil society. Whether or not the Internet otherwise may be a threat to Cuba's own democratic aspirations, it is surely so perceived by the government. Rather than producing an ideology whereby the system of information is perceived as open, accessible, and responsive to individual needs, the Cuban government has instead designed an infrastructure of technology creating the idea of socially responsible use of digital media. The negotiation of the competing ideas of social responsibility and individual needs will be key in the transformation of Cuban culture over the next millennium.

Exile communities demonstrate that the Internet plays an important role in reimagining longing and in constructing what, in another instance, Cuban journalist Luis Ortega has called a "portable homeland."[3] As postcolonial scholar Homi Bhabha has pointed out, "the organic or biological metaphor through which the concepts of community and communication are constituted . . . does not permit the lifeworld of cyberspace to reach beyond the homogenous empty time of the imagined community of the nation and its largely consensual, unitary peoples."[4] If the virtual community shares the temporal structure of the modern nation, then, he asks, what would prevent it from replicating the worst excesses of xenophobia and nationalism? This question is particularly probing for Cuban virtual communities because of how history has defined the tenor of their national and exile politics. The exiles who arrived in the United States after the revolution found unprecedented economic and social support from their new host country, which, through its immigration policies, helped to construct a replacement "nation" intended to help return Cuba one day to its prerevolutionary character. This is no longer possible. The Miami community in particular makes it clear that visions of political homogeneity have eroded. As political commentator David Reiff argues, the seeds of change may actually come from political challenges to the established power brokers of the Cuba lobby in the U.S. Congress.[5]

Of significance to Cuba has been the development of close economic relations with Venezuela under its president Hugo Chavez, a populist, socialist force in the Southern Hemisphere. The new regional assemblages formed among Cuba, Bolivia, Argentina, Ecuador, Brazil, China, and nations in the Middle East reorient power and economic determinations away from the United States hegemony over the hemisphere. Socialism in the twenty-first century, in part defined by the Bolivarian alternative, a defiant response to neoliberalism, and inspired by the liberation leader Simón Bolivar's unrealized dream of Latin American unification, negotiates and establishes new approaches to markets. The political and economic changes occurring through improved economies and regional integration are transferring the work of the social imagination to alternative interactions, positions, and futures. The Internet and digital tools, along with knowledge and imagination, bring information, overcome isolation, stimulate new research, present dangers and challenges to sovereignty, and generate new, individual spaces of communication and unprecedented lifeworlds. Discoveries regarding the digital dilemmas, their components and their effects, ultimately reveal a potential to assist Cuban adaptation in a rapidly changing economic and political world.

An old Cuban joke tells about the returning CIA spy (sent by Nixon, or Reagan, or Clinton): "Mr. President, there is no unemployment, but no one works. No one works, but statistics show that all the production goals are met. All production goals are met, but there is nothing in the stores. There is nothing in the stores, but everyone eats. Everyone eats, but they all complain constantly that there is no food. People complain constantly, but they all go to the Plaza of the Revolution to cheer Fidel. Mr. President, we have all the facts and no conclusion." The "joke" both ridicules constant attempts by the United States to assess what is really going on in Cuba and paints a bleak picture of life under the Castro regime. It also underscores the defiant characteristic of Cuban identity that at once reveals and prevents a full understanding of the people's social interactions.

If the Special Period encountered an analogue Cuba, the first decade of the twenty-first century has featured a Cuba where digital technology is a major part of the cultural fabric. Legal reforms to information policy in 2009 point to greater Internet "accessibility" for Cuban citizens as the state slowly expanded the mechanism of public access to all citizens. As I have insisted throughout, official policies and popular depictions of the Internet in Cuba resonate against a broader context of national and international events. The entry of the Internet—which, as one Cuban said, "was designed by the enemy, but we have to take advantage of it"—takes its adaptations from the current flow of politics and history.

Notes

INTRODUCTION

1 NBC News, "Listening post in Lourdes/Cuba," October 24, 2003, http://www .geocities.com/dulfkotte/lourdescuba.html (accessed June 10, 2008).

2 For instance, Ciudad Libertad, which became a major educational center, was formerly the Columbia Military Base in Marianao, a symbol of military rule under Batista.

3 Leticia Martínez and Orfilio Peláez, "Salto hacia la soberanía tecnológica," *Granma Internacional*, October 7, 2007, http://www.granma.cubaweb.cu/2007/10/07/ nacional/artico6.html (accessed October 5, 2009).

4 Anna T. Sing, *Friction: An Enthnography of Global Connection* (Princeton, NJ: Princeton University Press, 2005), 15. See also A. Hughes, "Retailers, Knowledges, and Changing Commodity Networks: The Case of the Cut Flower," in *Blackwell Cultural Economies Reader*, ed. Ash Amin and Nigel Thrift (Malden, MA, and Oxford: Blackwell Publishing, 2004), 210–230.

5 Joseph S. Nye, *Soft Power: The Means to Success in World Politics* (New York: Public Affairs, 2004), 11.

6 Tariq Ali, *Pirates of the Caribbean: Axis of Hope* (London: Verso, 2006), 111.

7 The government's crackdown saw the arrest and jailing of seventy-five independent journalists, in a raid that became known as "Black Spring." See "Las damas de blanco: La primavera negra," 2003, http://www.damasdeblanco.com/prima vera/primavera2003.asp (accessed July 27, 2008). Many of the arrested remain political prisoners, accused by the Cuban government of treason.

8 Martínez and Peláez, "Salto hacia la soberanía tecnológica."

9 Bert Hoffman, "Cuba's Dilemma of Simultaneity: The Link between the Political and the National Question," in *Debating Cuban Exceptionalism*, ed. Bert Hoffman and Lawrence Whitehead (New York: Palgrave Macmillan, 2007), 101.

10 Ibid., 102.

11 Jas Gawronski, "Castro Views U.S. Administration, Socialism," interview with President Fidel Castro, *La Stampa*, Hamburg, December 23, 1993, http://lanic .utexas.edu/project/castro/db/1993/19931228.html (accessed November 29, 2008).

12 Jules Marshall, "Cuba Faces the Web Revolution," *The Guardian*, July 22, 1999, http://www.guardian.co.uk/theguardian/1999/jul/22/technologyguardian/ technology (accessed January 2, 2009).

13 Armand Mattelart, *Networking the World, 1794–2000* (Minneapolis: University of Minnesota Press, 2000), viii.

14 Arturo Escobar, *Encountering Development: The Making and Unmaking of the Third World* (Princeton, NJ: Princeton University Press, 1995), 4.

15 Mattelart, *Networking the World*, 59.

16 Michel Foucault, "Governmentality," in *The Essential Foucault*, ed. Paul Rabinow and Nikolas Rose (New York and London: The New Press, 2003), 229–245.

17 Raymond Williams, *Television Technology and Cultural Form* (Hanover and London: Wesleyan University Press, 1974, 1992), 13.

18 Enrique Gonzalez-Manet, "Internet: Espejismos y promesas de la cultura electronica," unpublished essay, 1998.

19 Errol Pierre-Louis, "Berners-Lee: Future of Web Is a Semantic One," *PC Magazine*, June 12, 2008, http://www.pcmag.com/article2/0,1217,2319807.asp (accessed July 21, 2009).

20 Nicholas Carr, "Is Google Turning Us into Stooped?" *The Atlantic* (July/August 2008): 36.

21 Wendy Hui Kyong Chun, *Control and Freedom: Power and Paranoia in the Age of Fiber Optics* (Cambridge, MA: MIT Press, 2006).

22 Oficina Nacional de Estadísticas, ICT, Republica de Cuba, http://www.one.cu/aec2008/esp/20080618_tabla_cuadro.htm (accessed July 17, 2009).

23 John Coté, "Cubans Log On behind Castro's Back," in *Capitalism, God, and a Good Cigar*, ed. Lydia Chavez (Durham, NC: Duke University Press, 2005), 161.

24 Patrick Symmes, "Che Is Dead," *Wired* (February 1998): 145.

25 Restrictions are not the sole territory of the Cuban state. Cuban technology critic Amaury del Valle inquires, "Does Google Block Cuba?" since Cuban users attempting to access various Google products—Google Earth, Google Code, and others—find their access blocked on the basis of country of origin. See Amaury E. del Valle, "¿Google bloquea Cuba?" *Memoria* (November 2007): 35–36.

26 See Louis A. Perez Jr., *On Becoming Cuban: Identity, Nationality and Culture* (Chapel Hill: University of North Carolina Press, 1999).

27 Esther Whitfield, *Cuban Currency: The Dollar and the "Special Period" Fiction* (Minneapolis: University of Minnesota Press, 2008).

28 Fidel Castro, "Castro Gives Speech at Moncada Barracks Anniversary," transcript of Radio Havana Cuba, Havana, July 27, 1993, http://lanic.utexas.edu/project/castro/db/1993/19930727.html (accessed November 29, 2008).

29 Joy Gordon, "Cuba's Entrepreneurial Socialism," *The Atlantic* (January 1997): 18–30, http://www.theatlantic.com/issues/97jan/cuba/cuba.htm.

30 Jorge I. Dominguez, "Cuba's Many Faces: Not Quite the New Millennium," *DRCLAS News* (Winter 2000): 3.

31 Many gross domestic product statistics for Cuba in the 2000s are estimated. These statistics are from *latinamericadatabase, NotiCen: Central American & Caribbean Political & Economic Affairs*, including Cuba 10, no. 9 (March 3, 2005), http://www.cubaupdate.org/cuo404_22.htm (accessed July 16, 2007). (ISSN 1089–1560.)

32 Silvia M. Domenech, *¿Cuba: Socialismo o capitalismo? Hacia el Tercer Milenio* (La Habana: Editora Politica, 1998), 71.

33 CIA Factbook, Cuba statistics from 2007, https://www.cia.gov/library/publications/the-world-factbook/geos/cu.html (accessed November 29, 2008).

34 Luz Marina Fornieles Sanchez, "The State of Cuban Tourism with Statistics," *Havana Journal*, http://havanajournal.com/travel/entry/the-state-of-cuban-tourism-with-statistics/ (accessed July 6, 2008).

35 USDA Foreign Agricultural Service, "Trade with Cuba," http://www.fas.usda.gov/itp/cuba/cuba.asp (accessed November 29, 2008).

36 Eloy Rodriguez, "Zonas francas y parques industriales," *Granma Internacional Edicion Digital*, May 7, 1997, http://www.cubanet.org (accessed May 8, 1997).

37 Mark Fineman, "Caribbean Nations Warm Up to Cuba with Economic Ties," *Los Angeles Times*, December 27, 1997, A2.

38 Homero Campa, "Al estilo capitalista: Por primera vez, desde el inicio de la Revolución, en Cuba se cobraran impuestos," *Proceso*, 1002, January 15, 1996, 49–51.

39 *The Economist*, September 23, 1999, 37, referenced in Susan Eckstein, "Dollarization and Its Discontents in the Post-Soviet Era," *Reinventing the Revolution: a Contemporary Cuba Reader* (UK: Rowman and Littlefield Publishers, 2008), 186.

40 Homero Campa and Orlando Perez, *Cuba: Los años duros* (Barcelona: Plaza y Janés, 1997), 18–30. The *habanazo* occurred in August 1994 in the dilapidated area of Old Havana along the Malecón. Thousands of people crowded into the streets yelling "Down with Fidel!" "Liberty!" At the height of the violence, dollar stores and tourist hotels in the area were looted and vandalized. Work brigades, police, and Fidel himself, when he showed up, brought the situation under control. One interesting aspect was that none of the opposition groups (such as those proclaiming human rights, democracy) participated in the disturbance. In other words, the event was a spontaneous popular uprising.

41 Elián Gonzalez, a six-year-old Cuban boy, was rescued at sea near the coast of Florida on Thanksgiving Day in 1999. His mother and ten others, who, along with the boy, had left Cuba on a raft, all perished at sea. An international custody case was unleashed when his Miami relatives claimed the child and refused to return him to his father in Cuba.

42 Chun, *Control and Freedom*, 66.

43 Mario Coyula, "Havana Always: Preserving the Soul of the City," *DRCLAS News* (Winter 2000): 28.

44 Coyula, "Havana Always," 28.

45 Mario Coyula, "El Trinquenio Amargo y la ciudad distopica: Autopsia de una utopia," in *La política cultural del período revolucionario: Memoria y reflexión*, ed. Eduardo Heras León and Desiderio Navarro (La Habana: Centro Teórico-Cultural Criterios, 2008), 47–68.

46 Taxes on income earned in dollars are one way the government is attempting to halt illicit enrichment; another is the centralized control of economic development.

47 Dominguez, "Many Faces," 177.

48 Jorge I. Dominguez, *Cuba: Order and Revolution* (Cambridge, MA: Belknap Press of Harvard University Press, 1978), 148.

49 Ibid.

50 See Victor Fowler, "Dialogar sobre cambios y esencias," *Foro: La UNEAC en Congreso*, April 1–4, 2008, La Habana, Cuba, http://www.foroscubarte.cult.cu/read.php?6,940 (accessed July 28, 2008).

51 Robert Siegel, All Things Considered, "Miami Fund Invests for Cuba's Post-Castro Era," http://www.npr.org/templates/story/story.php?storyId=10819094 (accessed July 28, 2008).

52 Greg Allen, "Digital Tools Bolster Property Claims against Cuba," June 7, 2007, NPR Technology report, http://www.npr.org/templates/story/story.php?storyId=10817208 (accessed July 28, 2008).

53 Manuel Vázquez Montalbán, Y Dios entró en la Habana (Madrid: Aguilar, 1998). Montalban's book weaves together fascinating interviews from persons representing competing visions of contemporary Cuba and ranging from Eusebio Leal, in charge of rebuilding and historicizing the city, to Cuban officials, ministers, cardinals, and generals, to Spanish politicians, diplomatic, and economic ministers, and to exiled Cubans in both Spain and Miami. Montalbán concludes with an interview with Rigoberta Mechu, the Guatemalan indigenous rights leader and Nobel laureate, and with letters the author exchanged with Subcomandante Marcos to propose that, in Cuba, the next Atlantis be mixed-race or black. The conversations were inspired by the visit of John Paul II in January 1998 and the author's view of the visit's significance for Cuba's future.

54 For his reformist views, Payá has met resistance from the Cuban government and is considered a dissident in Cuba. He received the Sokurov Prize in 2003, internationally recognizing his work on human rights.

55 Father Felix Varela, a Cuban priest revered for his efforts as a social reformer, represents the convergence of socialist and Christian ideas. Varela called for equality in the education of women and for an end to slavery. His antislavery stance led to his exile in the early 1800s to New York City, where he worked for the rights of the immigrant community. He died in St. Augustine, Florida, praised in speeches by Jose Martí as the first man who embraced new Cuban ideas. Exalted also by Pope John Paul II during a visit to Cuba in 1998 and seen as an important symbol of the possibility of religious reconciliation, Varela represents Cuban-ness for Cubans on and off the island.

56 Nelson P. Valdés, "The Varela Project and the Clash within the Catholic Church in Cuba," http://www.progresoweekly.com/RPW_Archives/RPWeekly080102/neighborsValdesVarelaProject080102.htm (accessed April 15, 2006).

57 Raisa Pagés, "A Transcendent Yes," Granma Internacional, June 17, 2002, http://www.latinamericanstudies.org/cuba/constitution-changed.htm (accessed July 21, 2009).

58 Jorge G. Castañeda, Utopia Unarmed: The Latin American Left after the Cold War (New York: Alfred A. Knopf, 1993), 73.

59 Ibid.

60 Ibid., 74.

61 Quoted in Vázquez Montalbán, Y Dios, 375.

62 The Gray Years. Others in Cuba have used the term Black Decade. These were the euphemisms for the period during the 1970s of severe censorship against what hard-line conservatives in the Castro regime perceived as, and termed, weaknesses and deviations in character or political conviction. This language of "weakness" and "deviation" would be used in attacking many citizens, but especially notable were cases against artists and homosexuals. Artists were banned, jailed, or made to perform public self-repudiations. Labor camps were

used to "reform" homosexual men. Politically, the country was adhering to Soviet pressure to follow bureaucratic and factionalist practices.

63 Vázquez Montalbán, *Y Dios*, 384. There are those who see Fidel's powerful paternalist and authoritarian role as a result of an independence that never was. Emilio Ichikawa suggests that, because Cuba never had a leader that consolidated its independence from Spain, the nation had not, since 1898, expressed its essence and unity—until Fidel came to power. He fulfilled this role with great charisma. See Emilio Ichikawa, "Tres notas sobre la transición," *Encuentro de la cultura Cubana* (Madrid: Ediciones la Palma, primavera/verano 8/9, 1998), 5–15.

64 Manuel Calviño, "Psicologia, marxismo, y posmodernismo: Notas de una primera impresión." unpublished manuscript, October 1998, 20.

65 Vázquez Montalbán, *Y Dios*, 386.

66 Margarita Mateo Palmer, "Postmodernismo y criterios: Prólogo para una anología y para un aniversario," in *El postmoderno, el postmodernismo y su critica en Criterios*, ed Desiderio Navarro (La Habana: Centro Teórico-Cultural Criterios, 2007), 7–8.

67 Ibid., 9.

68 Desiderio Navarro, "Cuantos años de qué color? Para una introducción al Ciclo," *La polítical cultural*, ed. Heras León and Navarro, La Habana: Centro Teórico-Cultural Criterios, 2008: 17.

69 Mateo Palmer, "Postmodernismo," 8.

CHAPTER 1 — INVENTING, RECYCLING, AND DEPLOYING TECHNOLOGIES

1 Radio Habana Cuba was founded in 1961 by the Cuban revolutionary leadership, and is an international government radio broadcast station.

2 Arnaldo Coro, personal interview, August 1998.

3 Ibid.

4 Maria Grant, "Was the Telephone Invented in Havana?" *International Granma*, April 4, 1999, 2. Also, José Altshuler y Roberto Díaz Martín, eds., *Los días cubanos de Antonio Meucci y el nacimiento de la telefonía* (La Habana: Empresa de Telecomunicaciones de Cuba S.A. y Sociedad Cubana de Historia de la Ciencia y la Tecnología, 1998). Altshuler and Díaz Martín explain how the development of telecommunications is further intertwined with Cuba. They pay tribute to the preliminary work done by the Florentine Antonio Meuci in 1849, when he accidentally discovered the electric transmission of the human voice. While living in Cuba in 1835, Meuci worked at the Tacón Theater in Havana as a mechanic, but he also did research on electricity and its medical applications, apparently gaining fame in the city for providing electrical treatments for rheumatism. His important discovery came when a patient, who had electrical conductors attached to his mouth, yelled when the charge was applied. Through a closed door and in an adjoining room, Meuci, also holding electrical conductors, heard the patient's voice "through the wires" and recognized that he had obtained the transmission of the human voice. In 1850, not long after his discovery, Meuci traveled to the United States, where he spent the rest of his life trying to develop his discovery.

5 Manuel Moreno Fraginals, *El ingenio: Complejo económico social cubano del azúcar*, quoted in Armand Mattelart and Hector Schmucler, *Communication and*

Information Technologies: Freedom of Choice for Latin America?, David Buxton, trans. (Norwood, NJ: Ablex Publishers, 1985), 41–42 (pages 24–26 in the 1964 edition).

6 Yeidy M. Rivero, "Broadcasting Modernity: Cuban Television, 1950–1953," *Cinema Journal* 46, no. 3 (Spring 2007): 3–25.

7 Manuel A. Alvarez, "History of Cuban Broadcasting," Old Radio Web site, 1995, http://www.oldradio.com/archives/international/cuban.html (accessed July 8, 2008). Autobiographical sketch of Cuban Broadcast history. Alvarez's father was another early pioneer of radio broadcasting in Cuba.

8 Alvarez, "Cuban Broadcasting," 2.

9 John Sinclair, *Latin American Television: A Global View* (New York: Oxford University Press, 1999), 13.

10 Ibid.

11 For an account of media wars in pre-Castro Cuba see Michael B. Salwen, *Radio and Television in Cuba: The Pre-Castro Era* (Ames: Iowa State University Press, 1994).

12 Joe Cohen, "Cuba's New Ch. 10 Just as Yanks Like It—Flock to US Pix; Mould's Slated to Grab Mestre's NBC Label," *Variety*, August 6, 1958, quoted in Salwen, *Radio and Television*, 58 (1994):1.

13 Cuban technical staff, for example, were instrumental in the nascent Colombian television industry in the 1960s and 1970s. Writers like the legendary Delia Fiallo helped generate an industrial process that is the commercial backbone of Latin American television enterprises.

14 Jeremy Turnstall, *The Media Are American* (New York: Columbia University Press, 1977), 293, quoted in Ana M. Lopez, "Our Welcomed Guests: Telenovelas in Latin America," in *To Be Continued: Soap Operas around the World*, ed. Robert C. Allen (London: Routledge, 1995), 264.

15 Alvarez, "Cuban Broadcasting," 3.

16 Enrique C. Betancourt, *Apuntes para la historia: Radio, television, y farandula de la Cuba de ayer* (Puerto Rico: Ramallo Bros., 1986).

17 Richard Bunce, *Television in the Corporate Interest* (New York: Praeger, 1976), 81, quoted in Sinclair, "Television," 14.

18 Manuel A. Alvarez, e-mail correspondence, August 10, 1999.

19 Salwen, *Radio and Television*, 135.

20 Jose López Villaboy, *Statistical Abstract: Motivos y culpables* (Puerto Rico: Editora El Prin, 1958, 1973), quoted in Alvarez, "Cuban Broadcasting."

21 López, "Welcomed Guests," 264. López has commented on the attitudes toward *telenovelas* after the revolution. The genre was criticized for reflecting only the interests and values of American consumer imperialist culture. After being a leader in the creation of *telenovelas*, Cuba stopped production and consumption of the serial form, and it was not until the 1980s that there was again realization of the popularity of this genre. Cubans began importing Brazilian *telenovelas* and later began producing them again in Cuba.

22 Mattelart and Schmucler, *Communication and Information*, 46.

23 Enrique Gonzalez-Manet, "La cibernetica en Cuba," *Granma*, November 6, 1969. (Photocopy obtained from author, no page number available.)

24 Ibid.

25 Manuel Castells, *The Rise of the Network Society* (Malden, MA: BlackwellPublishers, 1999), 43–44. Castells retells in detail the convergence of the technological axes that made the "information age" possible.

26 Mattelart and Schmucler, *Communication and Information,* 71.

27 Coro interview, 1998.

28 Larry Press, "Cuban Telecommunications Infrastructure and Investment," Association for the Study of the Cuban Economy conference, Miami, FL, electronic document, August 1996, http://som.csudh.edu/fac/lpress/devnat/nations/cuba/asce.htm (accessed July 9, 2008).

29 Ibid., 3.

30 Larry Press, "Cuba, Communism, and Computing," *Communications of the ACM* 35, no. 11 (November 27–29, 1992): 112. The second generation computers were based on Digital's PDP-11.

31 Alfedo Luis del Valle, "Cuba, Internet y la politica exterior de EE.UU," unpublished paper, 12th Congreso de la Asociación Mexicana de Estudios Internacionales, Puebla, Mexico, October 17, 1998.

32 Manuel Castells, *The End of Millennium* (Malden, MA: Blackwell Publishers, 1999), 35.

33 Ibid., 29.

34 Ibid., 30–31.

35 Enrique Gonzalez-Manet, "Cibernética, política y desarrollo," *Granma,* November 3, 1969, La Habana, Cuba. (Photocopy of original obtained from author, no page number visible).

36 Gonzalez-Manet, "Politica y desarrollo," 1969.

37 Enrique Gonzalez-Manet, "Qué es la cibernética? *Granma*, November 1, 1969.

38 Enrique Gonzalez-Manet, "Cibernetica, politica y desarrollo, parte 2," *Granma,* November 3, 1969. (Photocopy of original obtained from author, no page number visible).

39 Orfilio Peláez, "Dos decadas de capacitación en las técnicas de computación," *Granma*, December 5, 1997, 4.

40 Press, "Communisim and Computing," 27.

41 Castells, "Network Society," 44.

42 Cuba joined the CMEA, or Comecon, an economic organization of communist states, in 1972. The organization was dissolved in 1991.

43 Press, "Communism and Computing," 27.

44 Ibid., 28.

45 Nelson P. Valdés and Mario A. Rivera, "The Political Economy of the Internet in Cuba," Cuba in Transition (conference), ASCE 1999, http://www.lanic.utexas.edu/la/cb/cuba/asce/cuba9/valdes.pdf (accessed July 8, 2008).

46 Nelson P. Valdés, "Cuba, The Internet, and U.S. Policy," Cuba Briefing Paper Series, no. 13, March 1997: 3–6, http://www.trinitydc.edu/academics/depts/Interdisc/International/Caribbean/20Briefing/20Papers.htm (accessed July 8, 2008).

47 Ibid., 3–6.

48 UNESCO, Consejo Ejecutivo, 151st reunion, "Declaration of the CAC Regarding Universal Access and Basic Information and Communication Services," 151EX/16 Addendum Paris, May 20, 1997: 4. *My translation.*

49 Gopher systems had file-like arrangements that allowed information to be stored hierarchically, and were simple to use. Given the nation's financially strapped situation when it began using the Internet, Cuba used "gophers" while its strategy was still in its infancy (in, that is, the early 1990s).

50 Center for Genetic Engineering and Biotechnology Web site, main page, http://gndp.cigb.edu.cu/ (accessed July 9, 2008).

51 Larry Press, "Cuban Networking Update," *OnTheInternet* (January-February 1996): 46–49, http://som.csudh.edu/fac/lpress/devnat/nations/cuba/update.htm (accessed July 8, 2008).

52 Jesús Martinez, personal interview, July 1998.

53 Ibid.

54 Larry Press and Joel Snyder, "A Look at Cuban Networks," http://som.csudh.edu/cis/lpress/devnat/nations/cuba/cuba3.htm (accessed August 15, 2007).

55 Valdés, "Cuba, the Internet," 7.

56 Susana Lee, "Aprueban decreto sobre acceso a redes informáticas de alcance global," *Granma*, June 20, 1996 (no page number available). *My translation.*

57 Decree 209/96, http://www.aladi.org/NSFALADI/ecomerc.NSF/61010aafa547414e03256eb50058640e/20b65b2e5de3357303256e1d004ac116/$FILE/Dec-No-209–96.pdf (accessed July 9, 2008).

58 Naghim Vázquez, "Cuba in the Internet Window," unpublished master's thesis (copy in author's possession), Universidad de La Habana, La Habana, Cuba, 1998. Cuba has a class B license, which means that CENIAI initially distributed 256 IP real numbers to a subnetwork, and in turn that network created another 256 class C providers.

59 In 2009 there were 215 com.cu domain names registered to companies in Cuba, which are the most likely to do effective e-commerce as it becomes a viable business option. This is further evidence of the way the nation prepares a business environment for Cuban firms. See *http://www.nic.cu/* (accessed July 21, 2009).

60 CITMATEL is the corporate entity that sets monthly charges for Internet connections and provides a variety of services including Web hosting and design, teleconferencing, and production of multimedia business and educational tools.

61 Edda Diz Garcés, "La red de redes más universal," *Trabajadores*, August 12, 1996, 5.

62 Lee, "Aprueban decreto."

63 Julio Garcia Luis, *Cuba en la era de Internet y las autopistas electronicas: Una entrevista con Enrique Gonzalez-Manet* (La Habana: Pablo de la Torriente Editorial, 1997), 10–11.

64 History of Informática, conference, http://www.informaticahabana.com/?q=en/node/38 (accessed July 29, 2007).

65 Marc Eisenstadt, "Cuba's Other Revolution," Eisenblog, http://eisenstadt.wordpress.com/2004/12/08/cubas-other-revolution/ (accessed July 9, 2008).

66 Cubaweb portal, http://www.cubaweb.cu/esp/main.asp (accessed August 14, 2007).

67 Nam June Paik, "TV Bra for Living Sculpture, Shock of the View," Walker Art Center, http://www.walkerart.org/archive/5/B85391323C41DD836167.htm (accessed July 9, 2008).

68 Jorge Barata, personal interview, August 1998. Often, Cubans are reluctant to offer the names of their business partners, in fear of reprisals from Helms-Burton legislation. This company has apparently found a way to circumvent this problem.

69 Prensa Latina Web site, main page, http://www.prensa-latina.cu/ (accessed July 8, 2008).

70 InfoMed Web site, "Acerca de," available at http://www.sld.cu/red/acercade/ (accessed July 8, 2008).

71 Pedro Urra González, personal interview, August 1998.

72 José A. de la Osa, "Creada red nacional de telemedicine," *Granma*, June 6, 1998.

73 USA-Cuba InfoMed Web site, main page, http://www.cubasolidarity.net/ (accessed July 8, 2008).

74 Jorge I. Dominguez, "Cuba's Many Faces: Not Quite the New Millennium," *DRCLAS News* (Winter 2000): 4.

75 Coro interview, 1998.

76 UNESCO, Human Development Reports, 2007–2008, http://hdrstats.undp.org/countries/data_sheets/cty_ds_CUB.html (accessed July 21, 2008).

77 Valdés, "Cuba, the Internet," 8.

78 On the transformation of Cuban film culture in the 1990s, see Cristina Venegas, "Filmmaking with Foreigners," in *Cuba in the Special Period: Culture and Ideology in the 1990s*, ed. Ariana Hernandez-Reguant (New York: Palgrave Macmillan, 2009), 37–50.

79 Human Development Report, "International Cooperation at a Crossroads" (2005), http://hdr.undp.org/en/reports/global/hdr2005/ (accessed July 21, 2008).

80 Domenech, *¿Capitalismo o socialismo?*, 71.

CHAPTER 2 — MEDIA TECHNOLOGIES AND "CUBAN DEMOCRACY"

1 See YouTube video at http://youtube.com/watch?v=vgj3gPbLE4g&feature=related (accessed June 26, 2008).

2 "Videos Hint at Public Discontent in Cuba," CNN.com News, http://www.cnn.com/2008/WORLD/americas/02/07/cuba.videos/ (accessed July 13, 2008); "Students Challenge Regime in Rare Video," *Miami Herald*, February 7, 2008, A13; "People in Cuba Are Becoming More Vocal in Their Calls for Change," NBC6, http://www.nbc6.net/news/15271697/detail.html (accessed July 13, 2008).

3 Jean Franco, *The Decline and Fall of the Lettered City: Latin America in the Cold War* (Cambridge, MA: Harvard University Press, 2002), 101.

4 Martí-an refers to the ideas of Cuban independence leader Jose Martí. In his long essay "Our America," he attempts to unify the Americas under their differences toward a common goal of liberty. While in exile in the United States, he founded a political party and a newspaper that were instrumental in disseminating and organizing the struggle and its ideas. He was killed in Cuba in 1895, in an early battle of the War of Independence.

5 David Held and Heikki Patomäki, "Problems of Global Democracy: A Dialogue," *Theory, Culture, and Society* 23, no. 5 (2006), http://tcs.sagepub.com (accessed April 4, 2007).

6 Anna L. Tsing, research symposium hosted by Department of Sociology, University of California, Santa Barbara, March 2007. Earlier, Tsing had discussed the ways that disastrous global projects might appear ordinary links in a global chain, but turn out to be links with features that have ramifying effects. See also Anna Tsing, *Frictions* (Princeton, NJ: Princeton University Press, 2005), 15.

7   See Sonia Alvarez, Evelina Dagnino, and Arturo Escobar, eds., *Culture of Politics, Politics of Culture: Revisioning Latin American Social Movements* (Boulder, CO: Westview Press, 1998).

8   "Support for a Democratic Transition in Cuba," electronic document found at GlobalSecurity.org, http://www.globalsecurity.org/wmd/library/news/cuba/970128-transition.htm (accessed August 28, 2007).

9   For example, the highly contested 2008 congressional elections in the state of Florida, where both Lincoln and Mario Diaz-Balart, Castro nephews and anti-Castro hardliners, fought a virulent political campaign against Raul Martinez and Joe Garcia, two Cuban American candidates who campaigned on ending the U.S.–Cuba embargo.

10   Dietrich Rueschemeyer, Evelyn Huber Stephens, and John D. Stephens, *Capitalist Development and Democracy* (Chicago: University of Chicago Press, 1992), 43. The authors offer a thoughtful discussion of the complexities of defining democracy, given the myriad varieties of democracies worldwide.

11   Held and Patomäki, "Global Democracy," 116.

12   Daniel Cohen, *Globalization and Its Enemies* (Cambridge, MA: MIT Press, 2006), 117.

13   Toby Miller and George Yúdice, *Cultural Policy* (London: Sage Publications, 2002), 134.

14   Jeffrey Belnap and Raúl Fernández, *José Martí's "Our America": From National to Hemispheric Cultural Studies* (Durham, NC: Duke University Press, 1998), 3.

15   Larry Press, "Cuban Telecommunication Infrastructure and Investment," paper presented at the Conference of the Association for the Study of the Cuban Economy, Miami, Florida, August 1996, http://som.csudh.edu/fac/lpress/devnat/nations/cuba/asce.htm.

16   U.S. Department of State, "U.S.–Cuba Relations," http://www.state.gov/p/wha/rls/fs/2001/2558.htm (accessed August 18, 2007).

17   This includes Caribbean nations that have long sided with the U.S. government. Although Jamaica has had an embassy in Cuba for a quarter of a century, it is only since 2000 increasing investment in the Cuban tourist sector. Other Caribbean nations, e.g., Barbados and St. Lucia, have forged economic and diplomatic agreements with Cuba in the face of threats from the United States to curtail financial assistance, threats that many in those nations see as meaningless since U.S. aid to their countries is negligible and since globalization presents new challenges and opportunities, such as trade with Cuba.

18   Philip Scranton and Janet F. Davidson, eds., *The Business of Tourism: Place, Faith, and History* (Philadelphia: University of Pennsylvania Press, 2007), 231–232. On the Helms-Burton international controversy, see also Paolo Spadoni, "The Impact of Helms-Burton Legislation on Foreign Investment in Cuba," *Cuba in Transition*, Volume 11, online document of the papers and proceedings of the Eleventh Annual Meeting of the Association for the Study of the Cuban Economy, Miami, August 2–4, 2001: 25–32.

19   Report by Center for International Journalism, Florida International University, Miami, n.d.

20 Cuba Working Group, U.S. House of Representatives, "A Review of U.S. Policy Toward Cuba," Washington, DC, May 15, 2002, http://lexingtoninstitute.org/970.shtml (accessed August 19, 2007).

21 U.S. Broadcasting Board of Governors, annual report, electronic document, 2005:16, http://www.bbg.gov/bbg_press.cfm (accessed August 19, 2007).

22 Center for International Policy, Cuba program, "Report on Radio and TV Martí," June 28, 2007, http://ciponline.org/cuba/marti.dwt (accessed August 19, 2007).

23 Joel del Rio, "Producto memorable de la industria audiovisual norteamericana," *Juventud Rebelde,* August 5, 2007, http://www.juventudrebelde.cu/cultura/2007-08-05/un-producto (accessed August 19, 2007).

24 Lisa Parks, *Cultures in Orbit: Satellites and the Televisual* (Durham, NC: Duke University Press, 2005), 49.

25 Gillian Gunn, quoted in Larry Press, "Cuban Computer Networks and Their Impact," paper presented at ASCE Cuba in Transition Conference, Havana, Cuba, 1996: 341, www.lanic.utexas.edu/la/cb/cuba/asce/cuba6/43press2.fm.pdf (accessed July 13, 2008).

26 U.S. Government Accountability Office, "Foreign Assistance: U.S. Democracy Assistance for Cuba Needs Better Management and Oversight," GAO 07–147, November 2006, http://www.gao.gov/new.items/d07147.pdf (accessed August 28, 2007).

27 Pascual Serrano, "Cuba in the Sights of the United States," *Granma International* (from *Le Monde Diplomatique*), September 22, 2003, http://granmai.cubasi.cu/ingles/2003/septiembre03/lun22/38lemon.html (accessed July 12, 2008).

28 Carlos Lage Dávila, vice president of the Cuban State Council, Convención y Feria Internacional Informática 2000, May 22–27, 2000, Havana, Cuba.

29 Cohen, *Globalization,* 113.

30 Morris H. Morley, *Imperial State and Revolution: The United States and Cuba, 1952–1986* (Cambridge: Cambridge University Press, 1987). Excerpted in Aviva Chomsky, Barry Carr, and Pamela Maria Smorkaloff, eds., *The Cuba Reader: History, Culture, Politics* (Durham, NC: Duke University Press, 2003), 323.

31 Radio Rebelde Web site, Historia, http://www.radiorebelde.com.cu/historia.htm (accessed July 13, 2008).

32 Robin D. Moore, *Music and Revolution: Cultural Change in Socialist Cuba* (Berkeley and Los Angeles: University of California Press, 2006), 103.

33 Ambrosio Fornet, "El Quinquenio Gris: Revisitando el término," in *La política cultural,* ed. Heras León and Navarro, 25–46.

34 Gabriel García Márquez, "Fidel, el oficio de la palabra," *Areito* 2, nos. 5–6 (July 1989): 14, http://www.juventudrebelde.cu/cuba/2006–08–13/el-oficio-de-la-palabra-hablada/ (accessed July 13, 2008).

35 Ibid.

36 "Reflexiones de Fidel," http://www.granma.cubaweb.cu/secciones/ref-fidel/index.html (accessed July 13, 2008).

37 Fidel Castro Ruz, "Autocrítica de Cuba," *Granma Digital Internacional,* July 11, 2007, http://www.granma.cu/espanol/2007/julio/mier11/refexiones.html (accessed September 1, 2007). ("La falta real y visible de igualdad y la carencia de información pertinente da lugar a opiniones críticas, sobre todo en los sectores más necesitados.")

38 Cristina Venegas, "Will the Internet Spoil Fidel Castro's Cuba?" in *Democracy and New Media*, ed. Henry Jenkins and David Thorburn (Cambridge, MA: MIT Press, 2003), 179–201.

39 Desiderio Navarro and Eduardo Heras León, "Para una cronología," in *La política cultural*, ed. Heras León and Navarro, 5.

40 Victor Fowler, "Pavonato, uno de los nombres del autoritarismo," *Encuentro en la Red*, http://www.cubaencuentro.com/es/encuentro-en-la-red/cultura/temas/tema-la-exaltacion-de-ex-comisarios-politicos/pavonato-uno-de-los-nombres-del-autoritarismo-29904 (accessed July 22, 2009). This online publication from outside Cuba provided space for discussion and covered the Pavón debate.

41 Arturo García Hernandez, "La política cultural de Cuba, sin dogmas ni sectarismos," *La Jornada* online, February 26, 2007, http://www.jornada.unam.mx/2007/02/26/index.php?section=cultura&article=a10e1cul (accessed July 13, 2008).

42 Decades earlier, another controversy over a short film, *PM* (Orlando Jimémez and Sabá Cabrera Infante, 1961), led to Fidel's "Words to the Intellectuals," which became the cultural policy of the period.

43 Desiderio Navarro, "¿Cuantos años de qué color? Para una introducción al Ciclo," in Heras León and Navarro, *La política cultural*, 17.

44 To normalize its relations with Cuba, the U.S. government has required, and requires, that the Cuban government hold free elections. See Institute for Democracy in Cuba, "Support for a Democratic Transition in Cuba," Washington, DC, January 28, 1997, www.somosuno.org (accessed July 28, 2008).

45 Leonardo Avritzer, *Democracy and the Public Space in Latin America* (Princeton, NJ: Princeton University Press, 2002), 5. For example, in Argentina the displaced workers' movement recovered companies laid idle by their owners and set the facilities into production again, under fair working conditions.

46 Partido Revolucionario Institucional (PRI), Partido de Acción Nacional (PAN), and Partido Revolucionario Demócratico (PRD).

47 The widely published writings of Subcomandante Marcos on the Internet challenged the Eurocentric historical view of the Mexican nation in its institutionalized exclusion of indigenous citizens by putting their demands for full representation in Mexico on the global agenda.

48 See the official Web site of the National Assembly of Popular Power for a full description of the structure of the Cuban government, http://www.asanac.gov.cu/ (accessed September 5, 2007).

49 Fidel Castro press conference, December 4, 1971, Guayaquil, Ecuador, in Castro Speech Database UTLANIC, http://lanic.utexas.edu/project/castro/db/1971/19711205–3.html (accessed November 15, 2008).

50 Carolee Bengelsdorf, *The Problem of Democracy in Cuba: Between Vision and Reality* (New York: Oxford University Press, 1994).

51 Joel C. Edelstein, "The Future of Democracy in Cuba," *Latin American Perspectives* 22, no. 4 (Fall 1995): 7–26.

52 Jesús Martín-Barbero, *Communication, Culture, and Hegemony: From Media to Mediations* (London: Sage Publishers, 1993), 6–22. In this impressive work, Martín-Barbero traces the concept of *the people* as it was used from the era of Romanticism and the Enlightenment, and how it was later adopted, with changes in meaning, by anarchists and Marxists.

53 Agencias [no further identification provided], "Proyectan el documental *PM* prohibido desde hace 33 años," *La Jornada*, December 3, 1994, 26.

54 Campa and Perez, *Los años duros*, 289–290. This book reproduces some portions of the closed-door sessions that candidly point to the extreme entrenched perspective of the Communist Party.

55 Ibid., 288.

56 Edward Said, *Culture and Imperialism* (New York: Vintage Books, 1993), 291.

57 Bengelsdorf, *Problem of Democracy*, 4.

58 Cuban government Web site, http://www.cubagov.cu (accessed August 31, 2007).

59 Chun, *Control-Freedom*, 151.

60 Christopher R. Kedzie, quoted by Larry Press in "Cuban Computer Networks and Their Impact," paper, ASCE Cuba in Transition Conference, Havana: Cuba, 1996, 340, http://www.lanic.utexas.edu/la/cb/cuba/asce/cuba6/43press2.fm.pdf (accessed July 13, 2008).

61 As Cuba acquired connectivity, Cuban exiles flooded networks with anti-Castro propaganda. Perceived as abuses by the Cuban leadership, the actions are said to have originated through America OnLine in 1996.

62 Jorge I. Dominguez, *Democratic Politics in Latin America and the Caribbean* (Baltimore, MD: Johns Hopkins University Press, 1998), 184.

63 Ibid., 183.

64 Tad Szulc, "When the Pope Visits Castro," *Los Angeles Times Parade Magazine*, December 14, 1997, 6.

65 Manuel Castells, *The Information Age: The Rise of the Network Society* (Malden, MA: Blackwell Publishers, 1996), 199.

CHAPTER 3 — TOURISM AND THE SOCIAL RAMIFICATIONS OF MEDIA TECHNOLOGIES

1 Joseph L. Scarpacci, Roberto Segre, and Mario Coyula, *Havana: Two Faces of the Antillean Metropolis* (Chapel Hill: University of North Carolina Press, 2002), 300–301.

2 For an account of Sol Meliá's corporate history, see http://www.answers.com/topic/sol-meli-s-a?cat=biz-fin (accessed July 10, 2008). The Meliá hotel name refers to hotels of the highest level of luxury service. Sol Meliá are standard hotels.

3 Lázaro J. Blanco Encinosa, "Apuntes para una historia de la Informática en Cuba," electronic document, http://www.sld.cu/galerias/doc/sitios/infodir/apuntes_para_una_historia_de_la_informatica_en_cuba.doc (accessed July 10, 2008).

4 Pérez Jr., *On Becoming Cuban*, 166.

5 Ibid., 167.

6 Scarpacci, Segre, and Coyula, *Havana: Two Faces*, 64–65.

7 Ibid.

8 Ibid., 290. Prerevolutionary levels of tourism reached 304,711—a number not attained again until 1990.

9 Chinese Central Television (CCT) signed an agreement with the Cuban Institute of Radio and Television in February 2008 for an exchange of programming, opening the door for future cooperation. Three Chinese channels then began airing on Cuban television. Cuban programming will also be broadcast into China and into China's hotel networks.

10 Speech by Ramiro Valdés Menéndez, minister of informatics and communications, at the opening of the twelfth Information Technology Convention and Fair, February 12, 2007, http://embacu.cubaminrex.cu/Default.aspx?tabid=3006 (accessed July 10, 2008).

11 Minerva Hernández Basso, "Propicia avance de la telefonía pública," 24 June 2007, http://www.opciones.cubaweb.cu/leer.asp?idnuevo=2866 (accessed July 10, 2008).

12 Marvin D'Lugo, "Transparent Women: Gender and Nation in Cuban Cinema," in *Mediating Two Worlds: Cinematic Encounters in the Americas*, ed. John King, Ana M. López, and Manuel Alvarado (London: BFI, 1993), 279–290.

13 Cubanacan is the main Cuban tour operator. Cubanacan Web site, main page, http://www.cubanacan.cu/index.php?lang=en (accessed July 10, 2008).

14 Ana María Dopico, "Picturing Havana: History, Vision, and the Scramble for Cuba," *Nepantla: Views from the South* 3, no. 3 (2002): 451.

15 Ibid., 452.

16 Patricia Rodríguez Alomá, *Viaje a la memoria: Apuntes para un acercamiento a la Habana Vieja* (La Habana: Oficiana del Historiador de la Habana Vieja, Cuba, 1996), 10.

17 Patricia Rodríguez Alomá with Alína Alomá Ochoa, *Desafío de una utopia: Una estrategia integral para la gestión de salvaguarda de la Habana Vieja* (La Habana: Oficina del Historiador de la Ciudad de la Habana, Cuba, 1999), 43.

18 See, for example, the review of *Buscándote Habana* (Alina Rodríguez Abreu, 2007), a documentary about existing inequalities among provinces in Cuba. The review features a preview clip, also located on YouTube, http://www.cubaencuentro.com/ (accessed July 10, 2008).

19 Claire Voeux and Julien Pain, "Going Online in Cuba: Internet under Surveillance," Reporters Without Borders Web site, October 19, 2006, http://www.rsf.org/Going-online-in-Cuba-Internet.html (accessed July 22, 2009).

20 Wikipedia on *Wikipedia*, definition, http://en.wikipedia.org/wiki/Wikipedia (accessed July 9, 2008).

21 Pablo Bachelet, "War of Words: Website Can't Define Cuba," Miami Herald. com, http://www.miami.com/mld/miamiherald/news/world/cuba/14485633.htm (accessed May 3, 2006), and http://www.cubanet.org/CNews/y06/mayo6/10e4. htm (accessed July 9, 2008). See also part of the editorial discussion on the Cuba entry under Talk:Cuba at http://en.wikipedia.org/wiki/Talk:Cuba (accessed July 9, 2008).

22 See http://wi-fitv.com (accessed August 2, 2007).

23 "Live TV and News from Cuba to Cubans around the Globe," Government Technologies news report, August 3, 2006, http://www.govtech.com/gt/articles/100415 (accessed August 14, 2007).

24 Mary Speck, "Prosperity, Progress, and Wealth: Cuban Enterprise during the Early Republic, 1902–1927," *Cuban Studies* 36 (2005): 58.

25 Mattelart, *Networking the World*, 11.

26 Moreno Fraginals, *El ingenio*, Comisión Nacional Cubana de la UNESCO, La Habana: Cuba, 1964, quoted in Mattelart and Schmucler, *Communication and Information*, 41–42.

27 Speck, "Prosperity," 58.

28 The film *El otro Francisco* (Sergio Giral, 1975) shows how the English promoted emancipation to better market their technology.

29 Antonio Benítez-Rojo, *The Repeating Island: The Caribbean and the Postmodern Perspective*, trans. James E. Maraniss (Durham: Duke University Press, 1992), 114.

30 Jorge F. Pérez-López and José Alvarez, *Reinventing the Cuban Sugar Agroindustry* (London: Lexington Books, 2005), 1.

31 Nubia Piqueras Grosso, "Fiber Optics to Link Cuba, World," *Prensa Latina*, http://www.plenglish.com/media/OpticalFiber/Index.html (accessed July 22, 2007).

32 Mattelart and Schmucler, *Communication and Information*, 104.

33 Pedro Urra González, "Infotelecomunicaciones," in *Cuba: amanecer del tercer milenio*, ed. Fidel Castro Díaz-Balart (Madrid: Editorial Debate, 2002), 221.

34 Mattelart and Schmucler, *Communication and Information*, 104.

35 Domenech, *¿Capitalismo o socialismo?* 164.

36 Domenech, *¿Capitalismo o Socialismo?* 163.

37 For example, Mexican entrepreneur Carlos Slim, owner of Teléfonos de Mexico (Telmex) and America Móvil, was officially the world's richest man in 2007. See news article at http://business.guardian.co.uk/story/0,,2117330,00.html (accessed August 14, 2007).

38 Mattelart and Schmucler, *Communication and Information*, 5.

39 Jeffrey Ryser, "The Return of the Yanqui," *Global Finance*, November 1996, http://findarticles.com/p/articles/mi_qa3715/is_199611/ai_n8751032 (accessed July 29, 2007).

40 In the case of México, advantageous policies and cooperation between the government and telecommunications entrepreneurs has been facilitated by trade agreements that restructure the geography of media technologies. See David C. Chaffe, *Building the Global Fiber-Optics Superhighway* (New York: Kluwer Academic / Plenum Publishers, 2001), 57–59.

41 Helen Mayer Harrison and Newton Harrison, "Seventh Lagoon: The Ring of Water," *Structure and Dynamics: eJournal of Anthropological and Related Sciences* 1, no. 4 (2006), http://repositories.cdlib.org/imbs/socdyn/sdeas/vol1/iss4/art5 (accessed August 14, 2007).

42 La revolución cubana, YouTube video, http://www.youtube.com/watch?v=QgAfcUCtzr4 (accessed July 23, 2007).

43 Modesto Arocha, *Chistes de Cuba*, Miami: Alexandria Library, 2003. Nicolás Guillén's poem "Ahora sí, ahora sí, ahora Varadero es para ti y para mí," http://www.alexlib.com/chistes/libro-promo.pdf (accessed July 10, 2008).

44 Raymond Williams, *Television Technology and Cultural Form* (Hanover, NH: University Press of New England, 1974, Wesleyan University Press, 1992), 7–9.

45 Benítez-Rojo, *Repeating Island*, 18–19.

46 In the film sector, it happened in the 1980s as part of the NGO movement/ phenomenon.

47 Chun, *Control and Freedom*, 49.

48 Mattelart and Schmucler, *Communication and Information*, 7.

49 Online research on the uses of the Internet in Latin America. The findings exhibit certain problems, including the language barrier (since the research was carried out in English) and self-selection.

50 Enrique González-Manet, "Internet: Espejismos y promesas de la cultura electrónica," unpublished manuscript, Havana, Cuba, 1998.

51 Benítez-Rojo, *Repeating Island*, 18. "Caribbean rhythm" is a metarhythm encompassing the forgotten foundation of multiple forms of knowledge that preceded the postindustrial world and continue in Caribbean culture.

52 Susan Eckstein, "Resistance and Reform: Power to the People?" *DRCLAS News* (Winter 2000): 9–12.

CHAPTER 4 — FILM CULTURE IN THE DIGITAL MILLENNIUM

1 Arjun Appadurai, *Modernity at Large: Cultural Dimensions of Globalization* (Minneapolis: University of Minnesota Press, 1996), 52.

2 Gerardo Chijona, personal interview with author, July 2005.

3 *Granma*, "Carta de la UNEAC about Alicia en el pueblo de Maravillas," June 18, 1991.

4 Alfredo Guevara would step down from the ICAIC in 2000 to preside over the Havana International Film Festival; he would be succeeded at the ICAIC by Omar González Jimenez, the first nonfilmmaker to head the institution. Guevara's departure marked an important bureaucratic separation of the film festival from the ICAIC; the two had been joined since 1979, when the festival was founded, under the leadership of another contemporary filmmaker, Julio García Espinosa.

5 There were thirty-one features produced during the period, as well as thirty-eight shorts (documentary and fiction), six feature-length documentaries, and many shorts by the students of the film school at San Antonio de los Baños (EICTV) and at the Instituto Superior de Arte (ISA). (These are approximate statistics derived from the Web site for ICAIC.)

6 In referring to Cuba's model of production as industrial cinema, I do not mean to suggest that this industrialization follows a Hollywood model. It should be considered an autochthonous model of production, fostering an industrial process based on Cuba's needs and conditions post-1959. Given the amount of "independent" production taking place today, it is fair to refer to this earlier mode and style of production as industrial.

7 Alfredo Guevara, "Para presentar cincuenta años de arte nuevo en Cuba," *Cine Cubano*, no. 142 (1998): 5–14.

8 Julio García Espinosa, "For an Imperfect Cinema," in *New Latin American Cinema: Theory, Practices, and Transcontinental Articulations*, vol. 1, ed. Michael T. Martin (Detroit: Wayne State University Press, 1997), 75.

9 Julio García Espinosa, *Un largo camino hacia la luz* (La Habana: Casa de las Américas, 2002), 116–123.

10 Julio García Espinosa, personal interview with author, September 1999. See also García Espinosa, *Largo camino*, 189–197.

11 Miguel Coyula, e-mail communication with author, July 19, 2008.

12 Miguel Coyula, interview in "Making of *Red Cockroaches*," *Red Cockroaches* DVD, Heretic Films, 2005.

13 Coyula, interview "Making of *Red Cockroaches*."

14 For a comprehensive historical account of Cuban cinema, see, among others: Michael Chanan, *Cuban Cinema* (Minneapolis: University of Minnesota Press, 2004); Ana M. López, "Cuban Cinema in Exile: The 'Other' Island," *Jump Cut*, no. 38 (June 1993): 51–59; Juan Antonio García Borrero, *Guía crítica del cine cubano de ficción* (La Habana: Editorial Arte y Literatura, 2001); Julianne Burton, "Revolutionary Cuban Cinema," *Jump Cut*, no. 19 (December 1978): 17–20; Marvin D'Lugo, "Transparent Women," in *Mediating Two Worlds*; Catherine Benamou, "Cuban Cinema: On the Threshold of Gender," in *Redirecting the Gaze: Third World Women Filmmakers*, ed. Diana Robin and Ira Jaffe (New York: SUNY Press, 1999), 68–97; Anne Marie Stock, *On Location in Cuba: Street Filmmaking during Times of Transition* (Chapel Hill: University of North Carolina Press, 2009).

15 Specifically, the work of the British filmmaker John Grierson (his work at the post office), Dutch filmmaker Joris Ivens, and Russian filmmaker Alexandr Medvedken (his cine train).

16 Humberto Solás, "Manifiesto de Cine Pobre," http://www.cubacine.cu/cinepobre/espanol/manifiesto.htm (accessed October 3, 2007).

17 García Espinosa, *Largo camino*, 195.

18 Solás, "Cine Pobre" Web site.

19 Fernando E. Solanas and Octavio Getino, "Towards a Third Cinema"; Julio García Espinosa, "Imperfect Cinema"; Glauber Rocha, "An Aesthetic of Hunger"; Fernando Birri, "Cinema and Underdevelopment"; Tomás G. Alea, "The Viewer's Dialectic"; Jorge Sanjinés, "Problems of Form and Content in Revolutionary Cinema," in *New Latin American Cinema: Theory, Practices, and Transcontinental Articulations*, vol. 1, ed. Michael T. Martin (Detroit: Wayne State University Press, 1997), 33–108.

20 See Esther Whitfield, *Cuban Currency*.

21 Of note is the experimental first video feature *El plano* (1993), directed by Julio García Espinosa. Produced in conjunction with EICTV, the film investigates the evolution of film language, as well as its relationship to narrative conventions and technology.

22 The official Web site for the Muestra de Cine Jóven has an alphabetical listing of the young filmmakers presenting their work during the past seven years. The listing shows that many women are part of this generation of filmmakers. See "Nuevos Realizadores," Instituto Cubano de Arte e Industria Cinematográfica, www.cubacine.cu/muestrajoven/ (accessed May 10, 2006).

23 Festival Internacional de Cine Pobre, "Memorias," http://www.cubacine.cu/cinepobre/memorias/ (accessed May 18, 2006).

24 Dean Luis Reyes, "El sollozo del hombre nuevo," unpublished essay, http://redcockroachesmovie.com/light/article_weeping.htm. (This is a review essay by a Cuban film critic, posted on the reviewed film's Web site, accessed November 23, 2008).

25 See festival program, http://www.cubacine.cu/muestrajoven (accessed July 20, 2008).

26 Loss Pequeño Glazier, Electronic poetry Web site, "Territorio Libre," 2003, http://epc.buffalo.edu/authors/glazier/e-poetry/Territorio/ (accessed July 20, 2008).

27 Glazier, "Territorio Libre."

28 Solás, "Manifesto."

29 Ibid.

30 Mauricio Vincent, "Aires de apertura en La Habana," *El Pais.com,* July 5, 2007, http://www.elpais.com/articulo/cultura/Aires/apertura/Habana/elpepuint/20070507elpepicul_5/Tes (accessed July 5, 2007).

31 The following newspapers/journals have online digital versions: *Adelante, Ahora, Escambray, Guerrillero, Granma Nacional, Granma Internacional, Habanero, Giron, Invasor, Victoria, La Demajagua, Periódico 26, Sierra Maestra, Trabajadores, Tribuna de la Habana, Venceremos, Vanguardia, 5 Septiembre,* AIN, *Prensa Latina,* and *Bohemia.*

32 Ariana Hernandez-Reguant, "Radio Taino and the Cuban Quest for Identi . . . que?" in *Cultural Agency in the Americas,* ed. Doris Sommer (Durham, NC: Duke University Press, 2006).

CHAPTER 5 — DIGITAL COMMUNITIES AND THE PLEASURES OF TECHNOLOGY

1 Loss Pequeño Glazier, "Code as Language," *Leonardo Electronic Almanac* 14, no. 5–6 (September 2006), http://leoalmanac.org/journal/vol_14_n05–06/lpglazier.asp (accessed July 25, 2008).

2 Ibid., 1.

3 Hamid Naficy, *Home, Exile, Homeland: Film, Media, and the Politics of Place* (New York: Routledge, 1999), 4.

4 E. Gabriella Coleman and Alex Golub, "Hacker Practice: Moral Genres and the Cultural Articulation of Liberalism," *Anthropological Theory* 8, no. 3 (2008): 255–277.

5 Dan Schiller, *Digital Capitalism: Networking the Global Market System* (Cambridge, MA: MIT Press, 2000).

6 Elián Gonzalez Web site, http://www.elian.cu/ (accessed July 25, 2008).

7 *Granma International* Web site, http://www.granma.cu (accessed July 25, 2008).

8 The current Cuban chamber of commerce was created in February 1, 1963, replacing the previous chamber of commerce, established in 1927. See current Web site at http://www.camaracuba.cu/ (accessed November 24, 2008).

9 Wayback Machine Internet Archive, http://web.archive.org/web/20031218042239/http://www.libertyforelian.org/ (accessed July 25, 2008).

10 The National Committee to Free the Cuban Five Web site, http://www.freethefive.org/index.htm (accessed November 24, 2008).

11 NoCastro Web site, only available through Wayback Machine Internet Archive, http://web.archive.org/web/20070811100648/http://nocastro.com/ (accessed July 25, 2008).

12 Hamid Naficy, "Exile Discourse and Televisual Fetishization," *Quarterly Review of Film and Video* 13, nos. 1–3 (1991): 86.

13 Ibid., 87.

14 Cristina Garcia, *Dreaming in Cuban* (New York: Ballantine Books, 1992), 3.

15 Celedonio Gonzalez, quoted in Hector Tobar, "An Era of Exiles Slips Away," *Los Angeles Times*, September 14, 1999, A-18.

16 Max Lesnick, quoted in Tobar, "Era of Exiles ."

17 In *Cuba Confidential,* Ann Luise Bardach argues for reading the complexity of the intransigent political dispute between the United States and Cuba in part as a family standoff.

18 See Jorge I. Dominguez, *Cuba and Power* (Cambridge and London: Belknap Press of Harvard University Press, 1978); Gustavo Perez-Firmat, *Life on the Hyphen: The Cuban-American Way* (Austin: University of Texas Press, 1994); and Maria Cristina García, *Havana, U.S.A.: Cuban Exiles and Cuban Americans in South Florida, 1959–1994* (Berkeley and Los Angeles: University of California Press, 1997).

19 Silvia Pedraza, *Political Disaffection in Cuba's Revolution and Exodus* (New York: Cambridge University Press, 2007), 110–126.

20 Maria Cristina Garcia has studied the South Florida community and discusses, at length, the first three periods of migration. See her *Havana, U.S.A.*

21 Maria Cristina Garcia's in-depth study identifies the influence of the *Miami Herald, El Herald*, and the hundreds of small newspapers that emerged out of the heated ideological climate. The now extensive literature of the first and second generation of exiles delves into the psychic nature of this rupture and the kinds of memories that Cubans rely on for emotional survival. Ruth Behar's *Bridges to Cuba* is also important, in that it calls attention to the different experience of exile felt by men and by women.

22 There is a growing fiction and nonfiction literature by Cuban exiles, and second-generation Cuban Americans in the United States, Europe, and Latin America. For instance, Perez-Firmat, *Life on the Hyphen*, and David Rieff, *The Exile: Cuba in the Heart of Miami* (New York: Touchstone, 1993), as well as novelists Cristina García, Zoe Valdez, Jesús Diaz, Reinaldo Arenas, and Severo Sarduy.

23 First-generation Cubans often define themselves in relation to "old" Cuba, and must reconcile with the "new" world; the generation born in exile, belonging to the "new" world, must reconcile itself with "old" Cuba. Those born in Cuba but who went through adulthood in the United States experience the identity split of belonging neither to the one place nor to the other. They have been called the one-and-a-half generation. See Perez-Firmat, *Life on the Hyphen*.

24 See www.bpicuba.org/, as well as the Committee to Protect Journalists' Cuba coverage at http://www.cpj.org/attacks96/countries/americas/cubalinks.html (accessed July 26, 2008).

25 By 2006, reports from independent journalists could be found on many sorts of Web sites operated outside Cuba. See CUBANET, www.cubanet.org, www.puenteinfocubamiami.org/ (Puente Informativo Cuba-Miami), www.cpj.org (Committee to Protect Journalists), www.rsf.org)Reporters without Borders), (all accessed July 9, 2008).

26 Ernesto J. De la Fé, personal Web site, http://www.delafe.com/cardenas/ (accessed July 26, 2008).

27 De la Fé, http://www.delafe.com/cardenas/homes.htm (accessed July 26, 2008).

28 De la Fe, "City of Cardenas: Images of the present, under Castro," http://www.delafe.com/cardenas/imgprese.htm (accessed July 26, 2008).

29 Guije.com Web site available at http://www.guije.com/index.htm (accessed November 24, 2008).

30 Beam Radio, Inc., Web site, "News," http://www.beamradio.com/news.htm (accessed July 26, 2008).

31 Manuel A. Alvarez, "A History of Cuban Broadcasting," Oldradio.com, http://www.oldradio.com/archives/international/cuban.html (accessed July 26, 2008).

32 Cuban American National Foundation, http://www.canfnet.org/ (accessed July 26, 2008); Brothers to the Rescue, http://www.hermanos.org/ (accessed July 26, 2008); Coalition of Cuban American Women, http://coalitionofcubanamericanwomen.blogspot.com/ (accessed July 26, 2008).

33 See Hector Tobar, "An Era of Exiles Slips Away," *Los Angeles Times*, September 14, 1999, A1, A18. Jorge Mas Canosa's son, Jorge Mas, is president of a telecommunications infrastructure company that plays a significant role in the telecommunications of the region. Already in 1985, Mas Canosa owned twenty companies with a combined worth of $80 million. His company, MasTec (http://mastec.com), specializes in the installation of networks and fiber-optic cable. It has a relationship with Sintel, an affiliate of Telefónica in Spain, which specializes in selling telecommunications equipment. It made an advantageous business deal with the Felipe González government of Spain to purchase the company, which the Spanish state then spent a fortune to improve. Mas Canosa downsized the company, releasing most of the Spanish work force and deciding that Cuban American youths could take over the vacancies. He posited, in Manuel Vazquez Montalban's *Y Dios entró en la Habana*, "If they had created Miami, they could certainly rebuild Cuba." Later, with the death of its director, MasTec sold 87 percent of Sintel to Spanish investors, but continues to operate it in North America and Latin America.

34 Cuba Free Press Project's Web site, http://www.cubafreepress.org/ (accessed July 26, 2008). See Manuel David Orrio, "La gorra del Viejo Habana," CPI-CubaNet, http://www.cubanet.org/CNews/y99/sep99/09a1o.htm (accessed July 26, 2008).

35 Reuters, "Cuban Blogger Wins Spanish Journalism Prize," April 4, 2008, http://uk.reuters.com/article/internetNews/idUKN0440148520080404 (accessed July 31, 2008).

36 Achille Mbembe, "At the Edge of the World: Boundaries, Territoriality, and Sovereignity in Africa," in *Globalization*, ed. Arjun Appadurai (Durham, NC: Duke University Press, 2001), 25.

37 Yoani Sanchez, Generación Y (blog), July 21, 2008, http://desdecuba.com/generaciony/?m=200807 (accessed July 26, 2008). See also Revista Convivencia (blog), http://www.convivenciacuba.es (accessed July 23, 2009) and numerous other blogs linked from Generación Y.

38 "Habeas Data," on Sanchez, *Generación Y*, February 12, 2008, http://desdecuba.com/generaciony/?m=200802, accessed July 26, 2008.

39 "Isolated Cuba Begins to Inch into the Internet Age," *Los Angeles Times*, November 19, 2006, A5. Written by an anonymous correspondent whose entrance into Cuba the Cuban government had not authorized.

40 See Lengua Suelta, on Habana Elegante, http://www.habanaelegante.com/Lengua/Lengua.html (accessed July 25, 2008); and see La isla en peso, http://www.uneac.org.cu/LaIslaEnPeso/ (accessed July 31, 2008).

41 "Variación jaula," on Victor Fowler, Oppiano's Coctel (blog), May 2008, http://oppianos.wordpress.com/2008/05/ (accessed July 27, 2008).

42 "Cuba y arte porno: Los caminos futuros," on Fowler, Oppiano's Coctel (blog), June 2008, http://oppianos.wordpress.com/2008/06/ (accessed July 27, 2008).

43 For example, the films *Perfecto amor equivocado* (Gerardo Chijona, 2004); *Flores de otro mundo* (Icíar Bollaín, 1999); *Cosas que dejé en la Habana* (Manuel Gutierrez Aragón, 1997); *Habana Blues* (Benito Zambrano, 2005); *Life Is to Whistle* (Fernando Perez, 1997).

44 See Cuban marriage Web site, http://www.cubanmarriage.co.uk/, accessed November 26, 2008.

45 See GoCubaPlus Web page, "Weddings," http://www.gocubaplus.net/onsitesrv/marriage.asp (accessed July 27, 2008).

46 Joanne P. Cavanaugh, "Cuba's Marry-Go-Round," *Johns Hopkins Magazine*, April 1, 1998, http://www.jhu.edu/~jhumag/0498web/wedding.html (accessed July 27, 2008).

47 Victor Fowler, personal interview with author, July 2005.

48 See the video of Bian Rodriguez of rap group Los Aldeanos, available on YouTube, http://www.youtube.com/watch?v=TRIAePTmb4Y (accessed July 22, 2009).

49 Gerardo Mosquera, "Alien-Own/Own-Alien: Globalization and Cultural Difference," *boundary 2*, no. 29: 3 (2002): 168.

50 Eugenio Valdés Figueroa, "Trajectories of a Rumor: Cuban Art in the Postwar Period," in *Art Cuba. The New Generation*, ed. Holly Block (New York: Harry N. Abrams, Inc., 2001): 19–21. Quoted on "Espacio Aglutinador," http://www.thing.net/~7Ecocofusco/espacioag.html (accessed July 27, 2008).

51 Espacio Aglutinador is hosted on Cuban American artist Coco Fusco's Web site, http://www.cocofusco.com (accessed July 27, 2008) and http://www.thing.net/~7Ecocofusco/espacioag.html (accessed July 27, 2008).

52 Victor Casaus, "Cuba Arte Digital," *Centro Pablo de la Torriente Breu*, May 3, 2007, http://www.artedigitalcuba.cult.cu/ (accessed July 27, 2008).

53 Ibid.

54 Luisa Marisy, "Exposiciones de videoarte cubano," *La Jiribilla*, June 24–30, 2006, http://www.lajiribilla.cu/2006/n268_06/268_03.html (accessed July 27, 2008).

55 Ibid. *Fast-Forward I* showed works by Raul Cordero, the undisputed pioneer of this art in Cuba, as well as works by Alexander Arrechea and Eduardo Moltó. *Fast-Forward II* included works by Luis Gómez, Ernesto Leal, Sandra Ramos, René Francisco Rodríguez, Lázaro Saavedra, and José Angel Toirac.

56 Victor Fowler, email correspondence with author, August 1, 2005.

57 Howard Rheingold, *Smart Mobs* (Cambridge: Perseus Publishing, 2003), xv.

CONCLUSION

1 Mark Lacey, "At a Fork in the Road, Cuba Follows Two Paths," *New York Times* online, Americas, July 31, 2008, http://www.nytimes.com/2008/07/31/world/americas/31cuba.html (accessed November 27, 2008).

2 Raul Castro, July 26, 2008, speech available on Radio Rebelde, http://www.radiorebelde.com.cu/english/cuba/nacionales1–280708-eng.htm (accessed November 27, 2008). Also see Raul Castro, "Discurso pronunciado por el compañero Raúl Castro Ruz, Presidente de los Consejos de Estado y de Ministros, en las conclusiones de la sesión constitutiva de la VII Legislatura de la Asamblea Nacional del Poder Popular," Palacio de las Convenciones, La Habana, February 24, 2008, "Año 50 de la Revolución," *Granma*, http://www.granma.cubaweb. cu/2008/02/24/nacional/artic35.html (accessed July 31, 2008).

3 Luis Ortega, *Cubanos en Miami* (La Habana: Editorial de Ciencias Sociales, 1998), 11.

4 Homi K. Bhabha, "Arrivals and Departures," in *Home, Exile, Homeland*, ix.

5 David Reiff, "Will Little Havana Go Blue?" *New York Times*, on NYTimes.com, July 13, 2008, http://www.nytimes.com/2008/07/13/magazine/13CUBANS-t.html (accessed July 31, 2008).

BIBLIOGRAPHY

PUBLICATIONS

Alea, Tomás G. "The Viewer's Dialectic." In *New Latin American Cinema: Theory, Practices, and Transcontinental Articulations*, vol. 1, ed. Michael T. Martin. Detroit: Wayne State University Press, 1997.

Ali, Tariq. *Pirates of the Caribbean: Axis of Hope*. London and New York: Verso, 2006.

Altshuler, José, and Roberto Díaz Martín, eds. *Los días cubanos de Antonio Meucci y el nacimiento de la telefonía*. La Habana: Empresa de Telecomunicaciones de Cuba, S.A., y Sociedad Cubana de Historia de la Cienci y la Tecnología, 1998.

Alvarez, Sonia, Evelina Dagnino, and Arturo Escobar, ed. *Culture of Politics, Politics of Culture: Revisioning Latin American Social Movements*. Boulder, CO: Westview Press, 1998.

Appadurai, Arjun, ed. *Globalization*. Durham, NC: Duke University Press, 2001.

Arocha, Modesto. *Chistes de Cuba*. Miami: Alexandria Library, 2003. http://www.alexlib.com/chistes/libro-promo.pdf. Accessed July 10, 2008.

Avritzer, Leonardo. *Democracy and the Public Space in Latin America*. Princeton, NJ: Princeton University Press, 2002.

Bardach, Ann Louise. *Cuba Confidential: Love and Vengeance in Miami and Havana*. New York: Random House, 2002.

Belnap, Jeffrey, and Raúl Fernández. *José Martí's "Our America," From National to Hemispheric Cultural Studies*. Durham, NC: Duke University Press, 1998.

Benamou, Catherine. "Cuban Cinema: On the Threshold of Gender." In *Redirecting the Gaze: Third World Women Filmmakers*, ed. Diana Robin and Ira Jaffe. New York: SUNY Press, 1999.

Bengelsdorf, Carollee. *The Problem of Democracy in Cuba: Between Vision and Reality*. New York: Oxford University Press, 1994.

Benítez-Rojo, Antonio. *The Repeating Island: The Caribbean and the Postmodern Perspective*. Trans. James E. Maraniss. Durham, NC: Duke University Press, 1992.

Betancourt, Enrique C. *Apuntes para la historia: Radio, television, y farándula de la Cuba de ayer*. Puerto Rico: Ramallo Bros, 1986.

Bhabha, Homi K. "Arrivals and Departures." In *Home, Exile, Homeland: Film, Media, and the Politics of Place*, ed. Hamid Naficy. New York: Routledge, 1999.

———, ed. *Nation and Narration*. London: Routledge, 1990.

Birri, Fernando. "Cinema and Underdevelopment." In *New Latin American Cinema: Theory, Practices, and Transcontinental Articulations*, vol. 1, ed. Michael T. Martin. Detroit: Wayne State University Press, 1997.

Blanco Encinosa, Lázaro J. "Apuntes para una historia de la Informática en Cuba." http://www.sld.cu/galerias/doc/sitios/infodir/apuntes_para_una_historia_de_la_informatica_en_cuba.doc. Accessed July 10, 2008.

Burton, Julianne. "Film and Revolution in Cuba: The First Twenty-Five Years." In *Cuba: Twenty-five Years of Revolution, 1959–1984*, ed. Sandor Halebsky and John M. Kirk. Westport, CT: Praeger Publishers, 1985.

———. "Revolutionary Cuban Cinema." *Jump Cut: A Review of Contemporary Media*, no. 19 (December 1978):17–20.

Calviño, Manuel. "Psicología, marxismo, y posmodernismo: Notas de una primera impresión." Unpublished manuscript. October 1998.

Campa, Homero. "Al estilo capitalista: Por primera vez, desde el inicio de la Revolución, en Cuba se cobrarán impuestos." *Proceso* 1002, January 15, 1996: 49–51.

———, and Perez Orlando. *Cuba: Los Años Duros*. Barcelona: Plaza y Janés, 1997.

Carr, Nicholas. "Is Google Turning Us into Stooped?" *The Atlantic* (July/August, 2008): 36.

Castañeda, Jorge G. *Utopia Unarmed: The Latin American Left after the Cold War*. New York: Alfred A. Knopf, 1993.

Castells, Manuel. *The Information Age: Economy, Society, and Culture*. 3 vols. Malden, MA: Blackwell Publishers, 1996.

Castro, Fidel. "En Cuba, revolución, socialismo, o independencia están indisolublemente unidos." *Proceso 684*, December 11, 1989.

Cavanaugh, Joanne P. "Cuba's Marry-Go-Round." *Johns Hopkins Magazine,* April 1, 1998. http://www.jhu.edu/~jhumag/0498web/wedding.html. Accessed July 27, 2008.

Centro de Estudios e Investigación, Facultad de Humanidades. *Cuba: De la utopia al desencanto*. Mexico: Universidad Autónoma del Estado de México, 1993.

Chaffe, David C. *Building the Global Fiber-Optics Superhighway*. New York: Kluwer Academic/Plenum Publishers, 2001.

Chanan, Michael. "Cuba and Civil Society, or Why Cuban Intellectuals Are Talking about Gramsci." *Nepantla* 2, no. 2 (2001).

———. *Cuban Cinema*. Minneapolis: University of Minnesota Press, 2004.

———, ed. *Twenty-five Years of Latin American Cinema*. London: BFI, 1983.

Chavez, Lydia. *Capitalism, God, and a Good Cigar: Cuban Enters the Twenty-first Century*. Durham, NC: Duke University Press, 2005.

Chomsky, Aviva, Barry Carr, and Pamela Maria Smorkaloff, eds. *The Cuba Reader: History, Culture, Politics*. Durham, NC: Duke University Press, 2003.

Chun, Wendy Hui Kyong. *Control: Freedom, Power, and Paranoia in the Age of Fiber Optics*. Cambridge, MA: MIT Press, 2006.

Cohen, Daniel. *Globalization and Its Enemies*. Cambridge, MA: MIT Press, 2006.

Coleman, E. Gabriella, and Alex Golub. "Hacker Practice: Moral Genres and the Cultural Articulation of Liberalism." *Anthropological Theory* 8, no. 3 (2008): 255–277.

Coté, John. "Cubans Log On behind Castro's Back." In *Capitalism, God, and a Good Cigar*, ed. Lydia Chavez. Durham, NC: Duke University Press, 2005.

Coyula, Mario. "El Trinquenio Amargo y la ciudad distopica: autopsia de una utopia." In *La política cultural del período revolucionario: Memoria y reflexión*, ed. Eduardo Heras León and Desiderio Navarro. La Habana: Centro Teórico-Cultural Criterios, 2008.

———. "Havana Always: Preserving the Soul of the City." *DRCLAS News* (Winter 2000): 28.Cuba Working Group, U.S. House of Representatives. "A Review of U.S. Policy toward Cuba." Washington, DC, May 15, 2002. http://lexingtoninstitute.org/970.shtml. Accessed August 19, 2007.

del Valle, Amaury E. "¿Google bloquea Cuba?" *Memoria* (November 2007): 35–36.

del Valle, Alfredo Luis. "Cuba, Internet, y la politica exterior de EEUU." Paper presented at the twelfth Congreso de la Asociación Mexicana de Estudios Internacionales, Puebla, Mexico, October 17, 1998.

D'Lugo, Marvin. "Transparent Women: Gender and Nation in Cuban Cinema." In *Mediating Two Worlds*, ed. John King, Ana M. López, and Manuel Alvarado. London: BFI, 1993.

Domenech, Silvia M. *Cuba: ¿Capitalismo o socialismo? Hacia el tercer milenio.* Havana: Editora Politica, 1998.

Dominguez, Jorge I. *Cuba and Power.* Cambridge and London: Belknap Press of Harvard University Press, 1978.

———. *Cuba: Order and Revolution.* Cambridge, MA: Belknap Press of Harvard University Press, 1978.

———. "Cuba's Many Faces: Not Quite the New Millennium." *DRCLAS News* (Winter 2000): 3.

———. *Democratic Politics in Latin America and the Caribbean.* Baltimore, MD: Johns Hopkins University Press, 1998.

Dopico, Ana Maria. "Picturing Havana: History, Vision, and the Scramble for Cuba." *Nepantla* 3, no. 3 (2002).

Eckstein, Susan. "Resistance and Reform: Power to the People?" *DRCLAS News* (Winter 2000).

Edelstein, Joel C. "The Future of Democracy in Cuba." *Latin American Perspectives* 22, no. 4 (Fall 1995).

Escobar, Arturo. *Encountering Development: The Making and Unmaking of the Third World.* Princeton, NJ: Princeton University Press, 1995.

Fernandes, Sujatha. *Cuba Represent! Cuban Arts, State Power, and the Making of New Revolutionary Cultures.* Durham, NC: Duke University Press, 2006.

Fornet, Ambrosio. "El Quinquenio Gris: Revisitando el término." In *La politica cultural del período revolucionario: Memoria y reflexión*, ed. Eduardo Heras León and Desiderio Navarro. La Habana, Cuba: Centro Teórico-Cultural Criterios, 2008.

Foucault, Michel. "Governmentality." In *The Essential Foucault*, ed. Paul Rabinow and Nikolas Rose. New York and London: The New Press, 2003.

Fowler, Victor. "Pavonato, uno de los nombres del autoritarismo." *Encuentro en la Red.* http://www.cubaencuentro.com.

Fraginals, Moreno. *El ingenio, complejo economico social cubano del azúcar.* Vol. 3. La Habana, Cuba: Editorial de Ciencias Sociales, 1978.

Franco, Jean. *The Decline and Fall of the Lettered City: Latin America in the Cold War.* Cambridge, MA: Harvard University Press, 2002.

Garcia, Cristina. *Dreaming in Cuban.* New York: Ballantine Books, 1992.

García, Maria Cristina. *Havana, U.S.A.: Cuban Exiles and Cuban Americans in South Florida, 1959–1994*. Berkeley and Los Angeles: University of California Press, 1997.

García Borrero, Juan Antonio. *Guía crítica del cine cubano de ficción*. La Habana, Cuba: Editorial Arte y Literatura, 2001.

García Canclini, Nestor. *Hybrid Cultures: Strategies for Entering and Leaving Modernity*. Trans. Christopher L. Chiappari and Silvia L. Lopez. Minneapolis: University of Minnesota Press, 1995.

García Espinosa, Julio. "Cibernautas de todos los países periféricos, uníos!" In *Un largo camino hacia la luz*. La Habana, Cuba: Casa de las Américas, 2000.

———. "For an Imperfect Cinema." In *New Latin American Cinema: Theory, Practices, and Transcontinental Articulations*, ed. Michael T. Martin. Vol. 1. Detroit: Wayne State University Press, 1997.

———. "For an Imperfect Cinema, Twenty-five Years Later." In *La doble moral del cine*. Bogotá, Colombia: Voluntad Editores, 1995.

García Luis, Julio. *Cuba en la era de Internet y las autopistas electronicas: Una entrevista con Enrique Gonzalez-Manet*. La Habana, Cuba: Pablo de la Torriente Editorial, 1997.

García Márquez, Gabriel. "Fidel, el oficio de la palabra." *Areito* 2, nos. 5–6 (July 1989).

Getino, Octavio. *Cine latinoamericano: Economia y nuevas tecnologias audiovisuales*. La Habana, Cuba: Fundación del Nuevo Cine Latinoamericano, 1987.

Glazier, Loss Pequeño. "Code as Language." *Leonardo Electronic Almanac* 14, no. 5–6 (September 2006).

Gonzalez-Manet, Enrique. *Informatics and Society: The New Challenges*. Norwood, NJ: Ablex Pub., 1992.

———. "Internet y promesas de la cultura electronica." La Habana, Cuba, 1998. Unpublished manuscript.

Guevara, Alfredo. "Para presentar cincuenta años de arte nuevo en Cuba." *Cine Cubano*, no. 142 (1998): 5–14.

———. *¿Y si fuera una huella?* La Habana, Cuba: Ediciones Autor Festival del Nuevo Cine Latinoamericano, 2008.

Held, David, and Heikki Patomäki. "Problems of Global Democracy: A Dialogue." *Theory, Culture, and Society* 23, no. 5 (2006).

Hernandez-Reguant, Ariana. "Radio Taino and the Cuban Quest for Identi . . . que?" In *Cultural Agency in the Americas*, ed. Doris Sommer. Durham, NC: Duke University Press, 2006.

———. "Return to Havana: Adió Kerida and the Films of the One-and-a-Half Generation." *Journal of Latin American Anthropology* 9, no. 2 (Fall 2004).

———. "Socialism with Commercials: Consuming Advertising in Today's Cuba," *ReVista*, DRCLAS News (Winter 2000).

Hoffman, Bert. "Cuba's Dilemma of Simultaneity: The Link between the Political and the National Question." In *Debating Cuban Exceptionalism*, ed. Bert Hoffman and Lawrence Whitehead. New York: Palgrave Macmillan, 2007.

———. *The Politics of the Internet in Third World Development: Challenges in Contrasting Regimes, with Case Studies with Costa Rica and Cuba*. New York: Routledge, 2004.

Hughes, A. "Retailers, Knowledges, and Changing Commodity Networks: The Case of the Cut Flower." In *Blackwell Cultural Economies Reader*, ed. Ash Amin and Nigel Thrift. Malden, MA: Blackwell Publishers, 2004.

Ichikawa, Emilio. "Tres notas sobre la transición." *Encuentro de la Cultura Cubana* 8/9 (Primavera/Verano, 1998).

Jenkins, Henry, and David Thorburn, eds. *Democracy and New Media*. Cambridge, MA: MIT Press, 2003.

Le Fray, Martin. "Internet in Latin America Forum." Internet World 2000, Los Angeles, CA, May 3–7, 2000.

López, Ana M. "Cuban Cinema in Exile: The 'Other' Island." *Jump Cut: A Review of Contemporary Media*, no. 38 (June 1993): 2006: 51–59.

———."An 'Other' History: The New Latin American Cinema." In *Resisting Images: Essays on Cinema and History*, ed. Robert Sklar and Charles Musser. Philadelphia: Temple University Press, 1990.

———. "Our Welcomed Guests: Telenovelas in Latin America." *To Be Continued: Soap Operas Around the World*, ed. Robert C. Allen. London: Routledge, 1995.

López Villaboy, José. "1958 Statistical Abstract." In *Motivos y culpables*. Puerto Rico: Editora El Prin, 1973.

Martin-Barbero, Jesús. *Communication, Culture and Hegemony: From Media to Mediations*. London: Sage Publishers, 1993.

Mattelart, Armand. *The Invention of Communication*. Trans. Susan Emanuel. Minneapolis: University of Minnesota Press, 1996.

———. *Networking the World, 1794–2000*. Trans. Liz Carey-Libbrecht and James A. Cohen. Minneapolis: University of Minnesota Press, 2000.

———, and Hector Schmucler. *Communication and Information Technologies: Freedom or Choice for Latin America?* Trans. David Buxton. Norwood, NJ: Ablex Publishers 1985.

Mayer Harrison, Helen, and Newton Harrison. "Seventh Lagoon: The Ring of Water." *Structure and Dynamics: eJournal of Anthropological and Related Sciences* 1, no. 4 (2006). http://repositories.cdlib.org/imbs/socdyn/sdeas/vol1/iss4/art5. Accessed August 14, 2007.

Mbembe, Achille. "At the Edge of the World: Boundaries, Territoriality, and Sovereignity in Africa." In *Globalization*, ed. Arjun Appadurai. Durham, NC: Duke University Press, 2001.

Miller, Toby, and George Yúdice. *Cultural Policy*. London: Sage Publications, 2002.

Moore, Robin D. *Music and Revolution: Cultural Change in Socialist Cuba*. Berkeley and Los Angeles: University of California Press, 2006.

Moreno Fraginals, Manuel. *El ingenio: Complejo economico social cubano del azúcar*. La Habana, Cuba: Comisión Nacional Cubana de la UNESCO, 1964.

Morley, Morris H. *Imperial State and Revolution: The United States and Cuba, 1952–1986*. Cambridge: Cambridge University Press, 1987.

Mosquera, Gerardo. "Alien-Own/Own-Alien: Globalization and Cultural Difference." *Boundary 2* 29, no. 3, (2002): 163–173.

Naficy, Hamid. "Exile Discourse and Televisual Fetishization." *Quarterly Review of Film and Video* 13, nos. 1–3 (1991).

———. *Home, Exile, Homeland: Film, Media, and the Politics of Place*. New York: Routledge, 1999.

—————. *The Making of Exile Cultures: Iranian Television in Los Angeles.* Minneapolis: University of Minnesota Press, 1993.

Navarro, Desiderio. "¿Cuantos años de qué color? Para una introducción al ciclo." In *La politica cultural del período revolucionario: Memoria y reflexión,* ed. Eduardo Heras León and Desiderio Navarro. La Habana, Cuba: Centro Teórico-Cultural Criterios, 2008.

—————, and Eduardo Heras León. "*Para una cronología.*" In *La politica cultural del período revolucionario: Memoria y reflexión.* ed. Eduardo Heras León and Desiderio Navarro. La Habana, Cuba: Centro Teórico-Cultural Criterios, 2008.

Nye, Joseph S. *Soft Power: The Means to Success in World Politics.* New York: Public Affairs, 2004.

Ortega, Luis. *Cubanos en Miami.* La Habana, Cuba: Editorial de Ciencias Sociales, 1998.

Paranagua, Paulo-Antonio. "News from Havana: A Restructuring of Cuban Cinema." *Framework* 35 (1989).

Parks, Lisa. *Cultures in Orbit: Satellites and the Televisual.* Durham, NC: Duke University Press, 2005.

Pedrazza, Silvia. *Political Disaffection in Cuba's Revolution and Exodus.* New York: Cambridge University Press, 2007.

Pequeño Glazier, Loss. "Code as Language." *Leonardo Electronic Almanac* 14, no. 5–6 (September 2006). http://leoalmanac.org/journal/vol_14_n05–06/lpglazier.asp. Accessed July 25, 2008.

Pérez, Louis A. Jr. *On Becoming Cuban: Identity, Nationality, and Culture.* Chapel Hill: University of North Carolina Press, 1999.

Perez-Firmat, Gustavo. *Life on the Hyphen: The Cuban-American Way.* Austin: University of Texas Press, 1994.

Pérez-Lopez, Jorge F., and José Alvarez, eds. *Reinventing the Cuban Sugar Agroindustry.* London: Lexington Books, 2005.

Press, Larry. "Cuba, Communism, and Computing." *Communications of the ACM* 5, no. 11 (November 1992).

—————. "Cuban Computer Networks and Their Impact." http://www.lanic.utexas.edu/la/cb/cuba/asce/cuba6/43press2.fm.pdf.1996:344. Accessed July 21, 2009.

—————. "Cuban Networking Update." *OnTheInternet* (Jannuary/February 1996): 46–49. http://som/csudh.edu/fac/lpress/devnat/nations/cuba/update.htm. Accessed July 21, 2009.

—————."Cuban Telecommunication Infrastructure and Investment." Paper, conference of the Association for the Study of the Cuban Economy, Miami, Florida, August 1996. http://som.csudh.edu/fac/lpress/devnat/nations/cuba/asce.htm. Accessed July 21, 2009.

Press, Larry, and Joel Snyder. "A Look at Cuban Networks." http://som.csudh.edu/cis/lpress/devnat/nations/cuba/cuba3.htm. Accessed August 15, 2007.

Reyes, Dean Luis. "El sollozo del hombre nuevo." Upublished essay. http://redcockroachesmovie.com/light/article_weeping.htm. Accessed November 23, 2008.

Rheingold, Howard. *Smart Mobs.* Cambridge, MA: Perseus Publishing, 2003.

Rieff, David. *The Exile: Cuba in the Heart of Miami.* New York: Simon and Schuster, 1993.

Rivero, Yeidy M. "Broadcasting Modernity: Cuban Television, 1950–1953." *Cinema Journal* 46, no. 3 (2007).

Rocha, Glauber. "An Aesthetic of Hunger." In *New Latin American Cinema: Theory, Practices, and Transcontinental Articulations*, vol. 1, ed. Michael T. Martin. Detroit: Wayne State University Press, 1997: 59–61.

Rodríguez Alomá, Patricia. *Viaje a la memoria: apuntęs para un acercamiento a la Habana Vieja*. La Habana: Oficiana del Historiador de la Habana Vieja, Cuba, 1996.

Rodríguez Alomá, Patricia, with Alína Alomá Ochoa. *Desafío de una utopia: una estrategia integral para la gestión de salvaguarda de la Habana Vieja*. La Habana: Oficina del Historiador de la Ciudad de la Habana, Cuba, 1999.

Rueschemeyer, Dietrich, Evelyn Huber Stephens, and John D. Stephens. *Capitalist Development and Democracy*. Chicago: University of Chicago Press, 1992.

Ryser, Jeffrey. "The Return of the Yanqui." *Global Finance*, November 1996. http://findarticles.com/p/articles/mi_qa3715/is_199611/ai_n8751032. Accessed July 22, 2009.

Said, Edward. *Culture and Imperialism*. New York: Vintage Books, 1993.

Salwen, Michael B. *Radio and Television in Cuba: The Pre-Castro Era*. Ames: Iowa State University Press, 1994.

Sanjinés, Jorge. "Problems of Form and Content in Revolutionary Cinema." In *New Latin American Cinema: Theory, Practices, and Transcontinental Articulations*, vol. 1, ed. Michael T. Martin. Detroit: Wayne State University Press, 1997, 62–70.

Scarpacci, Joseph L., Roberto Segre, and Mario Coyula. *Havana: Two Faces of the Antillean Metropolis*. Chapel Hill: University of North Carolina Press, 2002.

Schiller, Dan. *Digital Capitalism: Networking the Global Marketplace*. Cambridge, MA: MIT Press, 1999.

Scranton, Philip, and Janet F. Davidson, eds. *The Business of Tourism: Place, Faith, and History*. Philadelphia: University of Pennsylvania Press, 2007.

Sinclair, John. *Latin American Television: A Global View*. New York: Oxford University Press, 1999.

Solanas, Fernando E., and Octavio Getino. "Towards a Third Cinema." In *New Latin American Cinema: Theory, Practices, and Transcontinental Articulations*, vol. 1, ed. Michael T. Martin. Detroit: Wayne State University Press, 1997, 33–58.

Spadoni, Paolo. "The Impact of Helms-Burton Legislation on Foreign Investment in Cuba." In *Cuba in Transition, vol. 11*: 25–32. Report by Association for the Study of the Cuban Economy, meeting in Miami, FL. August 2–4, 2001. http://lanic.utexas.edu/project/asce/pdfs/volume11/spadoni.pdf

Speck, Mary. "Prosperity, Progress, and Wealth: Cuban Enterprise during the Early Republic, 1902–1927." *Cuban Studies* 36 (2005): 58.

Stock, Anne Marie. *On Location in Cuba: Street Filmmaking during Times of Transition*. Chapel Hill: University of North Carolina Press, 2009.

Suckling, James. "Unforgettable Cuba." *Cigar Aficionado*, June 1999.

Symmes, Patrick. "Che Is Dead." *Wired*, February 1998, 145.

Szulc, Tad. "When the Pope Visits Castro." *Parade Magazine*, December 14, 1997.

Tsing, Anna. *Frictions*. Princeton, NJ: Princeton University Press, 2005.

Turnstall, Jeremy. *The Media are American*. New York: Columbia University Press, 1977.

UNESCO. Executive Council. 151st session. "Declaration of the CAC Regarding Universal Access and Basic Information and Communication Services." 151EX/16 addendum. Paris: UNESCO, May 20, 1997.

United States. Broadcasting Board of Governors. Annual report, 2005: 16. http://www.bbg.gov/bbg_press.cfm. Accessed August 19, 2007.

United States. Government Accountability Office. "Foreign Assistance: U.S. Democracy Assistance for Cuba Needs Better Management and Oversight." GAO 07–147, November 2006. http://www.gao.gov/new.items/d07147.pdf. Accessed August 28, 2007.

Urra González, Pedro. "Infotelecomunicaciones.",In *Cuba: Amanecer del Tercer Milenio*, Fidel Castro Díaz-Balart, ed. Madrid: Editorial Debate, and Cuba: Editorial Científico Técnica, 2002.

Valdés, Nelson P. "Cuba, the Internet, and U.S. Policy." Cuba Briefing Paper Series, no. 13, March 1997: 3–6. Washington, DC: Center for Latin American Studies, Georgetown University. .http://www.trinitydc.edu/academics/depts/Interdisc/International/Caribbean/20Briefing/20Papers.htm. Accessed July 8, 2008.

———, and Mario A. Rivera, "The Political Economy of the Internet in Cuba." *Cuba in Transition*. ASCE 1999. http://www.lanic.utexas.edu/la/cb/cuba/asce/cuba9/valdes.pdf. Accessed July 8, 2008.

Valdés Figueroa, Eugenio. "Trajectories of a Rumor: Cuban Art in the Postwar Period." In *Art Cuba. The New Generation*, ed. Holly Block. New York: Harry N. Abrams, Inc., 2001.

Vazquez, Naghim. "Cuba in the Window of the Internet." Master's thesis, Universidad de La Habana, Cuba, 1998.

Vazquez Montalbán, Manuel. *Y Dios entró en la Habana*. Madrid: Aguilar, 1998.

Venegas, Cristina. "Filmmaking with Foreigners." In *Cuba in the Special Period: Culture and Ideology in the 1990s*, ed. Ariana Hernandez-Reguant. New York: Palgrave Macmillan, 2009.

Voeux, Claire, and Julien Pain. "Going Online in Cuba: Internet under Surveillance." Reporters Without Borders website, October 19, 2006, http://www.rsf.org/Going-online-in-Cuba-Internet.html. Accessed July 22, 2009.

Whitfield, Esther. *Cuban Currency: The Dollar and the "Special Period" Fiction*. Minneapolis: University of Minnesota Press, 2008.

Williams, Raymond. *Television: Technology and Cultural Form*. Hanover, NH, and London: Wesleyan University Press, 1992 [1974].

WEBSITES

CENIAI, http://www.ceniainternet.cu/.

Center for Genetic Engineering and Biotechnology, http://gndp.cigb.edu.cu/.

Committee to Protect Journalists, http://www.cpj.org.

CUBANET, http://www.cubanet.org.

Cuban National Assembly of Popular Power, http://www.asanac.gov.cu/.

Cubaweb, http://www.cubaweb.cu/esp/main.asp.

Elián Gonzalez website, http://www.elian.cu/.

Encuentro de la cultura Cubana en la Red, http://www.cubaencuentro.com.

Genearación Y, http://www.desde.cuba.com/generacioy/.

Granma International, http://www.granma.cu.

InfoMed website, http://www.sld.cu/red/acercade/.

Institute for Democracy in Cuba, "Support for a Democratic transition in Cuba," http://www.somosuno.org.

Joven Club de Computación, http://www.jovenclub.cu/.

Manifiesto de Cine Pobre, http://www.cubacine.cu/cinepobre/espanol/manifiesto.htm.

Muestra de Cine Joven, http://www.cubacine.cu/muestrajoven.

Net for Cuba, http://www.netforcuba.org/.

Prensa Latina, http://www.prensa-latina.cu/.

Puente Informativo Cuba-Miami, http://www.puenteinfocubamiami.org/.

Radio Rebelde, http://www.radiorebelde.com.cu/historia.htm.

Reflexiones de Fidel, http://www.granma.cubaweb.cu/secciones/ref-fidel/index.html.

Reporters without Borders, http://www.rsf.org.

Revista Convivencia, http://www.convivenciacuba.es.

USA-Cuba InfoMed, http://www.cubasolidarity.net/.

INDEX

ABOUT THE AUTHOR

CRISTINA VENEGAS is an associate professor in Film and Media Studies at the University of California, Santa Barbara. Her teaching and writing focus on Latin American film and media, Spanish-language media in the United States, international cinema, and cultural studies.

3267

Gramley Library
Salem Academy and College
Winston-Salem, N.C. 27108